DELIVERANCE
THAT WORKS

DELIVERANCE
PRINCIPLES | PROCESSES | PRACTICES | PURPOSES

PATRICK ODIGIE

Copyright 2017 – Patrick Ighodalo Odigie

ISBN 13-978-0-9987923-0-9
ISBN 10-09-9987923-0-6

All rights reserved. This book is protected by the copyright laws of the United States of America. This book may not be copied or reprinted or reproduced or transmitted in any form or by any means, electronic, mechanical, and recording or any information storage and retrieval system for commercial gain or profit. The use of short quotations or occasional page copying for personal or group study is permitted and encouraged. Permission will be granted upon request. Unless otherwise stated, Scripture quotations are from the King James Version (KJV) of the Holy Bible.

First Printing – February 2017

Published by:
Prophetic Power House Inc. New York
For more copies of this book and all our messages and training materials:

CONTACT
Patrick I. Odigie
Post Office Box 830
Uniondale
New York 11553
516 499-2350
Email: propheticpowerhouse@yahoo.com
Website: www.patrickodigie.com

Contents

Dedication xiv
Acknowledgements xv
Foreword xviii
Endorsements xx
Preface xxiv
Introduction xxvii

CHAPTER 1
My Dysfunctional Early Years 30
Breakthrough Prophetic Deliverance Prayers 36

CHAPTER 2
My Introduction into Deliverance 39
Embarassing Dream Experience 41
My Deliverance Counseling and Cleansing 45
Breakthrough Prophetic Deliverance Prayers 46

CHAPTER 3
What is Deliverance? 48
Beyond casting out demons 51
Where can we find true Deliverance? 52
Two Kingdoms at War 54
The First Level of Deliverance 56
Prophetic Insight 57
Three Categories of People in Church 59

The Anointing Versus the Glory (The House of Joseph) 62
Fasting and the Glory Dimension of the Anointing 64
The House of Esau 65
Breakthrough Prophetic Deliverance Prayers 68

CHAPTER 4
The Deliverance Anointing 70
What is our basis of Deliverance? 70
Levels of Deliverance 71
Level One - Jesus Paid the Full Price for our Deliverance ... 71
Level Two – Counseling 74
Level Three - Proclaim Liberty 75
Level Four - Revelation of Divine Truths 79
Real Freedom - When does deliverance occur? 80
Who is a Free Person? 81
Breakthrough Prophetic Deliverance Prayers 83

CHAPTER 5
The Deliverance Process 84
Points of Contact 86
New DNA and Kingdom Transfer 86
The Spirit of Counsel 92
Breaking Evil Grips 95
No Alternative To God's Word 99
Three Phases of Deliverance 102
Salvation and Initial Counseling / Deliverance 102
Second Phase and Intense Warfare 102
Warfare 105
Life of Dominion 107

Breakthrough Prophetic Deliverance Prayers 113

CHAPTER 6
The God Who Delivers 115
The Covenant Keeping God 116
The Everlasting Covenant 118
Breakthrough Prophetic Deliverance Prayers 120

CHAPTER 7
The Origin, Fall and Career of The Devil 122
The Fall 124
Rebellion and Destruction 127
The Career of the Devil 130
The Career of the Devil Today 132
The Restoration Plans of God and the Defeat of the Devil .. 137
The Resurrected and Glorious Son of God is our pattern ... 141
Breakthrough Prophetic Deliverance Prayers 145

CHAPTER 8
Three Sources of Demonic Trouble 146
- The Congregation of the Dead 146
- Territorial Demonic Pollutions 157
- Personal Involvement/Flirtation with the devil 160
Breakthrough Prophetic Deliverance Prayers 163

CHAPTER 9
Some Signs of Demonic Oppression 165
- Exaggerated patterns of human behavior 165
- Addiction to chemical substances 165

- Mysterious illnesses 166
- Across-the-board horizontal family reverses 167
- Living below potentials 167
- Unexplainable delays 167
- Failure at the edge of success 168
- Unidentified moving objects 168
- Moods wings 168
- Unbridled religiosity 169
- Haunted homes and cursed items 169
- Hearing voices, seeing or being followed by people visible to you and not others 170
- The dream State 171

Breakthrough Prophetic Deliverance Prayers 172

CHAPTER 10
Other Demonic Doorways 174
- Through the religious activities of your parents 175
- From the womb 177
- Parental disobedience to God has implications on children 179
- Occult involvement 180
- Demonic Material possession 182
- Demonic transference from other people 182
- Sexual immorality 185
- Misguided deliverance 188
- Soul ties 191
- Demonic laying on of hands 193
- Fallen Generals 194
- Inherited family curses 196

Breakthrough Prophetic Deliverance Prayers 197

CHAPTER 11
Can A Christian be Demon-possessed? 199
A demon cannot possess a true Christian 202
Only Believers can receive deliverance 205
Believers carry God's DNA 208
Believers can have demons 209
Breakthrough Prophetic Deliverance Prayers 212

CHAPTER 12
Practical Deliverance Sessions 214
- Group Deliverance Services 214
- Faith Clinics 215
- Individual Counseling Sessions 217
- Self-Deliverance 219

Issues Addressed in a Practical deliverance Session 221
- Repentance 221
- Breaking Evil Covenants 222
- Authoritative Warfare 225
- The Holy Spirit Power and House Cleaning 226
- Deep Inner Cleansing 227
- The Word of God and Cleansing 229

Find a Teaching Ministry and Connect 233
The Flipside 234
- The fear of the Lord and cleansing 235

Benefits of spiritual Cleansing 240
- Freedom 240
- A Definite Promise 241
- Regain your Inheritance 241
  - Live out your Destiny 242

When Demons Are Expelled 243

People coming out of an Occult background 246
Breakthrough Prophetic Deliverance Prayers 248

CHAPTER 13
Three days of Deliverance prayer with fasting 250
Preparation to Start a Three-day shut 251
What can happen when demons are exiting 257
The much longer fast 259
Breakthrough Prophetic Deliverance Prayers 260

CHAPTER 14
Why Deliverance Cases Delay 261
Poorly identified background issues 261
- Previous Occult Involvement 262
- Misunderstanding of the Deliverance Process 263
- Impatience and Distractions 264
- Failure to Reckon with and work the
  Three Stages of Deliverance 266
Why Failure at the Edge of Success? 272
Power of Divine Encounters and Transformation 275
Breakthrough Prophetic Deliverance Prayers 278

CHAPTER 15
More Reasons for Delay in Deliverance Cases 280
- Need for a bigger vision 280
- Dealing with points of contact 282
- Categories of Points of Contact 283
- Jewelry, Literature, Video Materials and Music that
  are dedicated to satan 290
- Hidden Curses 290

Breakthrough Prophetic Deliverance Prayers 293

CHAPTER 16
Other Reasons for Delay in Deliverance 294
Hidden Altars 294
The Lawful Captive 298
- Demonic Cycles 302
- Illegal Collections 305
- Ancestral Spirits 306
Breakthrough Prophetic Deliverance Prayers 311

CHAPTER 17
The strongman of the house 312
Governmental Powers in the Spiritual Realm 314
Breakthrough Prophetic Deliverance Prayers 335

CHAPTER 18
Complicated Cases in Deliverance 336
Insanity and demonic delusions 337
The Holy Spirit versus psychic power 339
Authentic doorway into the spirit realm 341
Multi-dimensional approach 343
Need to have legal safeguards 345
Baiting the wicked 347
Need to build a team 351
Breakthrough Prophetic Deliverance Prayers 354

CHAPTER 19
Dreams and Deliverance 355
Divine Inspiration Dreams 356

Manipulation type dreams 368
Manifestation Dreams 377
Breakthrough Prophetic Deliverance Prayers 382

CHAPTER 20
Follow-up in Deliverance 384
The Place of Discipleship in Deliverance 387
First Things First 390
The Word of God is central 393
Power of testimony 394
Power of Personal Testimony 395
Overcoming the counter attacks 398
Breakthrough Prophetic Deliverance Prayers 400

CHAPTER 21
Preparation to Serve in Deliverance Ministry 403
Satan relies on smart strategies 404
The enemy is afraid of you 406
Fear and intimidation 408
Grace is not validation for sin 409
Sex trap 410
A vow dishonored brings reproach 413
The Desert School Experience 414
Breakthrough Prophetic Deliverance Prayers 417

CHAPTER 22
The Deliverance Minister 418
The Anointing of the Deliverance Minister 421
The Place of the Holy Spirit 425
The Power and Presence of the Holy Spirit 426

The Church needs this Power 428
Breakthrough Prophetic Deliverance Prayers 430

CHAPTER 23
The Deliverance Team 431
The Local Church Team 432
The Parachurch Deliverance Ministry Team 433
Character of an Effective Deliverance Team 434
Maintaining a Successful Deliverance Team 436
Breakthrough Prophetic Deliverance Prayers 438

CHAPTER 24
How to Answer the Call to Deliverance Ministry 440
The Call, Stages and Levels of Responses 441
Knowledge 441
Preparation 442
Theoretical level of training 443
Character level of training 444
Fulfilling Purpose 445
Breakthrough Prophetic Deliverance Prayers 447

CHAPTER 25
Some Deliverance Terms Explained 449
Covenant 449
Curses 451
Spiritual Marks 453
Tokens 455
Points of Contacts 456
The Strongman 458
Ancestral Spirits 458

Monitoring Demons	459
Familiar Spirit	461
Demonic Cycles	463
Demonic Reverses	464
Spells and Enchantments	465
Divination	465
Soul Ties	466
- Soul Ties in marriage	466
- Soul Ties in Covenant Friendship	467
- Negative or Demonic Soul Ties	468
- Samson the Deliverer	469
Breakthrough Prophetic Deliverance Prayers	471

CHAPTER 26
Seven urgent messages to the Church ... 472

Jesus Christ is the Message of the Entire Bible	472
Redemption is by the Blood	473
The Cross	474
Intimacy with God	475
- The Power of the Almighty	475
- Evangelism	476
- Eternity	477
Breakthrough Prophetic Deliverance Prayers	478

APPENDIX
Practical Deliverance Encounters ... 479

Case Encounter 1
A Case of Spiritual Confusion ... 480

Case Encounter 2
Confronting a Lifeless Young Woman 485

Case Encounter 3
Case of Delay in Marriage 488

Case Encounter 4
A Misleading Voice 491

Case Encounter 5
The Case of Demonic Manipulation 494

Case Encounter 6
Blood of God: A case of Deception 498

Case Encounter 7
A Case of the Boy without Father and Mother 501

Case Encounter 8
The Case of Vanishing Pregnancy 507

Case Encounter 9
A satanic Covenant of Destruction 511

Case Encounter 10
The Luciferian Marine Agent 514

About the Author 517

Bibliography 519

Dedication

To the one Eternal God, the Creator of all things, both visible and invisible; to the Lord Jesus who loves me completely; going all the way, He drank the full cup of the wrath of the Almighty God in my stead; and to the Blessed Eternal Spirit of grace, my Counselor, Teacher, and ever patient Coach, be all the glory always, now and forever! I love you till eternity my God.

Acknowledgements

In Africa, we say, "it takes a village to raise a child." To stay on the true path of life and attempting to share some beneficial truths through these series is made possible by three generations of generous human beings whose love, sacrifice and faith in me have greatly enriched my life's journey and purpose. Standing strong with me in love and mustering every ounce of energy to keep me moving is my precious wife, Pastor Mabel Odigie and of course, on our side, are three very loving and understanding children (Praise, Honor and Favor) both cheering us and bearing long with us in this tough undertaking called life. You are my earthly treasure, and I can't wait to share your noisy neighborhood in Heaven.

Faithful Friends, Mentors, and Destiny Helpers. Am told one of God's highest investment in life and destiny is people. They take you from here to there! I am immensely thankful for years of sacrifice and love invested in my family and me by the following God's generals; Pastor Jerome and Bola Obode, Dr Festus and Dr. Antonia Adeyeye, (Victoria Eto now with Jesus) Pastor Michael and Dr. Ronke Mordi, Rev. & Rev. (Mrs) James

Solomon, Rev. John and Prophetess Agnes Akinyemi, Pastors Vincent and Sarah Omusi, Pastors Nathaniel and Jumoke Saingbe, Dr. Paul and Rev Mrs Fakunle, Pastor Ajayi Adeniran and Pastor Yomi Oshikoya, Dr Abraham Akanni, Pastor Adeyokunnu, Bishop and Pastor Mrs. Awowoyin, Pastors Jacob and Margaret Afere, Dr. Samuel Malomo and a growing list of others. Your friendship gave me the platform to grow and practice these truths over the years; thank you!

My Anointed Warriors. God has greatly beautified my life with a long list of Spiritual children who gives me the highest reasons to stay in the fight and among them; Apostle Helen Godswill, Minister Omolara and Wale Olutumbi, Grace Edewede Iyochir, Olawumi Hamakim, Pastor Greg and Helen Eigbadon, Pastor Stephen and Funke Jagun, Pastors Yomi and Toyin Ademuwagun, Pastor John and Christine Arogbo, Omolara and Joshua Sodeinde, Krisie Mathews (Stanley), Ona and Chike Erike, Evangelist Emma and Ifeoma Unuigwe, Pastor Felix and Caro Odigie, Darvan and Nicole Dennis, Pastor Janet and Solomon Bakare, Larry and Chika Ezeani, Peter and Debbie Nwaobi, Jackie Sealy, Eti Ebewo, Eta Conteh and the list continues. If you don't see your name here, it's because we are a large family and simply too many, to accommodate in these short pages. Your love, prayer, and financial investment are here acknowledged and appreciated.

Finally, to my powerful editing team for these series, my most profound thanks. Ms. Nadine Thomas who did initial transcribing; my daughters Omolara Olutunbi and Praise Odigie for great editing work on this book. Further professional editing was done by Pastor Gbenga Showumi, Ola Aboderin, and Rosanda Richardson. Design and layout by Helen Uwana Bassey and cover design by Akinyanju Bodunrin. You have all labored so hard, thank you. The author accepts responsibility for any observable errors and welcomes your feedback.

Foreword

I consider it a great honor to be asked to write a foreword to this amazing book. I have known Rev. Patrick Odigie for over 30 years, both as a close friend, and co-minister in the service of God's Kingdom. Rev. Odigie is a widely respected minister of the Gospel with unusual teaching and prophetic insights. God has also blessed him with a special anointing to minister healing and deliverance to the sick and oppressed.

This book, Foundations for True and Effective Deliverance, has been written in response to the silent and vocal cries of many of God's people (including mine) for a balanced, insightful and inspirational reference on the subject of deliverance. The book lays a clear overview of the subject; it is also a fantastic resource and user guide covering varied and rarely addressed dimensions of the subject.

When Rev. Odigie made a decision to write this book, I was in no doubt about the scope, depth and clarity it will add to one of the most debated, yet all-important Christian subjects. In many respects, the author has made a new and scarce contribution to the topic, and I hope it will serve as an eye opener to the subject of deliverance- an area in which the devil has exploited the ignorance and laid-back attitude of God's people for too long.

For Christians who do not believe in deliverance ministry, I invite them to read this book with an open heart and have a rethink about their position. For believers who have unanswered questions about deliverance, this book will help clear the air and dispel many of the doubts in their hearts. And, for the rest of us who have absolute confidence that deliverance is God's will for His people, Foundations for True and Effective Deliverance, will provide additional learning and a reliable reference as we flip through its pages.

I have found this book a clear, rare and distinctive contribution to one of the most important aspects of Christianity. I strongly recommend it for everyone whatever your position, experience and calling in God's Kingdom. God bless as you read.

Jerome Obode
Senior Pastor, Global Impact Tabernacle,
London, United Kingdom.

Endoresements

This divinely inspired material is timely and needful in today's world where many are bound by sin, ignorance, forces of darkness, destructive habits and are crying out for liberty. This book is a balanced and comprehensive approach to deliverance that will not only enforce your deliverance but will empower you to stay delivered and even help others. The writer; Pastor. Patrick Odigie is a seasoned and anointed man of God with a strong apostolic grace that has liberated multitudes from the oppression of darkness across the globe. I strongly recommend this book as a divine material that will enhance the liberty of those that Jesus came to set free"

Festus Adeyeye D. Min.
Abundant Life Christian Center
www.alccwinnershouse.org
THE HOME OF GLOBAL TRANSFORMERS

Rev. Patrick has been a friend of mine for many years. It was an honor to endorse his book on Deliverance. In my friendship with Patrick over the years, I can attest to his fervent love for The Lord and his great desire to see the people of God free wherever he is opportune to minister. This book is the natural fruit of the Calling of God in his life. The knowledge he has gained and the lessons he has learned through his faithful walk with God are now at your fingertips.

I greatly encourage all Christians everywhere to avail themselves of this masterfully written book on Deliverance. It is an eye opener to truly live a worthy Christian life before God and men. The author has done a very extensive work under the leading of the Holy Spirit. Writing this book as a Prophet/Teacher of the Word, you can rest assured that the Good Hand of God is upon Him. His personal life testifies to the truth revealed in this book. You are encouraged to read and recommend it to everyone in your sphere of influence. The content of this book is biblically sound and the Lord Himself will not leave you without blessing your life now and always.

PASTOR MICHAEL C. MORDI
Pastor at Wind & Fire International Christian Center
Rochester, Minnesota USA

The author Dr. Patrick Odigie explains why people are dying prematurely through strange circumstances, many living an unfulfilled Christian life, some struggling to live a victorious Christian life, many losing their glory and vision like Samson. He emphasizes among other issues, the need for believers to understand how deliverance works when deliverance occurs, where the deliverance minister derives his authority. He gives never before heard explanation of the deliverance team, preparation to serve in deliverance ministry, the significance of dreams to deliverance, the Place of discipleship in deliverance and the power and presence of the Holy Spirit. Are you a man or a woman of God, called into the deliverance ministry? This manual is a great tool in your hands for a successful deliverance ministry.

This book "The Deliverance That works" is a book not only for the oppressed that needs deliverance but also for every minister especially the deliverance minister, counselors, the fivefold ministry and all Christian leaders. It will help equip the body of Christ with the knowledge to identify areas of the enemy's operation, what gives the enemy the legal ground to attack and how to fight the enemy. It is a great ministry manual, simple and straight forward yet full of insights.

Dr. Patrick Odigie is not only a deliverance minister he is also being used by God to function in the office of the prophet with very sharp prophetic accuracy. Through reading this book, I am encouraged as an apostle of prayer in the marketplace and the government and challenged with his important messages to the church. I encourage you to read and re-read this book. May the Holy Spirit breathe on you and open your eyes of understanding to the truths expatiated herein.

Apostle (Dr) Helen-Naomi Godswill
Esther Generation Prayer Ministries and Resource Centers
Alpharetta. Georgia. The United States of America

Preface

For many believers in Christ, addressing the myriad of internal conflicts, endless struggles, and contradictions that confront them daily, definitely, require spiritual grit and determination. There is also need to lift spiritual curtains and expose the secret layers of hidden demonic contaminations tucked away in a remote past of generational demonic influences and corruptions.

Hidden demonic covenants, curses, and a laundry list of self-inflicted wounds resulting from inappropriate interactions with controlling territorial demonic powers through ignorance and carelessness must be uncovered and cleared out.

To be sure, the ability to break free and live a meaningful, productive and fulfilling life calls for addressing critical issues in deliverance and aggressive warfare. Unfortunately, large sections of the Body of Christ are burdened with little understanding of effective deliverance training, and the devil's business thrives on ignorance. This needless darkness has proven to be problematic, leaving many genuine believers stuck at the crossroads of unidentified conflicts, delays, painful losses, and frustrations.

The Word of God declares, "*My people are destroyed for lack of knowledge*" (Hosea 4:6). The Holy Spirit, writing through the Apostle Paul, admonishes us to be abreast of Satan's devices:"*Lest Satan should get an advantage of us: for we are not ignorant of his devices*" (2 Corinthians 2:11).

There is indeed much to thank God for in Deliverance Ministry today. However, much of the practice of deliverance ministry in this generation on closer observation seem deficient of a real sound scriptural foundation. Just the other day, I heard a well-meaning and respectable Deliverance Minister define Deliverance as the act of casting out devils. This individual is a true laborer in the kingdom, but his incomplete understanding of the operational definition of deliverance like many other well-meaning servants of God engenders serious problems as it sets out on a faulty premise.

If we embark on a journey without knowing where we are headed, how can we know for sure that we have reached our destination ultimately? While the process of deliverance entails casting out of demons, it is far more than that; you cannot cast out sin, and while we are commanded to mortify the flesh, we can neither cast out the flesh nor the world we live in and these all impact on our deliverance from day to day.

The Preaching of deliverance is prevalent, and the true teaching of deliverance is scarce and much limited in scope. What is the implication of this? While preaching can warn and motivate a desire for the change of outcomes, it is sound teaching in all wisdom that can impart the actual know how to secure those desirable outcomes.

This is why every believer must be armed with an adequate knowledge of the principles, purposes, and processes of total deliverance from the works of the devil. What Christ purchased for us with His Blood is total freedom from everything that is contrary to God's desire for our lives. And until this is achieved, no true believer must relent.

It is in furtherance of this goal of absolute freedom in Christ that this book "Deliverance That Works" (also available as a three-volume book) has been written. This first section dwells on the meaning, necessity, and ramifications of deliverance, while the other two sections build on this foundation to explore other crucial issues and answer nagging questions on this very important subject. I expect that this book will be used by deliverance workers, spiritual warfare workers, and ministers of the gospel to help them understand the subject in depth. It is my prayer that as you read, you will experience Holy Spirit-inspired enlightenment that will position you for total emancipation from every bondage and limitation.

Introduction

Dear Reader, welcome, and congratulations. What you have in your hand is an explosive wealth of information about the ministry of Deliverance. I have carried these revelations in my heart and shared them as much as I could in the last thirty-some years. Thankfully, am finally able to present these truths to a wider audience after yearning for so long to do so. First, let me emphasize that all the works of our Lord are both profound and powerful in our lives. That said, the Ministry of Deliverance holds a special place in my heart for many important reasons.

The devil prefers to operate from behind the scene; unknown and undetected. That way, he can quietly destroy people leaving the victims groping in the dark for answers. On the other hand, when people somewhat realizes that he is behind their misfortune and struggles, he then tries to pass himself off as very powerful leaving his victims feeling obsessed and helpless. True knowledge of Bible-based Deliverance Ministry will dispel these lies any day. The Word of God declares, "My people are destroyed for lack of knowledge" and again, "we are not ignorant of the devices of satan lest he gains an advantage over us. The devil may have some power but he is a creature and a fallen one who has lost his position with God and can no longer maintain the originality of his power.

The Deliverance Ministry demonstrates in a visible manner, the complete triumph of our Lord Jesus Christ over the power and works of the devil. Understandably, the devil as of necessity fights this Ministry like no other. The devil presides over a vast Kingdom of fallen Angels, Demons and humans who, compared to the Kingdom of our blessed Savior are weak and very vulnerable. This results from the fact that even though satan has power, he lacks the authority to exercise power; because he is no longer in the service of the owner of 'All Power.' To survive his weak position, satan relies on smart lies called devices or strategies. Proper instruction in warfare exposes this weak aspect of our enemy and put in the open, things he would rather keep secret. This fact is one of the reasons I love Deliverance Ministry; it embarrasses the devil while instantly granting much-needed relief to the oppressed.

Purpose

There is indeed much to thank God for in Deliverance Ministry today. However, much of the practice of deliverance ministry

in this generation on closer observation seem deficient of a real sound scriptural foundation. The proclamation of liberty to the captives is, thankfully strong in many Church circles. Proclamation (preaching) may stimulate faith and a desire for the change of outcomes but it is solid teaching in all wisdom that will help God's people to reach those desirable outcomes. My purpose in this book is to address perceived gaps in the ministry of Deliverance Today.

Presentation
This is an ambitious attempt at dealing with the various aspect of the Deliverance Ministry in a single volume. The entire book can be conveniently divided into three sessions and readers may then choose their preferences as their need may determine from time to time. The first session, I will call the basic foundations. This aspect addresses the scriptural contexts in which proper Deliverance should be understood and practiced.

The second aspect of the book focuses on critical issues that must be properly understood and reckoned with to avoid painful delays in receiving the benefits of Deliverance. The third and final aspect of the book is intended to help those who may be sensing a call into this aspect of ministry. Deliverance Ministry is at the forefront of the battles of light against darkness. To succeed well in this ministry, certain fundamental principles of the Anointing, and training in Righteousness, Consecration, and Accountability and team building must be well understood and accepted. Finally, I have included some actual Deliverance Cases at the appendix and I believe they make interesting reading; check them out.

CHAPTER 1

My Dysfunctional Early Years

◆◆◆◆◆◆

I was born into a domestic war zone. My father had five wives and twenty-eight biological children. Because of this complicated polygamous setup, my father existed for all of his children, but each mother existed only for hers. Distrust ruled the household. Each woman went to desperate measures to sustain herself and sought out whatever local help was available in order to secure the survival of her children. And because the main sources of help they could access were demonic, witchcraft activity was inevitable. When my mother was pregnant with me, local witches in the area visited her and demanded my life. According to my mother, they visited physically and quietly informed her that she was pregnant with a male child and they gave her the option to either surrender me to them, or she would not be able to have another child. She opted to keep me, and so, I became her last born.

MY DYSFUNCTIONAL EARLY YEARS

As I grew up closely with my mother, I came to understand that she was involved in a marine-based religion; that is, she believed that she originated from a river spirit and raised an altar in our home to the marine goddess. My father himself was a medium, which I later realized was founded in a deep relationship with ancestral powers and the Leviathan spirit. As a child, I was often in my mother's company as she consulted with and patronized various traditional witch-doctors. The paraphernalia of witchcraft and their semi-prophetic ability left an outstanding impression on my young mind.

At a very early stage in life, I was introduced to sexual activities which opened the doorway for Satan to strengthen his hold on my life. Though I was fascinated by the more appealing faith of Christianity, my attempts to practice it were to no avail. I did not understand who Jesus was, and I certainly was not saved.

In 1975, my family (that is, my mother and her children) underwent a severe crisis that pushed my mother to join a syncretic movement called Celestial Church of Christ. It was a church that mingled biblical truths with practices bordering on the occult. This new form of worship was easy to transition to, as the same spirits that were active in our traditional occult practice and rituals were very active in the Celestial Church movement experience (i.e. the predictive tongue and the Seeing Eye that flows from Leviathan involvement and marine spirits).

My mother joined the movement in 1975, bringing all her children on board and going further to establish branches of the movement in our family and neighboring villages. This was where I called church until 1984 when I got saved through an encounter with the Lord Jesus. Before then, however, my entire life had come to revolve around Women, booze, and parties. I had reached a point where I decided that Christianity was not for me– not because Christianity was not valid, but because as a young man, I had become so entrenched in sexual perversion and felt helpless. Since I knew I couldn't combine wayward living with the tenets of Christianity, I let go of Christianity.

I would jokingly tell my friends back in those days: "I will have fun now and go to hell later." Once I made that decision, I gave into a riotous life. I partied and drank excessively anywhere the opportunity presented itself, and I would argue with anyone who dared to preach to me about Jesus Christ.

On February 28, 1984, at about 10:30p.m. at the University of Calabar, Hall 3, Room One, (in Nigeria) I was preparing to go to a party in town with my friend, Chris Morris when I overheard two young men talking about Jesus. I went over to argue with them as was my habit, mainly to prove to them that they did not know what they were saying. In the course of the argument, one of the young men, Lambert Ibe, dropped on his knees, looked me straight in the eye and started sobbing sorrowfully. That made an impression on me.

I remember thinking to myself, "Why is this man crying for me as if I am dead?" The second young man, Tony Onawakpo, whom I later regarded as my spiritual father, looked straight into my eyes and asked me, "Patrick, why don't you repent?" Those words went through me. I wanted to argue but I could not. For the first time, I found myself speaking from my heart, saying, "Yes, I know that Jesus is true; I know that the salvation experience is real, but I do not want to flatter myself because I know that I am incapable of sustaining a relationship with the Lord."

I imagined that my previous foray into "church" was equal to true Christianity and I thought that since I was frequently running after women, there was no way of sustaining that kind of relationship without offending God. I said to the young man: "Imagine that you commit a crime and go before the judge who then sets you free. You commit more crimes, and you are brought before the same judge again and he sets you free. Imagine that you keep coming and going like that for a season, but after a given point in time, you realize that you are not able to use the freedom." I told him I was better off as I was, and Jesus would be better off if I did not come to Him because I would frequently go back and break His heart.

"Patrick," Tony said to me, "The Bible says that we as human beings must forgive one another seventy times seven. That is, if an individual offends you 490 times, keep forgiving. If God can ask that kind of standard from mere humans, will He not forgive you so many more times, provided that right now you are truly repentant and sorry?" That went through me again. It was as if I could literally see the Father, Son, and Holy Spirit right there saying, "If you are prepared to repent now, your sins will be forgiven."

At that moment, I thought about the countless women in my life. I thought about the booze, I thought about the parties, and the words that came out of my mouth were "I cannot stand." Everything in me wanted me to say yes, but I knew I could not stand. I started to turn away and leave, but as I turned, my face connected with a poster on the wall. It was a poster of Jesus, with His bruised, battered, and bloodied Body. As my attention fell on that poster, I was arrested. I could not move. For the first time, the piece of paper and drawing became meaningful to me. *That was the Almighty God who loved me and was stripped naked on that wood.* As I looked at it, I could not turn away. I dropped on my knees, pointed at the poster and asked, "God, did you do that for me? Did you do that for me?"

Suddenly, the poster transformed and it was as if I was transported back in time, seeing Jesus on the Cross going through the horrors. He spoke to me, saying, "Patrick, not only did I do this for you, I did it without saying one word in My defense because I knew you could not stand on your own. All you have to do is to look at this love and say you do not want it, and I will not bother you again. But remember, I did this without saying one word in My defense knowing that you could not stand on your strength. Do you still say you cannot stand?" Somehow, a voice within me, and in spite of me, said: "Lord, I can stand." I fell on my face, weeping, sobbing over my sins, the life I had lived: my selfishness, my rottenness, the corruption.

When I got up, two and half hours later, a few things happened. My friend with whom I was going to the party got angry and left. The Christians surrounded me and were jubilating, singing joyfully to the Lord. As I wanted to get up, the power of God hit me, and I fell back. It was as if something was dissolving in my heart, and a movie of my life was passing by me. I felt so sorry for all that I had done. Then I was inflated with love for God. It was such deep love that filled me completely.

When I finally got up, a sense of peace and a new tenderness and love for God overwhelmed me. I got scared because I was reflecting on how I had wasted my life chasing shadows, not knowing that this was the real deal. Now that I had experienced it, I feared that I might wake up in the morning and find out it was a mere dream and I so badly wanted it to be for real. I stayed awake throughout that night. The following morning I was the first to arrive at the Protestant chapel.

That experience marked a dramatic turnaround in my life. I did not have to struggle to live a righteous life. All the women, all the booze, all the parties were instantly gone. I was saved, I was born again, I was happy in my Savior. Old things had passed away; all things had become new. I was set free by the Son of God, and I was free indeed.

Indeed? Well, at least, for a season I enjoyed unprecedented peace and love for the Lord. I would stay in my little corner, looking at my little poster that said: "Smile, Jesus Loves You." I skipped sleep many nights; I was so joyful that I just wanted to sing the praises of my Savior and Lord. In fact, my salvation caused a stir in the university because the people I used to hang out with immediately named me a fanatic, and the Christian community nicknamed me 'Holy Ghost Brother.'

BREAKTHROUGH PROPHETIC DELIVERANCE PRAYERS

1. Lord Jesus Christ, I know You are real! Make Yourself known to me in a deep, personal, and new way like never before.

2. Remove the veil of darkness (Religion, Demons, and Flesh) that stands in my way. Oh God, let the light of Your

glory in the face of Jesus burn away every form of darkness that seeks to hold me back from perfect knowledge and experience of who You truly are.

3. Lord God, I desire and pray to know You and be filled completely with Your love that far surpasses human ability to understand. I ask to be made complete in Your love.

4. Father of Love, life, and light, strip away from my life, every limiting self-imposed notions of You that are incorrect. Let Your perfect and complete love that heals set me free to be all that You created me to be.

5. Father of life, I surrender myself completely to You today. Let the River of Your Love and Joy overwhelm me and take me past my fears, hesitations, hurts, memories of abuse, pains and channel the currents of my life into meaning fulfillment of my destiny

6. Lord Jesus Christ, I pray that as I read this book on Deliverance, Faith and Love will be my guiding principle and Your Blessed Holy Spirit will bring me into unique understanding.

7. Finally, in the mighty name of Jesus Christ, I declare according to the Word of God that I am who God says I am

and that every devil in hell is subject unto me through the Mighty Name of my Lord and Savior Jesus Christ.

8. Give Him praise forever more.

CHAPTER 2

My Introduction into Deliverance

The Lord is very effective as a Shepherd. Psalms 78:70-72 shows us this truth:

> "He chose David also his servant, and took him from the sheepfolds: From following the ewes' great with young he brought him to feed Jacob, his people, and Israel his inheritance. So he fed them according to the integrity of his heart; and guided them by the skillfulness of his hands."

Here, the Lord is represented as David; that's why it says that He called David out to feed His inheritance, Jacob, and to lead His people Israel. And He fed them according to the integrity of His heart and guided them by the skillfulness of His hands.

Two powerful attributes of the Lord are portrayed here. He has complete integrity. In His integrity, He is thoroughly committed to us to the point of giving His life for ours. The Lord is also very skillful as a Shepherd. He knows how to guide each one of us. He does not throw everything at us at once.

Following my conversion, I spent some time basking in the euphoria of my newfound faith. I busied myself with writing gospel songs. I was on fire for God. You would have had to be in my situation to know the joy I felt at being free from the grip of sin, which, in my case, was a sexual perversion. My life had been so perverted that I would have a girlfriend and would go to bed with her sister, and with her friend. I would pick up prostitutes by the wayside, and supplement with masturbation. I would go to bed with a girl knowing that she was not faithful to me but would still sleep with her. So, just knowing that I was free from sexual bondage was a most beautiful experience for me.

I had thought that was all. Quite frankly, I poured myself completely into Christianity. (This is expected of every true believer, anyway). I acquired every faith material I could lay hands on, not minding the cost. I had been used to spending lots of money on booze and women, but this time I was buying Bibles and all kinds of faith materials. I was growing rapidly in the faith. Within the first six months of my salvation experience, one would have thought that I had been a Christian for years. I was like an ordained minister, due to the knowledge of the Word of God I had acquired just by zealously loving the Lord.

But, then, some things began to happen.

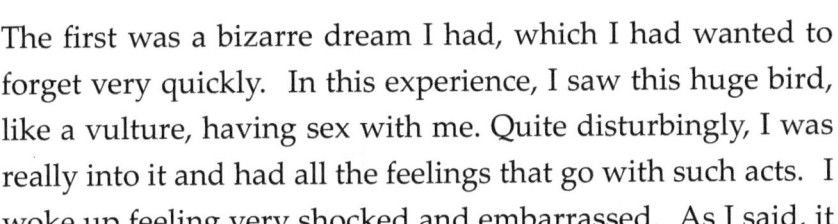
EMBARASSING DREAM EXPERIENCE

The first was a bizarre dream I had, which I had wanted to forget very quickly. In this experience, I saw this huge bird, like a vulture, having sex with me. Quite disturbingly, I was really into it and had all the feelings that go with such acts. I woke up feeling very shocked and embarrassed. As I said, it was an experience I had wanted to forget quickly, but it left a mark in my mind.

On another occasion, my friend and I had gone to minister Holy Spirit baptism to a fellow sister. As we were speaking in tongues, with our hands on her head, she suddenly slumped and began to foam at the mouth and twist like a snake. I beckoned to my friend and said, "This is a demon. We did not prepare for this. The Lord had told us to fast today, but we did not fast. The Bible says this kind does not go out but by prayer and fasting, but we did not fast." I was quickly talking my friend and myself out of faith while the sister was on the ground twisting.

But the Lord has a sense of humor. At that point, the demon manifesting spoke through the sister and said, "Lucifer, help me! Lucifer, help me!" That caused us to roar back to life. Really? *Was the demon calling Lucifer right where God the Father, the Son and the Holy Ghost were?* We went ahead and cast out the devil. So, right there, Brother Patrick cast out his first demon! But I soon forgot about the incident and continued to enjoy my newfound faith in God.

However, not long after this, I was on summer holiday and visited my village. As I was walking through a bushy area, I thought I heard some people praying in the bush. I was curious and went closer, only to find two young men praying for another young man. They belonged to a particular Pentecostal church. I asked them why they were praying for him in the bush and they replied that they were conducting deliverance and that two snails had already left and there was another one in there. That sounded very bizarre to me. *Snails?* I thought those young men just wanted to give Christianity a bad rap; so I stopped them and sent them away. They obeyed me and left, but now I believe that encounter was one of the first attempts the Lord had made to introduce me into deliverance ministry but I was not ready for it.

The next experience would be later on when I read a book written by the late Victoria Eto, titled, **The Forces of Darkness**. It was scary. The book was an exposition on Ephesians 6,

MY INTRODUCTION INTO DELIVERANCE

outlining in detail the structure of Satan's kingdom, namely, principalities, powers, rulers of darkness and spiritual wickedness in high places– and the powers that go with each. She was someone who had previously served Satan and was at one point in bed with Lucifer, and so had inside information into his kingdom. The book frightened me, so I put it aside.

After completing my first degree, the Lord led me to the northern part of Nigeria, which is predominantly Muslim, for my National Youth Service program. There, I led the Christian Youth Corps' Fellowship as the Prayer Secretary. I would fast and often pray at night. Within this period, I had some bizarre experiences. Often, when I interceded in the place of prayer, my spirit would be transported to pray in the spirit realm. On one of these occasions, as I prayed, the Holy Spirit transported me to a spiritual prison where people were in shackles. In this spiritual prison, Christians were being defiled, and all kinds of things bordering on satanic pollutions went on. One of the leaders of that satanic prison tried to get me compromised; but as I resisted, they threw me down, and I was soon back in my body, still praying.

While at the Christian Youth Corps' Fellowship, the power of God was strong at our meetings. People were being delivered. I was just now being introduced into deliverance. I had a lot of impacts there, but the light began to flash in my own spirit that I needed help. Suddenly, the sickness that I used to have as a child resurfaced. I was frequently having recurring episodes of fever, which were becoming protracted and interminable.

My old habits of quarreling and anger were also fast coming back. We would have quarrels and fights at the executive meetings of the Christian Youth Corps Fellowship. On top of that, I would continue to have bizarre dreams. I knew I was in trouble and that I needed help. But where would I find it? This was when I remembered the deliverance book I had read (*The Forces of Darkness*).I asked about the author and was told that a branch of her ministry was located some 500 miles away from my station. I was serving in Maiduguri, and the ministry was in Makurdi, all in Northern Nigeria.

At the end of the month, when I got my paycheck, I traveled down to Makurdi to seek my deliverance. My struggle for freedom intensified on the trip. Public transportation in those days was often overloaded, and it so happened that a young woman whom I had never met before sat by me on this trip. She threw her leg over mine, and I did not even make the least effort to resist. Instead, I was quietly enjoying the warm contact. I knew I was in deep trouble. Old habits and desires were making a comeback. However, in wisdom, I did not tell her who I was or where I was going. I did not give her any information about myself or ask anything of her. I was just waiting to disembark from the vehicle to go and get help. When we disembarked, I went and traced the ministry in a hurry.

 MY DELIVERANCE COUNSELING AND CLEANSING

When I got to my destination, the man of God I met there was used of the Lord to open the proverbial "Pandora's Box" of my life. He counseled me thoroughly. That counseling was the most probing interrogation of my life to date. All the rotten details of my past life, which I thought were no longer relevant being then a born-again Christian– he dug them all up and wrote them down. After that, he formed a prayer list and assigned two young men to pray for me.

I was disgusted when I saw those assigned to pray for me. *What could such young men know?* I was like Naaman, the Syrian, in the Bible story. I was so determined not to let them touch me. They, apparently, sensed my pride and did not try to touch me. They called me aside and prayed a very simple prayer, pleading the Blood of Jesus. They still did not touch me, but as they were pleading the Blood of Jesus, it was as if something hit me. I felt as if I was under anesthesia. I felt dizzy and began to foam at the mouth. At the same time, I was coughing up phlegm.

For one hour, I could not stop bringing up these things as these simple young men prayed. At the end of the prayer, I felt washed from within. It was as if I had been scrubbed from within. I felt clean; I felt pure. I asked, "Do you guys have any books on this thing?" They brought three books written by the leader of the ministry. They were entitled, *The Forces of Darkness; How I Served Satan Until Jesus Delivered Me* (which is a testimony book); and *Exposition on Water Spirits*. I read all of them within one week and went into fasting as I desperately wanted to know more about this phenomenon.

This is what launched my deliverance ministry. Soon after this experience, I went straight ahead into helping other people. Every other thing that happened, all the crises that were to follow– indeed the warfare that was to follow were intense and severe– but the Lord trained and sustained me. This was how I entered into deliverance ministry in 1985 to this present day.

BREAKTHROUGH PROPHETIC DELIVERANCE PRAYERS

1. Lord God my Savior, I love and adore You. I completely renounce all hidden things of darkness in my life and destiny in the mighty Name of Jesus Christ, my Lord.

2. Precious Father of light, let Your light expose and rebuke every layer of darkness in my life in Jesus name.

3. Lord God, in the precious Name of Jesus, I invite You to confront any hold of darkness in my life and set me free

from satanic yokes, burdens, and limitations in the mighty name of the Lord Jesus Christ.

4. I receive the God kind of faith to confront and defeat every satanic investment in my body, life, and destiny in the mighty name of Jesus.

5. I apply the blood of Jesus Christ to neutralize every satanic covenant in my life and declare such evil covenants nullified, broken and destroyed in the mighty name of Jesus.

CHAPTER 3

What is Deliverance?

Deliverance is the action of being rescued or set free; the act of delivering or the condition of being delivered. It means liberation, release, delivery, discharge, rescue, emancipation, salvation or bail out. (Oxford Dictionary).

The following Scripture verses reveal some useful insights into what deliverance entails.

> "But upon mount Zion shall be deliverance, and there shall be holiness; and the house of Jacob shall possess their possessions. And the house of Jacob shall be a fire, and the house of Joseph a flame, and the house of Esau for stubble, and they shall kindle in them, and devour them; and there shall not be any remaining of the house of Esau; for the LORD hath spoken it. And saviors shall come up on mount Zion to judge the mount of Esau; and the kingdom shall be the LORD's."

(Obadiah 1:17, 18, 21).

Deliverance is total liberation and freedom from factors and agents that hinder or seek to hinder a man or a woman from enjoying the full benefits of their covenant relationship with God in Christ Jesus. (late Victoria Eto with my emphasis on the covenant dimension) ..2 In other words, deliverance is a focused subject, predicated upon a covenant. I say *focused* in the sense that an individual seeker cannot benefit from the true experience of deliverance without embracing a committed relationship with the true and living God who alone delivers. Some people are deceived into thinking that they can just use God to resolve their issues and move on to live as they wish, but true deliverance entails committing to God in a covenant relationship, and that is freedom indeed. God will not deliver, except an individual takes hold of His covenant. Similarly, the devil cannot bind anyone, except there is some sort of covenant. The enemy actively seeks to bring people consciously or unconsciously into different types of binding covenant relationships, whereby he can exploit, oppress, suppress, defraud, kill, and destroy them. But for an individual to experience true deliverance, they have to take hold of God's covenant.

The entire Bible itself is, broadly speaking, divided into two covenants, called the Old Covenant (first covenant between Jehovah God and the nation of Israel) and the New Covenant (offered to the whole world through the sacrifice of our Lord Jesus Christ). The revelation of covenants in the Scriptures is both profound and progressive, but the consummation of all and by far the most powerful covenant is that between the Father and the Son on behalf all mankind. This is referred to as the "Blood of the Everlasting Covenant." **Hebrews 13:20 speaks of this:** *"Now the God of peace that brought again from the dead our Lord Jesus, that great shepherd of the sheep, through the blood of the everlasting covenant."*

In other words, in eternity past, God saw that man would fall from grace and become a victim of crafty and wicked spirits; therefore He prepared a covenant before laying the foundation of the earth. That is why the Bible says in **Revelation 13:8** that the Lord Jesus Christ is the Lamb of God slain from the foundation of the earth. In other words, Calvary, even though a reality some 2000 years ago, is nevertheless a manifestation of a divine reality in eternity past. The only valid way for a man and woman to experience true freedom is to enter into this covenant that God the Father had with the Son, which was consummated on Calvary through the death, burial, and resurrection of our Lord Jesus Christ.

> *"If we cast out a demon from an individual, we have not delivered him or her as yet. We have only given the person temporary relief."*

BEYOND CASTING OUT OF DEMONS

When dealing with the subject of deliverance, people mostly focus on getting rid of demons. This is basic, but getting rid of demons is not in itself deliverance. If we cast out a demon from an individual, we have not delivered him or her as yet. We have only given the person temporary relief. True deliverance deals with the factors that validate and empower the enemy's presence in the life of an individual. Such factors include sin, the flesh, and worldliness.

There are many doorways that the enemy exploits in order to sneak into people's lives. These will be dealt with in a later part of the book. It must, however, be emphasized that when the enemy has gained entrance into an individual, he doesn't come to play. He busies himself reproducing his evil nature in the character of the oppressed person. This is why demonic intentions or manifestations are often hidden behind the exaggerated behavior of the flesh in certain aspects of the human soul or personality.

When it comes to effective deliverance, you have to address the flesh also. You cannot cast out the flesh even though you can cast out demons. You also cannot cast out sin. Sin is a transgression against God, and it is what gives the enemy legitimacy. Anything that is not in agreement with God is a sin, and sin requires repentance. Where there is repentance of sin and denial or crucifixion of the flesh, the authority of the Holy Spirit will become available to force out the devil and to keep him out of the individual. This is what I mean by dealing with factors in addition to casting out the demon spirits.

WHERE CAN WE FIND TRUE DELIVERANCE?

Again, Obadiah 1:17 says, *"Upon Mount Zion there shall be deliverance."* Where do we find deliverance? It is upon Mount Zion. Mount Zion refers to the presence of God's Holy Spirit and power. Why do I say this? There are two opposing kingdoms – the Kingdom of God and the kingdom of Satan. Man is at the center or focus of these two kingdoms. When the power of God confronts the power of the enemy, we immediately see that which had been hidden begin to come to the surface. Mount Zion refers to God's stronghold, God's power-base, and it is activated when true believers in Jesus Christ gather together in true fellowship or worship.

There is also a historical side to this. In the time of King David of Israel, the people had been living in the Promised Land without actually possessing the **full** inheritance. When the territory of Canaan was conquered and divided by Joshua, there were pockets of places within the Promised Land which were still under the enemies' occupation. These were strongholds that had not yet been overthrown. One of such places was Jerusalem, inhabited by the Jebusites. They were so strong and the city so fortified that they had thought nobody could assail them. When David's generals received the mandate to take over territories within the Promised Land, the Jebusites boasted and said, "Look, we do not need to have able-bodied men to guard our cities, even our lame and blind are enough to ward you off because our gates are so fortified that nobody can penetrate anyway."

However, David challenged his mighty men to break through and conquer the city. After that, David reconstructed it and made it his own stronghold. So Zion became the power-base of the capital in Jerusalem where he ruled physically.

> *"And the king and his men went to Jerusalem unto the Jebusites, the inhabitants of the land: which spake unto David, saying, Except thou take away the blind and the lame, thou shalt not come in hither: thinking, David cannot come in hither. Nevertheless David took the strong hold of Zion: the same is the city of David. And David said on that day, Whosoever getteth up to the gutter, and smiteth the Jebusites, and the lame and the blind, that are hated of David's soul, he shall be chief and captain. Wherefore they said, the blind and the lame shall not come into the house. So David dwelt in the fort, and called it the city of David. And*

David built roundabout from Millo and inward. And David went on, and grew great, and the LORD God of hosts was with him." (2 Samuel 5: 6-10).

What is true physically is also true spiritually. There is a spiritual Zion. The Bible tells us about the spiritual Zion in **Hebrews 12:22-24**. We see the constituents of the spiritual Zion, which the Bible tells us are the company of innumerable angels. The church of the firstborn whose names are written in heaven, the presence of God the Father as the Judge of All, the presence of the Lamb of God, as the mediator between God and man, and the blood of sprinkling that speaks better things.

So, we have the blood of the Lamb, which is the legal basis, the legal ground, on which God delivers; we have the firepower of God's Holy Spirit that compels compliance and obedience from the enemy; we have the angels, innumerable ones the Bible says, that cannot be numbered.

TWO KINGDOMS AT WAR

So we immediately see that any time there is a confrontation, two kingdoms are at war – one is weak, and the other is strong..3 (Derek Prince notes of Spiritual Warfare) The stronger one is the Kingdom of Jesus Christ, of course. As strong as Satan's kingdom may pretend to be, before the power of the Living God, it is a very weak kingdom. That becomes

WHAT IS DELIVERANCE

> *"There is no point in trying to minister deliverance to a man or a woman who is not prepared to surrender to the Lordship of Jesus Christ."*

quickly visible when there is a confrontation. This is why Satan hates deliverance. It brings into the open things he would rather keep secret; besides, it reveals the superiority of the firepower and the Kingdom of our Lord Jesus Christ over his. So, the will to deliver, the power to deliver, the covenant that conveys the deliverance, the legal grounds of the Blood of Jesus— all of these God has provided, and man can access them through faith in the Lord Jesus Christ.

Unless people are willing to surrender to the authority of the Lord Jesus Christ, they really cannot be delivered. There is no point in trying to minister deliverance to a man or a woman who is not prepared to surrender to the Lordship of Jesus Christ. The Scripture tells us that such cases will lead to even more complications. We understand from **Matthew 12:43-45** that when an unclean spirit is gone out of a man, it goes about seeking rest and, finding none, it says, "I will go back to my house where I was evicted." And it goes back and gets seven more wicked spirits and they invade that man or woman, and the state of that person is worse than at the beginning.

This is to say that unless somebody is prepared to renounce the devil and submit to the Lordship of Jesus Christ, any attempt to minister deliverance to such an individual will be both a waste of time and a complication of an already existing bad situation.

THE FIRST LEVEL OF DELIVERANCE

The first level of deliverance is to surrender to the Lordship of Jesus Christ. In fact, I often say you cannot deliver somebody who is not already delivered. In other words, the basis on which you and I, as deliverance ministers, can administer deliverance to an individual is that they are already delivered or already under the covenant of Jesus Christ.

> *"By the force of translation... every act of aggression or oppression by the devil becomes illegal and therefore can be judged and destroyed through application of the Word of God and the power of the Holy Spirit in deliverance ministration."*

Colossians 1:13 says that we have redemption through the Blood of Jesus, having been translated by the Father from under the dominion of the kingdom of Satan and darkness, into the Kingdom of His dear Son. In other words, by receiving Jesus Christ, we enter into the benefit of divine translation. We are immediately removed from under the rule, dominion, and government of Satan, and grafted into the rule and government of the Lord Jesus Christ.

By the force of translation, we are moved from the state of the fallen man, past the fallen angels, even past the elect angels, and grafted into God's intimate family as sons and daughters of the Living God. Because of this, every act of aggression or oppression by the devil becomes illegal and therefore can be judged and destroyed through the application of the Word of God and the power of the Holy Spirit in deliverance ministration.

PROPHETIC INSIGHT

Still in Obadiah 1:17-18; it says *"and there shall be holiness and the sons of Jacob shall possess their possessions."* Immediately, we begin to see that deliverance should lead to something; it should lead to holiness. Another word for holiness is "wholeness" or "completeness." Everything and anything in your life and in my life that makes us not to feel whole or complete, the power of the Holy Spirit wants to apply the Blood of Jesus and deal with that fragmentation in order to bring wholeness or completeness or holiness in us.

Not only does deliverance lead to holiness or completeness, but the Bible also says *"the sons of Jacob shall possess their possessions."* In other words, deliverance is one of God's

> *"You have to go after the enemy eyeball to eyeball, shoulder to shoulder, and cut him down."*

methods of transmitting the benefits of our inheritance in Christ to us as believers. Your deliverance is directly related to your inheritance. You have a certain inheritance in God, and the enemy wants to seize this. He is an aggressor, a ruthless, devious one, who does not play fair. That is why he has to be compelled by the power of God to yield his ground.

For male, female, old, young, new converts, ministers of the gospel– anything that infringes upon your inheritance is calling for divine attention and retribution. It means that what Jesus died to give you, the enemy wants to steal from you. You have to go after the enemy, eyeball to eyeball, shoulder to shoulder, and cut him down. We have a right to possess our possessions in God. You must be really "angry" about any gap in your life, any lack of fulfillment in your life, any sickness in your life, any oppression in your life, and in your family. You must be so angry and go to war to correct the situation.

The enemy cannot be allowed to get away with his illegality. It is illegal for a blood-bought child of God to live under satanic oppression. Something more that is said in this beautiful prophetic chapter in Obadiah is, *"and the house of Jacob shall be fire, and the house of Joseph a flame, and the house of Esau for stubble, and they shall kindle together, and there shall not be any remaining of the house of Esau"*. What is it saying?

> *"It is illegal for a blood-bought child of God to live under satanic oppression"*

THE THREE CATEGORIES OF PEOPLE IN CHURCH

First, the passage mentions the House of Jacob. **What is the House of Jacob?** Jacob is the one with a promise; the covenanted child. He had done nothing of his own holiness or righteousness; neither have you, but by the fact that you are in Christ Jesus, you are in covenant with the Almighty God. All that Jesus is, all that He paid for, all that is available to Him is available to you. So, in Christ Jesus, we are a type of the sons of Jacob.

Why the emphasis on Jacob? This is very interesting. God is a God of redemption. Jacob means "the tricky one," "the supplanter." In other words, he had the promise of God and was covered by covenant, but he was not very straight. And that is how many of us are. In certain aspects of our lives, we are still work-in-progress. There are struggles; there are fleshly, carnal, and sinful behaviors. I am not excusing that, but I am simply saying that whatever contradictions there are in the character of a child of God cannot invalidate the covenant. There is still a covenant, and that covenant stands.

Jacob was the one who had the promise but often did things his own way. God promised to cover him with fire. Fire burns. Thank God for the fire of the Holy Spirit. It burns wickedness; it burns the devil, but the same fire preserves the believer in

Christ Jesus. The fire of God is in the house of the Lord, covering the children of God and protecting them. When the Israelites left Egypt, God covered them with a pillar of cloud by day and a pillar of fire by night.

In the church of the living God today, people are at various levels of grace that they are walking in. However, if you are an authentic member of the Body of Christ, who still believes in Jesus Christ, you are covered by that fire. It says, *"the house of Jacob shall be fire."* Fire burns sin from our lives. It burns circumstances that the enemy can try to use to destroy us.

> *"Contradictions… in the character of a child of God cannot invalidate the covenant."*

I want to emphasize that this is very wonderful and meaningful because as Jacob departed from his uncle, Laban, God confronted him on the way. He wrestled with God, and the Bible says God turned his name from Jacob to Israel, meaning he was no longer a cheat but a prince of God, having power with God and power with man. In that encounter, God changed his name and said to him, "Your name shall no more be called Jacob but Israel."

Hundreds of years later, God confronted Moses in the burning bush in the Sinai wilderness and commissioned him to go to Egypt. Moses wanted to know from God what to say to Israel in Egypt. God told Him *"I AM THAT I AM...Thus shalt thou say unto the children of Israel, The Lord God of your fathers, the God of Abraham, the God of Isaac, and the God of Jacob, hath sent me unto you: this is my name forever, and this is my memorial unto all generations"* (Exodus 3:14-15).

Notice that God did not say 'the God of Israel' but instead, the God of Jacob; amazing! He is still the God of Abraham, God of Isaac, and God of Jacob. The mere fact that God identifies himself as the God of Jacob is meaningful and liberating to the soul. Jacob is the imperfect one but covered by a perfect God with a covenant relationship. This means even though we are still a work in progress in many respect, the devil cannot lay hold on us because we are covered by the blood covenant God has with the Lord Jesus Christ.

So, are you a child of God today in the house of the Lord, and you find that you are still work-in-progress and the enemy is trying to lie to you, suggesting to you that, based upon certain things in your life, he has to have you under oppression? I want to say to you, no way! That is not the gospel.

Of course, God does not want us to continue in sin so that grace may abound. No! We have been delivered from the power of sin. You are not under the law; you are definitely under grace. You are covered by the fire of God. If you were around me, I would kick out that devil from you. I wouldn't waste any time;

I wouldn't struggle with you because I stand under the authority of God to kick that devil out of your life. You deserve to be free. That is the Word of God.

 THE ANOINTING VERSUS THE GLORY (THE HOUSE OF JOSEPH)

Obadiah says that the House of Joseph shall be for a flame. What is the difference between fire and flame? **Fire burns but flame cuts.** The superior blue flame will cut iron. Flame speaks of the glory of God. The House of Joseph here is a reference to those within the Body of Christ who dare to pay the price of separation. Joseph was the separated one. He was separated from his brethren. The Bible says *"Let the blessing come 'on the head of Joseph, And on the crown of the head of him who was separate from his brothers,'"* (**Deuteronomy 33:16, NKJV**).

Because Joseph was separated from his brethren, he brought the blessing to the rest. He presented them with posterity. I am saying prophetically also that God will raise up a people with the anointing of Joseph within the church of the Lord Jesus, who will embrace the authentic spirit of consecration, and they will stretch out before God and embrace the flame and the glory.

In the fire, the anointing functions; but in the flame the

> *"The end of man is the beginning of the glory of God!"*

glory functions. What is the difference? God can anoint a man or woman who can have the Holy Ghost and fire but does not go all the way, and the enemy can still function through their flesh. But in the glory, the flame, the enemy does not have any equipment to work with because in the glory God judges the flesh but then brings and unleashes a higher level of authority. So there are people who are consecrated; and you who are reading this book, you will be one of those vessels whom God will give the courage to love Him passionately, to go past the regular profession of Christianity; and to go deeper and more intimate with Him.

You are going to seek God in fasting and prayer. You are going to cry after Him. You want to be like Him, and get hold of Him. And guess what? It is going to happen. The flame will be upon you. I believe that the Lord Jesus best exemplifies this. From time to time, He moved in that glory, and the enemy saw it, and demons were terrified and began to scream, "We know You, we know who You are, the Holy One of God, have You come to torment us before the time?"

That's the realm of glory. And where are the Joseph of this generation? I summon you to rise up. Rise up! Because God wants to use you on the earth today. In the anointing, the gifted man is in evidence; but in the glory, we come to the end of the man. The end of man is the beginning of the glory of God.

FASTING AND THE GLORY DIMENSION OF THE ANOINTING

The Lord spoke to me through a vision in December 2001. I was visiting the United Kingdom, fellowshipping with my esteemed friend, Pastor Jerome Obode, at the time. We enjoyed robust times of prayer and fasting at very fulfilling and productive levels during this visit. We were excited for more of the Lord and decided to proceed on a twenty-one day complete fast. The fasting barely got underway when I had a very telling trance.

In the vision, I saw the late Archbishop Benson Idahosa on a large podium, kneeling and with his hands on the floor at the same time. There was an empty chair by his side and, in the meantime, Pastor Enoch Adeboye of the Redeemed Christian Church of God came and sat on the empty chair across from the Archbishop. Suddenly, he placed his two feet over the Archbishop and in a seemingly disrespectful manner pushed him out of the stage. Just then, my eyes were opened, while still wondering how the gentle Pastor could do that to the late Archbishop.

The Holy Spirit of God began to explain the meaning of the revelation to me. He said that the two men represented different phases of His program and moves on the earth. According to the Holy Spirit, the late Archbishop represented the charismatic move, while Pastor Adeboye represented the glory move. In the charismatic move, He said, He anointed gifted men who attracted a large following to the Kingdom. The late Archbishop represented this and brought great respectability and appeal to the gospel. However, under the charismatic gift, anointed or gifted men can still be corrupted and bring the cause of the gospel into disrepute.

The glory move is very different, however. According to the Holy Spirit, "in the glory move, I don't need the gift of a man; instead, I kill the man. The end of man is the beginning of the glory of God."

In the charismatic move, the anointed man can still carry the flesh around, and the devil will work with that to impose limitations, containments, and corruption. In the glory move, the flesh is crucified and the enemy has no equipment with which to work. Fasting, according to God, is one of the instruments of death to the flesh. He used the anointed ministry of the late Archbishop Idahosa to pioneer the charismatic move in Nigeria, but He is using the ministry of Pastor E. A. Adeboye to pioneer the glory move.

THE HOUSE OF ESAU

This is the third level or category of people (house) in the Church of God. This house is a bad one. It is called the House of

Esau. Esau, in the Bible, is referred to as the profane one. The Bible says *"Lest there be any fornicator, or profane person, as Esau, who for one morsel of meat sold his birthright"* (**Hebrews 12:16**). It says further that, afterward, when he would have inherited the blessing, he was rejected. He was rejected and he found no room for repentance even though he sought it carefully with tears.

The implication of this is that the choices we make are very important. Your choice today is shaping your tomorrow. It is affecting every person around you. It is affecting heaven, and it is even affecting time and eternity. Our choices are very important to God and man.

There are too many people today who play around. They give God sentimental or emotional commitments. But when it comes to time to really make decisions, they do not take the narrow road; they want the easy way out. They practice the kind of Christianity the devil does not respect. The Lord will not honor such because His desire for us is to be a committed people. So the house of Esau is the profane. And God says the fire of Jacob and the flame of Joseph shall combine and destroy profanity from the house. The Bible says, in fact, that there shall be none remaining of the house of Esau.

I am so glad that God is not going to leave us in this defeated and humiliated state of the Church. The anointing of God, the outpouring of God's Holy Spirit, will come upon the Body of the Lord, and a people will rise on the earth who will love God passionately. They will give God radical commitment and will do exploits. The devil does not stand a chance. They will demonstrate the complete defeat of the enemy as they move in their end-time authority of the sons of God and fulfill their ministry on the earth.

The Bible says finally in **Obadiah 1:21**, *"And saviors shall come up on mount Zion to judge the mount of Esau, and the kingdom shall be the LORD'S."*

Note that it doesn't say, savior but ***saviors***. It is plural. Here is what this means: God will anoint some consecrated men and women who will be radical, and they will carry governmental authority. This is one thing that will be increasingly important as we press further into these end times. God is going to raise men and women, old and young, and release the government of the Lord Jesus upon them. They will experience governmental authority to judge profanity on the earth, to break curses, to undo burdens, and to release many into liberty; and I believe you and I are called to be a part of this beautiful army of the Lord Jesus Christ. Hallelujah! Thank you, Lord.

BREAKTHROUGH PROPHETIC DELIVERANCE PRAYER

1. Thank the Lord for the understanding of what deliverance is.

2. Decree aloud: I have come to Mount Zion; today I embrace my deliverance and declare my deliverance a living reality in the Mighty name of Jesus.

3. I acknowledge, confess and renounce every sin that exposed me to defilement and I repent of them (name all known sins and receive forgiveness and cleansing in the Mighty name of Jesus Christ).

4. I renounce every evil covenant existing in my life, home, family; I release the fire of God to consume every token in my life, giving the enemy legal right over me in Jesus' name.

5. I declare I am a blood bought child of God and the Blood of the everlasting Covenant speaks on my behalf. (Hebrews 9:12 and Hebrews 13:20)

6. I stand on my Blood Covenant with the Lord Jesus Christ today to renounce any evil covenant upon my life. I denounce any satanic covenant and command the curse to be broken and lifted in the mighty name of Jesus.

7. Sovereign Lord, mark me this day with the true spirit of consecration and separation from sin.

8. I take my place as the 'Joseph' of my family and declare I am the curse breaker and the reproach remover in my family in the mighty name of the Lord Jesus Christ.

9. Give God some praise and celebrate your progress so far.

The Deliverance Anointing

The Spirit of the Lord God is upon me; because the Lord hath anointed me to preach good tidings unto the meek; he hath sent me to bind up the brokenhearted, to proclaim liberty to the captives, and the opening of the prison to them that are bound; To proclaim the acceptable year of the Lord, and the day of vengeance of our God; to comfort all that mourn; To appoint unto them that mourn in Zion, to give unto them beauty for ashes, the oil of joy for mourning, the garment of praise for the spirit of heaviness; that they might be called trees of righteousness, the planting of the Lord, that he might be glorified. **Isaiah 61:1-3**

WHAT IS OUR BASIS OF DELIVERANCE?

There is a legal basis of deliverance and this is based upon our Blood Covenant with God made possible by the sacrifice of the Lord Jesus Christ. Revelation 12:11, says, *"and they overcame him – (that is, the devil* parenthesis mine), *by the Blood of the Lamb and by the word of their testimony and they loved not their lives even to death."Furthermore,* the Book of Hebrews 2:14-15 also assures us; that, *"Forasmuch then as the children are partakers of flesh and blood, he also himself likewise took part of the same; that through death he might destroy him that had the power of death, that is, the devil; And deliver them who through fear of death were all their lifetime subject to bondage."*

LEVELS OF DELIVERANCE
Level One - Jesus Paid the Full Price for our Deliverance
"He has anointed me to preach good news..."

Jesus Christ became a man, took on flesh so that He could suffer death in the flesh. As God, He could not die, but as a man, the God-man, He could die in the flesh, and He did that. His death fully paid the penalty of sin and the liabilities under those broken laws. By Almighty God raising Jesus from the dead, God was declaring sinful men none guilty if they would put their faith in Jesus so that the curse could be broken. Jesus' Resurrection made the final statement that sin is dealt with and that the ultimate power of the enemy, which is death is destroyed.

The sacrifice of the Lord Jesus has completely rendered Satan incapable of fulfilling his original plan in the life of any person who receives Jesus Christ as personal Savior and Lord. Based on this understanding, the Holy Spirit comes to enforce compliance with the terms of that Blood Covenant. When the Blood of Jesus is raised, the Holy Spirit steps in and breaks any prevailing curse(s). *When I see the blood, I will pass over you or overshadow you with my Holy Spirit* – Exodus 12:13.
Let us see how this works in reality:

THE REALITY

"He has anointed me to preach good news ... It is finished." (Isa 61:1; John 1:30)

The good news is that Jesus, the perfect, sinless Son, has taken the place of the vilest offender in a divine substitution: No matter the sin we have committed, God put it all on Jesus and punished Him until He died. Since death is the end of punishment for all men, when Jesus died, that was the reality. He died and was buried to put our sins away.

The burial of Jesus signifies the putting away of our sins and God raising Him to a new life signifies divine justification for the believer in Jesus Christ – this is eternal hope for all men.

The death, the burial, and the Resurrection of Jesus are the operations of God in securing our eternal salvation, healing, deliverance, and well-being. When the good news of the gospel is preached, those who humble themselves (the meek), believe and submit to the gospel, come into the benefit of the first level of deliverance. According to Colossians 1:13, they are immediately translated and removed from under the dominion of darkness and transferred to the Kingdom of Jesus Christ. The Bible records that they are placed in heavenly places in Christ Jesus, far above all principalities and powers (Ephesians 1:21; 2:6). This is to say that when you are in Jesus Christ, you are moved away from the class of sinful men, past the class of fallen angels, past the class of elect angels, and become children of the living God. God's DNA is implanted in you in the new life, and you can cry, "Abba, Father." This is the first level of deliverance.

Since you are no longer in Satan's kingdom, you are not under his rulership anymore, and anything he does against you is illegal from that point on. This is the reason the Blood of Jesus and the power of the Holy Spirit can begin to enforce the rule, government, and standard of God to remove and restrict every satanic oppression.

From the preceding, notice that under the deliverance anointing, the preaching of the gospel is the first level of deliverance.

LEVEL TWO – COUNSELING
To bind up the broken hearted

The next level is "To bind up the broken-hearted." This portion of the deliverance anointing is what I call Counseling. When people come to faith in Christ Jesus, we all have an experience of having dealt with the devil at some point, and most of us do not even know the nature of the bondage we carry. We do not know the full extent of our hereditary spiritual liabilities – things from our ancestors up to the fourth generation – that may still have a negative impact on the life we live today. This is where careful and strategic counseling comes in. I am not talking about just filling out a card, but having a real, trained Deliverance Counselor take the counselee on an introspective journey of his or her life to unearthing secrets, hidden curses, evil covenants, grounds for satanic pollution, infestation and bondage, and probing open doors that need to be cleaned out and closed against the enemy. If this thorough work is done at the beginning, folks experience speed in the Christian life. On the contrary, you find years of running in circles of pain and containment is possible where the enemy can severely limit the believer's progress. Sometimes some shut-down pains are uncovered, dealt with, and the demons enforcing those pains overthrown where proper counseling is allowed to take place.

Many people have been scarred by their childhood experiences – physical, sexual, emotional abuse, and traumatic experiences of different kinds. There are things one may have done during growing up days that may have further opened the door to the enemy. So many things are locked in there which need to be searched out and cleaned out. Sometimes in the process of cleaning them out, we again experience pain. The effective counselor can take the counselee skillfully past the place of pain into the place of healing and wholeness so that the power of controlling demons that revisit these past pains can be completely eradicated.

LEVEL THREE - PROCLAIM LIBERTY

"...to proclaim liberty to the captives, and the opening of the prison to them that are bound. To proclaim the acceptable year of the LORD, and the day of vengeance of our God; to comfort all that mourn."

Then, of course, he talks about proclaiming liberty to the captives. The above Scripture points to the preaching of deliverance to the captive and the opening of the prison to the bound. This refers to both the preaching and ministering of deliverance.

Here we have a lot of problems because the deliverance ministry has often been immersed in controversies. One of the reasons this is so is because there is a lack of understanding and proper teaching in this area. There are the preaching and the teaching aspects of deliverance. In fact, there should be more of the teaching of deliverance.

Quite frankly, many people who are not called into this area of ministry tend to make statements that mischaracterize it. On the contrary, I think it is very prideful for anyone to think that God has to rely only on specific people to get His job done. God has apportioned the different areas of the Gospel to each and every one of His children to the intent that men may be drawn closer to Him. As such, whatever we do not understand, we must desist from making loud statements.

I have been a servant of God for over thirty years in ministry, and I cannot claim to know many things or everything – I know some and I do not know others. The truth is, there is no one person who knows and understands the entire Bible. The Bible is too big for you and me to understand fully. We will have the whole eternity to know Him but the portion that is validly delivered, if we stay with it and not make loud statements, we will surely reduce confusion.

A lot has been said about deliverance that is not true; for instance, the idea that you cannot cast out a demon from a real believer. On the flip side, it also not true that an individual Christian cannot have a demon in his or her life. Then again, there are some who are called into this ministry and have not been well groomed, have made some mistakes that have further compounded the issue, and, so many people in the Body of Christ seeking deliverance these days do not understand the context of deliverance and what they are seeking. All of these bring complications. I trust God to use this book to shed some light on the subject because deliverance is a very valid and important part of the Gospel.

If you look at the ministry of Jesus, He was constantly confronting the devil and casting out demons from people. The Bible says of Him in Acts 10:38, *"How God anointed Jesus of Nazareth with the Holy Ghost and with power: who went about doing good, and healing all that were oppressed of the devil; for God was with him."* Jesus is with us. Christ Jesus is with us. He has commissioned us to go out. He said, "cast out devils, heal the sick, cleanse the lepers, and raise the dead. Freely have you received, freely give" (Matthew 10:8).

Satan does not like the deliverance ministry for one clear reason: in everything he does, he hides his intentions behind the scenes. However, when there is confrontation such as you see in casting out devils, his secrets are brought to the open. Every time Jesus had to cast out a demon or a devil out of a person, the person immediately became aggravated. You see, there are two kingdoms at war, and one is stronger than the other. Of course, the Kingdom of God has more fire power. Satan is infinitely inferior when confronted by the authentic power of God. He hates that, so he tries to caricature the ministry of deliverance to scare people off. In fact, during the time of the ministry of Jesus, he claimed that Jesus was casting out devils through the prince of devils. However, we need to know that the deliverance ministry is a genuine experience to build on and not to be made light of.

Again, He said, **"to proclaim the acceptable year of the Lord and declare the day of vengeance"** (verse 2). I believe we are in that territory right now where God is using men and women as judges in the kingdom to declare vengeance on behalf of those who are so severely violated in this dispensation. I have seen some things being done which appear to be on edge but I also realize that these are the days of vengeance. Certain types of prayers are being prayed that only a few years ago would have seemed scandalous, but because this generation is extremely perverted, the enemy has taken his evil work to another level. So do not be surprised when you see God raising people (ministers) who are fierce with a warring mentality towards destroying the works of the devil and declaring judgment on the agents of darkness because this is a clash between light and darkness. For this, we must give God praise, and for what we do not fully understand, seek wisdom from the Holy Spirit rather than make statements that confuse the entire matter.

Let us look at Luke 4:17-18 where Jesus quoted this same Scripture in direct reference to Himself:

And there was delivered unto him the book of the prophet Esaias. And when he had opened the book, he found the place where it was written, "The Spirit of the Lord is upon me, because he hath anointed me to preach the gospel to the poor; he hath sent me to heal the brokenhearted, to preach deliverance to the captives, and recovering of sight to the blind, to set at liberty them that are bruised."

LEVEL FOUR – REVELATION OF DIVINE TRUTHS

"...and recovering of sight to the blind..."

Look at this – recovering of sight. Recovering denotes a progressive process. Physical blindness can be healed in this hour, but also more particularly regarding deliverance. There is a progressive encounter with the Word of God which will result in Deliverance. When people first come into the Kingdom and become born again, they are counseled, and demons cast out of them, but it should not stop there. They should enlist in a progressive encounter with the revelation of God's Word. There is a serious problem of poor communication of the Word in the Church. Even in the best local assemblies where deliverance is emphasized, people are recycling bondage – just beating the same old drum over and over.

After deliverance has been conducted and curses broken, people should proceed further to the teaching of the Word of God because the Word of God is God Himself (John 1:1). The Word imparts life. We should progress from ministering deliverance, casting out the devil, breaking bondages and curses to taking people to the real deal – the Word of God. There is no deliverance outside of the Word of God. Today if there is anything needed, personally, I believe it is the Word of God. Value for the Word of God needs to be rediscovered.

There is no way the Church of Jesus Christ will escape deception of the enemy if we do not re-emphasize the Word of God; we need to bring the Word of God into its proper place, with proper emphasis. The Word of God is the foundation for everything in Christianity – the Word holds everything together. People must know that true freedom can only be found in the Word of God: Deliverance itself is a spirit of justice executing the Word of God on the devil's rebellion to bring liberty to the people of God.

REAL FREEDOM

When does deliverance occur?

Does deliverance occur when the devil is cast out from someone? NO! It occurs when someone has received the Word, submitted to the Word such that because of his or her submission, he or she gains the authority of the Word to resist the devil personally and put him to flight. That is why the Bible says, "*Submit yourselves to God, resist the devil, and he will flee from you* (James 4:7).

WHO IS A FREE PERSON?

A free person is not the one from whom demons are cast out – that is a relief. A free person is one who has submitted to the Word, and because he or she has submitted to the Word in all aspects of his or her life, he or she has the authority, without the help of any other, to personally resist the devil and put him to flight. That is a free person. Someone may have a spirit of anger manifesting as excessive, uncontrollable anger, and that might be the ground on which the devil can violate him over and over. This individual can be prayed for, the Blood applied, the curse is broken, and the demon cast away. He experiences a level of liberty, but that liberty must immediately be followed up by discipleship in the Word. Why? Because when demons have lived in a person, they come to reproduce their evil nature. So it is not enough to cast out the devil. The Word of God has to rearrange the nature of this person who has been violated and thus become exaggerated. For instance, the Bible says in Ephesians 4:26, *"be angry and sin not, let not the sun go down upon your wrath."* What happens is that after the spirit of anger is cast out, the flesh still needs to be crucified. This is when he takes that Word and begins to meditate on it. Before you know it, he will discover 'be angry and sin not' written in it.

Meditation on this discovered Word will help him and deliver him from the deposits of anger in his life. Yes, the occasion will come to be angry when your sense of justice is violated, but the Spirit of God through the digested Word will deliver him from sin especially when he is willing to obey the Lord's gentle voice.

How does one sin in anger? One does so by justifying himself and by staying angry. Remember, the Word says, "let not the sun go down upon your wrath." When you are angry and do not humble yourself and stay angry, you immediately open the door to the devil. On the contrary, if this person will practice this Word, what happens? He will feel pain initially. That pain is the pain of transformation, of cleansing within, until the nature that was violated and demonized is restored. The Word of God recaptures, recovers lost ground and transforms such that the hold of that demon is broken. As such, even without the help of another minister or the brethren, when that demon of anger wants to jump on you, you can resist and put him to flight. This is how to be free – the Word of God is the medium. Jesus, in John 8:30-32, said it to His Jewish disciples who believed on Him this way: *"If ye continue in my word, then are ye my disciples indeed; And ye shall know the truth, and the truth shall make you free."*

The knowledge of the truth is a progressive encounter: the more revelation of truth you have, the freer you will be. Praise the Lord!

 BREAKTHROUGH PROPHETIC DELIVERANCE PRAYERS

1. Every power in me resisting and hating deliverance, be exposed and destroyed now by the Blood of Jesus.

2. Every grave clothes and evil objects the enemy is using as points of contact to oppress, suppress, depress and obsess me, catch fire now in Jesus' name. Amen

3. Every contamination in my life be cleansed with the Blood of Jesus.

4. My stolen, destroyed, or killed glory, I command you now to come alive in Jesus' name. Amen

5. My Father, preserve my spirit, soul and body blameless, unto the coming of our Lord Jesus Christ. Amen.

CHAPTER

The Deliverance Process

●●●●●●

There is a clear deliverance process revealed in the Scriptures. What do I mean by deliverance process? It is the process whereby God, the Holy Spirit, brings a believing person from satanic bondage to actual liberty. There is a process whereby He does *this* work.

I would like to reference this particular Scripture in Isaiah which depicts the whole anointing of deliverance:

> *"The Spirit of the Lord GOD is upon me; because the LORD hath anointed me to preach good tidings unto the meek; he hath sent me to bind up the brokenhearted, to proclaim liberty to the captives, and the opening of the prison to them that are bound; To proclaim the acceptable year of the LORD, and the day of vengeance of our God; to comfort all that mourn; To appoint unto them that mourn in Zion, to give*

THE DELIVERANCE PROCESS

unto them beauty for ashes, the oil of joy for mourning, the garment of praise for the spirit of heaviness; that they might be called trees of righteousness, the planting of the LORD, *that he might be glorified"* **(Isaiah 61:1-3).**

What this passage is saying, if you look at it and break it down a little bit, is that the process of deliverance begins with hearing the gospel message and receiving it in faith. This is critical because as I said before, there are two kingdoms that are reaching out for the souls of men. One is the kingdom of darkness that wants to destroy our souls in stages through life and eternity, and the other is the Kingdom of God, which has the original blueprint for destiny fulfillment and actualization of the human soul.

Every human being born into this world is dead on arrival. This has been so since the fall of Adam except your Parents are believers in which case you are sanctified by their faith until you reach the age of accountability; but when you come into Jesus Christ, you move from death to life. Of course, this raises the questions of what happens to all who die in their infancies. My response to that is that God is perfectly just and we can trust that he knows how to cover them.

> *Every human being born into this world is dead on arrival*

However, even though you are now out of the grave, the influences, decorations(meaning satanic emblems) deposited by demons, and implants conferred on you, while in the grave in a tomb of sin within the devil's camp, need to be dealt with. The reason is that these are the tools he uses and will continue to want to use even after you are born again.

POINTS OF CONTACT

There is something in deliverance called the points of contact. These are things Satan has planted in your life. He uses them against you when you have moved over to the Kingdom of Light. These are the things that people feel the constraints, the limitations, and the demonic containments that do not allow them to express themselves and be fulfilled in life. These challenges predispose the oppressed persons to seek answers. More detail on points of contact is provided in volume two of this series.

NEW DNA AND KINGDOM TRANSFER

In order to meaningfully address points of contact, a person first needs a kingdom change. That is why people must hear the Gospel, and the Bible calls it preaching the Gospel to the meek or those who are poor in spirit; that is, those who are humble enough to accept the simple message of the Cross.

The first thing that happens is that you receive a kingdom transfer **(Colossians 1:13)**, where you are transferred automatically from Satan's kingdom into the Kingdom of God, into the family of God. And there is also a blood transfusion in the spirit whereby the born again child of God actually receives God's DNA through the Blood or Life of the Lord Jesus Christ.

Sin is a spiritual thing in the nature of man. When someone carries the nature of the devil, being a sinner, they cannot cast Satan out of his property as it were. When you come to Christ, there is a spiritual blood transfusion in the spirit, and God's DNA becomes written into your system, and the life of God is given to you. You are then automatically transferred from Satan's kingdom. From this point, everything Satan does against you is illegal.

Being born again, being grafted into God's nature, is the first level of deliverance. The person who has not gained this level of deliverance has not yet begun the process. Anything the deliverance minister tries to do with such a person will only produce more confusion and more complications. That is why we find that a lot of people who go to deliverance meetings sometimes come out worse. It is putting the cart before the horse.

When people are born again, the next level in the deliverance process is counseling. It is referenced in Scripture as "binding up the brokenhearted" (Isaiah 61). Binding the brokenhearted requires skill. I hear people say there is nothing like deliverance ministry. I think that is a statement usually madein pride by an individual who does not fully understand what this ministry is all about. There is deliverance ministry. It is part of the Gospel. All are called to preach, but some people will be mandated by God to pay closer attention to certain aspects of the Gospel.We generally assume that we are called to preach the Bible. Nobody can preach the Bible. The Bible is a very big subject. God can give us a theme in the Bible and make us specialize in that theme.Still, all of us, put together, are preaching the Gospel.

Deliverance is a valid part of God's Word, and God in His wisdom does call people to pay more particular attention to this ministry because it requires skill more particularly when it has to do with binding up the brokenhearted. We call these people specialized, skillful spiritual counselors, who understand the nature of the human soul that has been violated by the wicked. People go through different levels of satanic violation, some as early as when they were in the womb, or in the formative years of their lives.

> *"People who carry invisible spiritual wounds are like a man at war within himself; so it requires counseling."*

In the process of my involvement in the deliverance ministry for the past 30 years, I have found out that the enemy always makes a desperate move to sexually violate children by the age of five. That is one of the fastest ways to put demons in them. We find that when children are sexually violated at the age of five, six or seven, the demons gain access but remain largely dormant, waiting for the opportune moment. By the time the children reach their teenage years, the demons fill them with inordinate curiosity and get them to indulge in activities that open them up more to evil. Eventually, they end up struggling to find purpose and fulfillment all through life.

People who are damaged may be well-dressed and look nice, but they have contradictions in their lives that they don't understand. Some are trying to serve God but cannot seem to break loose from certain habits and cannot understand what is going on. The spirit of counsel is an anointing of God that functions in prophets and, to a great measure, in those who are called by God to work in the deliverance ministry.

Specialized, skillful deliverance counselors are trained individuals who should be able to help those who are violated or are going through demonic oppressions and bring them into liberty. This is done through introspective investigations of their past lives to uncover where their souls have been violated and scarred, or where demonic infestations and wounds in the spirit have occurred so that they can skillfully work with them to clean them out.

There are many people who carry invisible spiritual wounds in the soul, and because their soul is deeply violated and fragmented, they cannot seem to get things together. It is like a man at war within himself; so it requires counseling.

In most deliverance encounters, the battles are lost or won depending on the skillfulness of the person doing the initial counseling. We often want to jump to the action side and kick the devil out. The devil enjoys that because it really is not effective. Yes, we will see the power of God and the weakness of demons. We probably get excited and carried away when we see the power of the Holy Spirit in action, knocking people down, with demons crying out and fleeing. But the ultimate goal is to ensure that the demons do not return.

To ensure that demons never return, the first step, as I pointed out earlier, is for the person to be born again. The next most important step is effective counseling, and that is what is called binding up the brokenhearted. You counsel the individual and probe deeply into their lives to find out what has really happened in the course of their lives. What are the things that have violated them? What activities, associations, and interactions have they been involved in? Sometimes it runs deep to include even their parents. It means that there may be things that they don't know about things that were done by their parents.

In some cultures, having a child is so significant that people go to all kinds of places to get one. When such a child is born, Satan already has a tag on them, and the demons are there to enforce the agreement that is on that child. The child is not even aware of it, and so the child goes through life and eventually comes to find out that there is something that is strange about him or her.

Although this example is very prevalent in African countries, I have found out that this happens even in the Western world. I was reading a book by a deliverance minister in America many years ago, and the main character in that book had an interesting story. The parents were poor, and the child was born with some disease condition and needed some help. A blood transfusion was done, the bills were paid for by an unknown benefactor, who turned out to be a satanic person, and the child was sold to the devil, and the battle commenced in her life.

Satan is alive and well all over the world. His demons are active; his agents are active; it is just that when it comes to the Western world, it is more sophisticated and rationalized, which really

"In most deliverance encounters, the battles are lost or won depending on the skillfulness of the person doing the initial counseling"

gives the devil a cover under which to function.

THE SPIRIT OF COUNSEL

The spirit of counsel is a major aspect of the anointing that was upon the Lord Jesus, the same anointing which we share. In the Scriptures, we see the seven-fold Spirit of the Lord Jesus Christ - the Spirit of the Lord, the Spirit of wisdom and understanding, the Spirit of counsel and might, the Spirit of knowledge and of the fear of the Lord (Isaiah 11:2).

It is instructive to note that in the above verse, *counsel* comes before *might*. Therefore, in conducting deliverance, before exercising *might* - which is to cast out the devil - we need *counsel*. This is how you can discover all that had happened; it is how you come to find out whether the individual you are ministering to has aided and given cover to the enemy to function in his or her life. I emphasize this because I am doing this book as a kind of theoretical analysis to help people understand the nature of deliverance; that is, how deliverance works because spiritual warfare and deliverance are a major part of God's end-time program on the earth. A lot of good is going on but, sorrowfully, too, a lot of misunderstanding, a lot of immaturities and a lot of confusion abound on the subject the result of which is that sometimes the wonderful works of God are caricatured, and the truth is left in contempt.

Essentially, the Spirit of counsel is part of what comes upon you as a worker in the kingdom to be able to sit with people and take an introspective journey into their lives and unearth the things that the enemy has done. That is why, sometimes, when I am doing deliverance for people, I do not want to jump into the prayer aspect. I try to put them in touch with the Lord and even recommend some days of fasting. Why? Because I want the Holy Spirit to meet with them and begin to signal some things in their lives.

People need to know that there is a deliverance process. Deliverance is not a magic wand where you just go to some meeting, and things are cast out of you. If you get something cheap, you will probably lose it very cheaply too. That is why most of what is done in deliverance is not sustained, and people have to come back again and again, with deliverance delayed in a cycle of confusion and frustration.

> *"It is instructive to note that in the above verse, counsel comes before might. Therefore, in conducting deliverance – before exercising might, which is to cast out the devil – we need counsel*

It is important that we know how the deliverance process works, and a major part of it is the counseling or the binding of the brokenhearted. In fact, it is through the process of counseling that wounds in the soul are uncovered and deep inner healing and deep inner cleansing can take place.

I will come back to the subject of deep inner cleansing within the deliverance process a little later on. However, I cannot overemphasize the area of counseling. The person desiring deliverance is first brought to the faith - they have to be willing to accept Jesus Christ as the basis for starting; but then once we are ready to go into deliverance proper, the next important step is counseling.

Binding up the brokenhearted is counseling going into the deep issues of their personal lives, seeking the wisdom and insight of the Holy Spirit to unearth how these people came into bondage. What kind of spirit is functioning? How has that spirit reproduced its character in the individual? When bondage occurs, demons do not come into the life of people to play games or to have a vacation. They seek a home in the oppressed person; they have a destructive nature which they will exercise in the life of the individual, and they have an evil character which they will also reproduce in the individual's life.

It is through the process of counseling that wounds in the soul are uncovered and deep inner healing and deep inner cleansing can take place.

For effective deliverance to happen, the afore mentioned must be followed. If not, you can eliminate the demon while his character or image is still inside the oppressed person. Eventually, the demon comes back and reoccupies. It is in counseling that we can show people what has happened; for example, the exaggerated aspect of their human character due to demonic corruption and the need to undergo crucifixion. It is like working with wounded people in a hospital, and this is why not everybody can succeed here. It is not about power - *even though power is required*; it is so much more about skill, training, and understanding how it works.

It is not merely running all over the place, knocking people down under the power of God and basically not caring about them. Our God wants to nurture His people back to health. He wants to bless them and break the curses on their lives. He wants to remove their wounds, heal them, make them whole and then they will be able to function in their true destiny.

BREAKING EVIL GRIPS

Another important component of the deliverance process after counseling is to literally apply the power of God and to *clean out* the individual. It is what I call the practical deliverance session.

During deliverance or cleaning out of an oppressed person, you must understand again that the ground for deliverance is the Blood. As I said earlier on in the definition, deliverance is based on the Blood Covenant that God has with Jesus, which we have come into by faith. As you counsel people, you will need to put them in touch with the Lord, while being yourself very sensitive to the Lord. You are very likely to discover the root causes, hidden curses and demonic covenants, which can now be broken by the application of the Blood.

Satan's aggression, human rebellion, and the conditions that produce bondage can be brought under judgment and remedied by application of the precious Blood of Jesus Christ. Again, it is *important* that we understand that the Blood of Jesus is the *legal* ground on which God delivers. He said, *"when I see the Blood I will pass over you"* (**Exodus 12:13**). The Blood of Jesus, validly applied, attracts the power and the presence of God.

There is also the firepower of the Holy Spirit. Because of the anointing, the yoke becomes destroyed (**Isaiah 10:27**). The anointing of the Holy Spirit comes when the Blood is validly applied to the situation. The power of the Holy Spirit comes and breaks the bondage.

Understanding the deliverance process is vital to those who work in this area and want to see good things happen. We must understand that there are different types of cases and scenarios. I will deal more on this when I start to talk about why some deliverance cases seem to delay. It is a challenge in this area of ministry because we want to see quick results as it often happened with Jesus. This is wonderful. I believe in anincrease of grace. But I must say that if God has us patiently take one person through this process effectively, that is a lot. We should be looking at the human being who is suffering.

> "... we tend to counsel people in a way which can only be explained as teaching them how to cohabit successfully with their demons. This is ridiculous! You cannot counsel demons; you cast out demons!"

We should also be looking at the fact that Jesus paid the price for people to be free. We should be patiently working to see people come to complete liberty.

Casting out demons is an important part of the deliverance process. At times, we tend to counsel people in a way which can only be explained as teaching them how to cohabit successfully with "their" demons. This is ridiculous! You *cannot* counsel demons; you *cast out* demons! If they are there - you locate them in the counseling session; but, after that, the power needs to come in to clean the person out.

> "It is one thing to kick a demon out, but it is another thing to keep it out."

I will not go into details now on how to recognize when demons are coming out and how to know when they are gone - we will look at those details later on - though as part of the process of casting out demons, it is very important. This is the part of the process that people focus their attention upon. Even for those who are coming to seek deliverance, initially, their whole focus is, "I just want to get rid of the demon, get this thing out of me."

Well, it is one thing to kick a demon out, but it is another thing to keep it out. To effectively kick it out and keep it out, we have to understand how the process works. Everything, both the natural and the spiritual, has a process. People do not get pregnant today and deliver a baby tomorrow. It takes a nine-month period of gestation within which people can prepare for the coming of the baby. It is the same with deliverance. It is a process.

Now, the next thing, after you have kicked out the devil, is to keep him out. How do you do that? The person who has been delivered has to be taught the Word of God. This is a crucial one. Remember, in deliverance, we bring the anointing of God, the Spirit of Justice, to release judgment on the devil and to give relief to the oppressed. Once the oppressed is cleaned up, we should teach them to be filled with the power of God's Holy Spirit. But we must remember that God's Holy Spirit only bears witness to God's Holy Word. Therefore, a major part of the deliverance process *is teaching and discipleship of people in the Word of God.*

Sadly, this is currently one big failure of deliverance ministries. We just recycle stuff, talk more and more about how to be free, cast out devils, bind this and bind that, all of which only brings marginal success.

NO ALTERNATIVE TO GOD'S WORD

If people do not embrace the Word of God in their lives, they really cannot enjoy true freedom. Jesus was speaking to believers in the Book of John: *"Then he said to some people who believed on Him"* see, they believed *"if ye continue in my word, then are ye my disciples indeed. And you shall know the truth, and the truth shall make you free"* (**John 8:30-32**). And when Jesus was restating His mission statement in **Luke 4:18,** He quoted Isaiah 61, saying, *"...and recovering of sight to the blind."*

Yes, the power of the Gospel can bring healing to blind people, but the worst form of blindness on earth today is ignorance of the Word of God. The progressive encounter of the revealed truth of God's Word brings people into various degrees of liberty. The more you know, the more you gain liberty; the more you know, the more your freedom increases. So, there is a need to know — to know the basics of our faith, to know the doctrines of sound faith.

> *"If people do not embrace the Word of God in their lives, they really cannot enjoy true freedom."*

We are so quickly producing a generation of emotional Christians who are very much in touch with the social media but have little time for the Word of God, yet there can be no freedom without the Word of God. The Word of God is given by a loving God to us to restore our violated and fragmented soul. It is through the revelation of that Word of God that we come into harmony with God - our nature, which had been violated from one degree to the other, being reclaimed, restored, and reconciled to God. As we become one with Him, His peace settles in us, and our heart is established with grace.

Nothing can replace the Word of God. In fact, deliverance is the execution of the Word of God against Satan's rebellion. If people who are seeking deliverance do not embrace the Word of God, or are not taught the Word of God and do not understand the centrality of the Word of God to their success, they cannot go very far. Satan will always be able to come around to steal, to kill, and to destroy them. **James 4:7 says,** *"Submit yourselves therefore to God. Resist the devil, and he will flee from you."*

How can you submit to a God you do not see? You can only submit to His Word. The Word of God is the same as God Himself. So when we submit to the Word, we become like Him, and Satan loses his hold. This point needs to be emphasized again and again. The failures that we see in deliverance ministry today are largely related to our inability to systematically train people in the Word of God.

There is an enemy out there. He is very much interested in our failure. But we do not have to fail because God has given us the tools to succeed. We can build our ministries around our gifts and anointing, but our gifts and our anointing only attract people to *us*. When people are attracted to us, the most they can do is to be like us; whereas, the Word of God will wean people from us and put them in touch with their eternal Creator.

The more people become like God, the further darkness will get away from them. The Bible says, *"Looking unto Jesus, the author and finisher of our faith"* (**Hebrews 12:2**). Seekers of deliverance cannot look unto Jesus if they do not know His Word. Yes, deliverance is real; warfare is real. But let us do it the right way. The Word of God is central and holds everything under creation together.

Once people embrace the Word of God, that Word goes deep and begins to correct satanic contradictions within them. Their scarred, disconnected, fractured nature begins to come together in wholeness. Then they will find out that they have inner peace and are unafraid. They can grow in love with God, for God and go ahead to fulfill their destiny. It takes a loving God and His Word to be strong enough to do exploits in this world.

THREE PHASES OF DELIVERANCE

Deliverance is in three phases. These include the past, the present, and the future. Let me explain it with these subheadings:
(1) Faith in the Lord Jesus Christ, repentance towards God and initial counseling and casting out of residual demons;
(2) Ongoing period of warfare, training and growth in the Word of God; and
(3) Maturing in spiritual authority and growth in Dominion

SALVATION AND INITIAL COUNSELLING/DELIVERANCE

The first phase of deliverance is embracing saving faith in the Lord Jesus Christ and renunciation of evil covenants. When you give your life to Christ and come into that beauty of God's deliverance, you are automatically removed from under the dominion of darkness to the dominion of light. In other words, you have moved from under Satan's authority and brought into God's Kingdom. Satan can only function illegally against you at that point. That is the first level of deliverance.

SECOND PHASE AND INTENSE WARFARE

The second phase is related to what the Holy Spirit is doing every day in your life in the present sense. The Lord is busy at work in each of His children every single day. We must identify what it is that the Lord is doing, to meaningfully connect with it. This again is important because deliverance is not the work of a deliverance minister. He is a vessel being used by the Holy Spirit. This means that your deliverance is not limited to the church or the deliverance minister.

Most of your deliverance can, in fact, happen between you and God, if you simply submit to the divine process and recognize that it is the Holy Spirit at work in you. This will enable you to continue to work with the Holy Spirit, and He will be doing things in your life. In fact, one of the reasons people are so disconnected is that they cannot understand what the Lord is doing in their lives in a present sense. If you do not know what the Lord is doing in your life at the moment, you will become distracted by what the devil is doing against you.

To further understand deliverance as a process that involves the past, the present, and the future, let's consider **2 Corinthians 1:8, where** Paul talks about how they came through some hardship in Asia. He says, *"for we would not, brethren, have you ignorant of our troubles which came to us in Asia that we were pressed out of measure, above strength, insomuch that we despaired even of life."*

Have you faced such pressure before to the point where you do not even know whether you want to live or die? This was what happened to Paul and his companions. But he says in verse 9, *"we had the sentence of death in ourselves so that we should not trust in ourselves, but in God which raises the dead."* In other words, in his pressures, difficulties, and fight with the enemy, he found meaning: he was under a sentence of death death to himself so that he would not trust in himself, but trust in the living God. Just that meaning alone gives him peace.

The implication of this for me, as a believer, is that in the midst of my trouble, whatever the enemy is doing, God is doing something within it. If I connect to that, I will be able to relate to whatever is happening around me from the place of strength.

The key message here is that if we are not connecting with what the Lord is doing within us at the moment, we will relate only to what the devil is doing outside against us and that only produces fear and hopelessness, and not faith. If I know my God is busy for me, even with the worst of the devil, whatever the devil is doing outside of me doesn't so affect me as to cause a breakdown. I will have the peace of mind, the presence of mind to stay with God, while He works in my life; and from the place of strength and authority, I can then go against the devil.

Verse 10 of the same passage says, *"Who delivers us from so great a death, and doth deliver; in whom we trust He will yet deliver us."* The full nature of deliverance is portrayed here He delivered us from so great a death; He doth deliver now; He will yet deliver. This confirms that deliverance is truly in three phases. He delivered us, He is delivering us now, and He will yet deliver us. A very dear wonderful man of God put it this way: "The first level of deliverance is to take us from the devil. You are saved, you are brought into the Kingdom, and the devil is kicked out of you. That is the first level." You are out of the devil, and the devil is out of you now, but he is still interested in you. You probably have some stuff in your life that he wants to use to destroy you, such as your family background, which brings us to the next level: warfare.

> "... if we are not connecting with what the Lord is doing within us at the moment, we will relate only with what the devil is doing outside against us and that only produces fear and hopelessness, and not faith."

WARFARE

Warfare is important. Warfare is taking authority. Then again, even that can be abused. We should be taking authority in faith, and we should be conscious that our prayer is having an impact. And let me say this: the greatest warfare does not consist in binding the devil, but *in knowing and*

> "The greatest level of warfare does not consist in binding the devil, but in knowing and fulfilling your purpose."

fulfilling your purpose.

If you want to disarm the devil, become knowledgeable about what you are called to do in life, about what your role is, and give attention to that. Once you give attention to your role, you come into meaning, you gain momentum, and your life becomes fruitful. If you do not know your role or you are not consciously fulfilling your role, while busy doing warfare after warfare, you are likely to become frustrated and hopeless. You will say, "I have been binding the devil all my life, and I do not see changes". Have you found your purpose? Are you fulfilling it? That is what will give you meaning more than anything. It is the best way to wound the devil.

But, having said that, warring is important. Paul said, "*I have fought a good fight, I have finished my course, I have kept the faith*" **(2 Timothy 4:7)**. These are the three things which are crucial. To run your race, you must fight the fight, but again your faith is more important than the fight. More importantly, your faith is the victory. It is the reason for the fight. If you are merely fighting because you want to survive, or want to have some extra money, it will be frustrating. But when you have a given purpose for which you are fighting, the fight becomes meaningful because the fight is part of the process and so you will be excited.

You are not scared of the devil. Why? Because now you are fighting for a reason. He is fighting a lost battle, but you are fighting for a reason. You are fighting for a dream. You have a purpose to your life.

LIFE OF DOMINION

As you go on warring, learning, becoming more like your Father, it brings you to the third level, which is dominion. You come into your dominion as a child of God. You come into an understanding of your exalted position in Christ. At this point in your journey, the presence of evil becomes meaningless and is no longer a threat to you. So when you are going through the process, there is no need to be confused; there is no need to become hopeless or frustrated; there is no need to begin to think that the devil is so powerful. No, he is not so powerful; he is a creature. God uses him too to fulfill purposes in our lives.

Your purpose is far more important than the threat of the devil. As you go through the process, you come to a place of dominion, which positions you to exercise Kingdom authority. After that, you are ready to help others, not just to seek help. Then you are in a position to know that the presence of darkness does not threaten light.

When light is shining, darkness will retreat. The presence of evil is not a threat to good. You are now in dominion. Satan is still an enemy - you still fight him, he still fights you - but he is not a threat to you. David said it this way, *"Thou preparest a table before me in the presence of my enemies. Thou anointest my head with oil, my cup runneth over"* **(Psalms 23:5)**. The presence of the enemy does not even stop you from enjoying the table of the Lord.

Here is a recap of the things I have said in this chapter. Understanding that there is a process to deliverance will help us to have the right frame of mind when we are going through that process. It will keep us from being confused. A lot of people become confused and frustrated because of a lack of understanding of the process of deliverance. If you meet someone who was oppressed and bound by the devil and you start to kick the demon out of them, the devil is going to fight back. The Bible puts it this way:*"When the unclean spirit is gone out of a man, he walketh through dry places, seeking rest, and findeth none. Then he saith, I will return into my house from whence I came out; and when he is come, he findeth it empty, swept, and garnished. Then goeth he, and taketh with himself seven other spirits more wicked than himself, and they enter in and dwell there: and the last state of that man is worse than the first..."* **(Matthew 12:43-45)**.

This means that when demons are in a human life, they regard that life as their home. When you kick them out, giving them an eviction notice and they become homeless, it affects their ability to manifest their evil nature, so they feel pain. Consequently, they will definitely seek to return; and when they do so and find their former abode empty, they solicit the help of seven other spirits even more wicked, and this means that when they find their way back into the person, his or her state becomes worse.

This is not a discouragement for deliverance; rather it is an encouragement for proper deliverance. The person being delivered has to be willing to come into the Kingdom of God, to receive Jesus Christ, and be born again. And we, who are ministering the deliverance, must carefully take that person through counseling. There is a time when you just don't want to keep knocking them down; you want to counsel, you want to go into the details and find out what has gone wrong with the people to whom you are ministering. Then, as part of that counseling process, you take the time to apply the power meaningfully. It takes power to break the curse, to break the yoke. Power breaks the yoke. Then you bring on the Word of God into the life of the person who is being delivered and they must be encouraged to develop a personal love for God's Word. God's Word is God Himself in print. As the person feeds on that Word, the Word cleanses and teaches reverence to God.

At this point, I will have to say more about the cleansing aspect, as I said I would earlier. The Book of **2 Corinthians 7:1-2** says, *"Having, therefore, these promises, dearly beloved, let us cleanse ourselves from all filthiness of the flesh and spirit, perfecting holiness in the fear of God."* In other words, there are two major aspects of cleansing that need to happen within the process of deliverance. The cleansing of contaminations in the spirit and the cleansing of contaminations of the flesh.

Let me explain it this way. The devil often seizes grounds in the spirit. He is an aggressor. He takes those grounds piece by piece. When we come into the Kingdom, we are restored to God's inheritance; however, it takes a gradual process to recover some things. It is like God bringing the children of Israel from Egypt through the wilderness into the land of Canaan - the land of promise, the land flowing with milk and honey, the good and large land. However, that land had to be taken territory by territory. The ability to take those territories also was predicated on their obedience to God.

This is the process. There is no magic wand. It is the process that works wonders. People who are seeking deliverance must be people who want to be like God, who want to end up in heaven - not just wanting to have an easier life here without caring about God or heaven. That is not real deliverance.

There is a lot of stuff out there that is not real deliverance. I call it recycled bondage. Real deliverance is cleansing and reclaiming the portions of an individual's life in the spirit realm, as well as dealing with the many physical doorways that were opened for the enemy to invade. Such doorways include doors of sexual sin, witchcraft, demonic inheritance or contaminated dwellings. I will give these details later on - but cleansing is a process, it is a major part of the process, and doesn't happen in just one day.

There are tools that are needed for thorough cleansing. We need the Word of God. And we need the Blood of Jesus because that is the legal ground. The Blood continues to be relevant, but the Word does the washing. We also need what the Bible calls the fear of the Lord. He says, *perfecting holiness* (that is maturing in holiness), *in the fear*(or out of fear)*of God*.

We need to know the fear of God. It is not a negative thing. It is one of the most beneficial aspects of our Christian heritage. It is our reverence for God - our personal choice to respect God in our life, conduct, and in the choices we make that will keep us purified in life. The Bible says,*"The fear of the Lord is clean, enduring fore*ver..." **(Psalm 19:9)**. The fear of the Lord as an attribute or character will keep us cleansed and purified from contamination with evil.

This is so important when demons are cast out of someone. As I mentioned before, demons will always *try* to come back. They will try to lure the individual by providing temptations that used to work effectively in the past. Most times, this approach doesn't work for those who have truly received the love of God. They can resist and not yield. But the demons won't give up easily. If you are not yielding to temptations, then they will try to persecute you, to make life difficult for you in other ways - in the hope that, by doing so, they can frustrate you and somehow open a doorway to return.

When this fails, they will try to blackmail and manipulate you through demonically generated dreams. The objective is to confuse you into thinking you are not delivered. Do not panic. Instead, immerse yourself in the atmosphere of worship and meditation in the Word of God. The devil will soon flee from you. Be steadfast and unmovable.

"Be sober, be vigilant; because your adversary the devil, as a roaring lion, walketh about, seeking whom he may devour: Whom resist stedfast in the faith, knowing that the same afflictions are accomplished in your brethren that are in the world. But the God of all grace, who hath called us unto his eternal glory by Christ Jesus, after that ye have suffered a while, make you perfect, stablish, strengthen, settle you. To him be glory and dominion for ever and ever. Amen" (1 Peter 5:8-11).

BREAKTHROUGH PROPHETIC DELIVERANCE PRAYERS

1. Heavenly Father, I thank You for the sacrifice of the Lord Jesus on my behalf. I declare with my mouth, what I now firmly believe in my heart that Jesus Christ is the sinless holy Son of God who came into this world to pay the price for my sin. I believe in His Virgin birth, atoning death, burial, and resurrection by the glory of the Father on the third day. I further declare Jesus as my personal Savior and the Lord of all my life.

2. Standing in faith before the Throne of God, the Father, Son, and Holy Spirit, the eternal witness of the Blood of Sprinkling, the elect Angels and all the hosts of heaven, I declare the Lordship of the Lord Jesus Christ over my life and destiny. I declare I am born of God and have His DNA.

3. I declare aloud before the entire kingdom of darkness, Satan, principalities and powers of darkness that I now belong to Jesus Christ and therefore renounce all allegiance to evil covenants and commitments. From this moment any satanic claims against me is made void by the Blood of Jesus and therefore illegal and subject to divine judgement and retribution.

4. I receive the spirit of wisdom and understanding regarding my role in life and destiny and full

understanding of the deliverance process and where I stand in God's victory in the mighty name of Jesus Christ.

5. Heavenly Father, strengthen me; train my hands to war, impart a victory mentality to me continually, and help me to abide in your love.

6. Lord God, help me to know Your purpose for my life and fill my soul with passion to fulfill it in the mighty name of Jesus.

7. Precious Father of light, help me to function at a spiritual level of understanding that effectively neutralizes satanic temptations, persecutions, and blackmail in the mighty name of Jesus Christ.

CHAPTER 6

The God Who Delivers

"Moreover he said, I am the God of thy father, the God of Abraham, the God of Isaac, and the God of Jacob. And Moses hid his face; for he was afraid to look upon God. And the LORD said, I have surely seen the affliction of my people which are in Egypt, and have heard their cry by reason of their taskmasters; for I know their sorrows; And I am come down to deliver them out of the hand of the Egyptians, and to bring them up out of that land unto a good land and a large, unto a land flowing with milk and honey; unto the place of the Canaanites, and the Hittites, and the Amorites, and the Perizzites, and the Hivites, and the Jebusites. Now therefore, behold, the cry of the children of Israel is come unto me: and I have also seen the oppression wherewith the Egyptians oppress them. Come now therefore, and I will send thee unto Pharaoh, that thou mayest bring forth my people the children of Israel out of Egypt" *(***Exodus 3:7-10)**.

THE COVENANT KEEPING GOD

Deliverance is a deliberate act of a loving God to rescue His people. I want you to see something in the above Bible passage, as revealed by the Almighty God. God, the Father of our Lord Jesus Christ, is the only authentic Savior and Deliverer. His redemptive works on the earth constitute an unfolding revelation of His love, compassion, and commitment to His creation.

Look at those words again: *"I have surely seen the affliction of my people which are in Egypt, and have heard their cry by reason of their taskmasters; for I know their sorrows; And I am come down to deliver them out of the hand of the Egyptians..."* Wow! He is the God that delivers.

Again, I want you to carefully take note of how He identifies Himself in this passage. He says, *"I am the God of thy father, the God of Abraham, the God of Isaac, and the God of Jacob".* Why does He identify Himself this way? Because there is a covenant in place. In this particular instance, it is a covenant referring to the children of Israel. It was a direct covenant with Abraham, which He repeated to Isaac and then to Jacob, to bind Himself to the Jewish people or to the descendants of Abraham. They had now been over 400 years in the land of Egypt and according to the terms of this covenant, God had not forgotten. He had come down to deliver them.

I believe that the children of Israel in that generation who were going through those severe trials, difficulties, pains, and oppression had not reckoned with the fact that they had a covenant that was covering them and that, by that covenant, God would act on their behalf as they cried out. Suddenly, their cry prevailed and God, on the basis of His covenant, came down to deliver them, through the ministry of Prophet Moses.

Here, again, I must emphasize that even though God will use human beings to bring help to other human beings, for that is His chosen method, we have to be careful to remember that God will not share His glory with anybody. It is God who delivers. And He does this because He loves us, His people.

You may be saying, "Well, He was available to deliver the Israelites because He had a covenant with Abraham, Isaac, and Jacob, and so He had to deliver the Jewish people." Of course, we also have a covenant. It is called the Everlasting Covenant – the eternal one – no beginning, no end. And that covenant is found in Jesus Christ, the Son of the Living God. *"Behold the Lamb of God that taketh away the sins of the world"* **(John 1:29)**.

Because of the sacrifice, the blood sacrifice of Jesus Christ, we have entered - both Jews and Gentiles - into a superior covenant. It is not a covenant based upon the blood of goats, calves, bulls, sheep or any other animal but upon the Blood of His only Begotten Son. As the Bible says, *"Neither by the blood of goats and calves, but by his own blood he entered in once into the holy place, having obtained eternal redemption for us"* **(Hebrews 9:12).**

THE EVERLASTING COVENANT

There is this one covenant that is eternal in scope and dimension that, today, men and women can plug into - and whatsoever be the curse or covenant that provided the enemy the avenue for oppression, it can be instantly broken as we exercise faith in the Lord Jesus Christ.

I really want to re-emphasize this because, often, when people are desperate to be free from their shackles, disease, and pain, they tend to focus on their situations to such an extent that would almost promote or elevate their unwanted conditions to the place of a god. Then, desperate to do anything prescribed by both authentic and non-authentic ministers or deliverers who are offering help, they can miss the whole point.

Deliverance comes from a God who cares. We cannot seek deliverance apart from a relationship of commitment to Him. He is committed to us and has made a way so that we can have the desire to know Him. The Bible says *"Then said Jesus to those Jews which believed on him, If ye continue in my word, then are ye my disciples indeed; And ye shall know the truth, and the truth shall make you free"* **(John 8:31-32).**

Progressive encounter with the truth of God's Word can only result from a committed relationship of true discipleship, and this, in turn, will impart liberty to the various components of our lives that the enemy has seized. The more we encounter God, the more we become free – free to be like Him and free to be whom we are called to be. People seeking deliverance must have a desire for God or must be encouraged to develop an appetite for God.

If people do not want God, they may want to pay for their deliverance. It is important to let them know that it doesn't work that way. Deliverance ministers are not magicians. Deliverance ministers do not act on their own authority. They have no power to act on their own authority. They have a term of reference. They are not allowed to go beyond the Word of God to do anything.

It is good to appreciate and celebrate the men and women who are anointed and called into deliverance ministry to help the multitudes of people, but it is very important as well to know that God is the One who delivers. One of the benefits of this realization is that deliverance will not end with the deliverance minister. Every day in your home, in your dream state, the Holy Spirit is busy enforcing your deliverance. In fact, David said, *"Thou wilt keep me from trouble while you encompass me about with songs of deliverance"* **(Psalm 32:7).** It is one thing to be delivered from a situation, but it is yet another to have your deliverance as a living reality because you are carrying God around.

God and bondage do not coexist. So, I encourage you to get rid of your demons, seek to grow in your character to become more and more like God and seek to love the Lord and follow Him.

"Every day in your home, in your dream state, the Holy Spirit is busy enforcing your deliverance."

BREAKTHROUGH PROPHETIC DELIVERANCE PRAYERS

1. Almighty Father of all spirits. You are the Lord God who alone delivers. I submit all aspects of my life to the glorious operations of your eternal Spirit. Release my soul and my life from every satanic yokes, weights and liabilities in the mighty name of Jesus.

2. Covenant Making and Keeping God; I invoke the power of your blood Covenant in my life to nullify any illegal claims the devil and his cohorts are seeking to enforce in my life and family.

3. My God and King, I fully recognize the operation of your hands in my life; so, build me up. Visit every aspect of my life with new mercies today in the mighty name of Jesus Christ.

4. Lord God, grant me a bigger picture of how big you are and help me to define and understand my purpose and role in my destiny and your kingdom.

5. I declare boldly that the light of the glorious gospel of the Lord Jesus Christ is shining brightly in my heart and every satanic lies and strongholds on my mind are exposed and destroyed permanently in the mighty name of Jesus Christ.

CHAPTER 7

The Origin, Fall and Career of The Devil

There is a treasury of information in the Word of God regarding the origin, fall, and the career of the devil. Just to put that into perspective, let us look at some Scriptures. We will start with **Ezekiel 28:11-13**

> *"Moreover the word of the Lord came unto me, saying, Son of man, take up a lamentation upon the king of Tyrus, and say unto him, Thus saith the Lord God; Thou sealest up the sum, full of wisdom, and perfect in beauty. Thou hast been in Eden the garden of God; every precious stone was thy covering, the sardius, topaz, and the diamond, the beryl, the onyx, and the jasper, the sapphire, the emerald, and the carbuncle, and gold: the workmanship of thy tabrets and of thy pipes was prepared in thee in the day that thou wast created"*

The above description, apparently, couldn't have been for a human being. First, while the man was made from the dust; this creature was made of precious stones. *Notwithstanding, it is clearly stated that the creature is not self-existing but was created.* Moreover, the Bible says that he was perfect in beauty and full of wisdom. In fact, he sealed up the sum. He represented what we could call perfect-perfect.

Not only that, of this creature, it is stated that music was imputed to him –organs, flutes, all kinds of music. What was the reason for God putting music into this very powerful, excellent being? It was because he was created to lead worship in heaven.

Verse 14 of the passage goes further to say: *"Thou art the anointed cherub that covereth; and I have set thee so: thou wast upon the holy mountain of God; thou hast walked up and down in the midst of the stones of fire."*

This being was in the very presence of God. He was a cherub, one of the highest levels of angels. He was an anointed cherub that covered the throne of God, a guardian angel. He covered the throne of God with worship, which means he was close to the heart of God. (Don't get disappointed when people who are close to you break your heart. Your Father went through it; you are not the first).

THE FALL

Up until this point, everything about this creature seems incomparable and irreproachable. But we must read further. Verses 15-17: *"Thou was perfect in thy ways from the day that thou was created, till iniquity was found in thee...Thine heart was lifted up because of thy beauty, thou hast corrupted thy wisdom by reason of thy brightness: I will cast thee to the ground, I will lay thee before kings, that they may behold thee.*

So we have the tragedy of this being, and the primary cause laid clearly before us. This powerful being fell. Why? His heart was lifted up because of his beauty. Pride came into his heart because of his beauty. This means that he started looking at himself, instead of looking at God who had made him.

This is where a fall would come from – self-focus and self-centeredness. It comes in all shapes and forms. Not only can you be tempted to keep looking at yourself to see how beautiful you are or how much you have accomplished, but you may also be tempted to focus on yourself, based upon your failures, inadequacies, and inabilities. Either way, it is still self-centeredness and can lead to a fall. The scriptural injunction is that we continually look unto Jesus the author and the finisher of our faith **(Hebrews 12:2)**.

So, the first problem of this angel was that he started to look at his beauty. Who created him beautiful? God. For who? God beautified him for Himself. But he became filled with pride, rather than giving glory to God. Moreover, the Bible says he corrupted his wisdom because of his brightness. *Brightness* here speaks of insight, intelligence, and inventiveness. This means that this angel was created with wisdom, with which he demonstrated exceptional intelligence. But he soon forgot who gave him the gift of wisdom and began to flatter himself. He thought himself omnipotent and illimitable; forgetting that being a created being, the One who created him would always be superior to him in every way. And, so, God told him:

> "...I will cast thee to the ground, I will lay thee before kings, that they may behold thee. Thou hast defiled thy sanctuaries by the multitude of thine iniquities, by the iniquity of thy traffic; therefore will I bring forth a fire from the midst of thee, it shall devour thee, and I will bring thee to ashes upon the earth in the sight of all them that behold thee" (Verses 17-18).

Note that even though Ezekiel was used to writing these lines, the conversation did not happen during his time. The things he recorded were things flowing out of the prophetic womb. I dare to think that he did not understand half of what he was saying but was just bringing forth a revelation.

One of the things God said about this being is that he had defiled his sanctuaries by the multitude of his iniquities and by the iniquity of his traffic. This means that not only did he have corrupt ideas, but he started pushing them to other angels to corrupt them. As he did, a third of the angels bought into it. That made God to pronounce judgment on him. God declared to him in **verse 19:** *"All they that know thee among the people shall be astonished at thee: thou shalt be a terror, and never shalt thou be any more."*

But what exactly is the name of this being? God brings it out clearly in **Isaiah 14:12-14:** *"How art thou fallen from heaven, O Lucifer, son of the morning! How art thou cut down to the ground, which didst weaken the nations! For thou hast said in thine heart, I will ascend into heaven, I will exalt my throne above the stars of God: I will also sit upon the mount of the congregation, in the sides of the north: I will ascend above the heights of the clouds; I will be like the most High."*

This being was called Lucifer. And we know that he had a throne, which he said he would exalt above the stars of God. Stars here refer to angels. Now, for Lucifer to say he would ascend to heaven means that he was coming from a place lower than heaven. This provides us with a number of insights. Could it be that, at this point in time, he was a delegate in a rulership capacity? Had God removed him from worship and given him another assignment, and could it be that it was there he began to scheme, saying, "I am not done with my career; I will ascend into heaven, I will exalt my throne above the angels, I will sit on the side of the north"?

The "north" is God's governmental seat. Lucifer's ambition was to take God's place. Not only had he defiled a third of the angels of heaven with his evil ambition but was thinking he could unseat the Almighty God. God's reaction to this is contained in verses 15–17: "*Yet thou shalt be brought down to hell, to the sides of the pit. They that see thee shall narrowly look upon thee, and consider thee, saying, is this man that made the earth to tremble, that did shake kingdoms; that made the world as a wilderness and destroyed the cities thereof; that opened not the house of his prisoners?*" God promised him a solid, resounding and permanent defeat.

REBELLION AND DESTRUCTION

I believe Genesis 1 contains some revelations as to the scope and impact of Lucifer's ambition on God's creation. Genesis 1:1 says, "*In the beginning, God created the heavens and the earth.*" "In the beginning" here refers to the eternal past. However, verse two speaks of chaos, and I believe that the rebellion of Lucifer occurred here.

In the Isaiah passage that we read earlier, he boasts, "I will ascend to heaven, I will exalt my throne above the stars, I will sit on the side of the north, and I will be like the Most High." He was already a defiled angel, pushing his idea. We know that God is patient, so none can really tell how many millions of years Lucifer had been faithfully serving God or when exactly he started nursing his ambition. Still, verse 2 tells us, *"And the earth was without form and void, and darkness was upon the face of the deep. And the Spirit of God moved upon the face of the waters."*

As I mentioned before, it is generally agreed by most sound Bible scholars that between verses one and two of Genesis chapter one was when Satan's rebellion took place; and at some point in time, there was angelic warfare which destroyed the elements of creation. God, then, withdrew light and everything froze. More on this subject can be read from Pastor Benny Hinn's book on "Demons and Angels."

In Genesis 1:3, God said, "Let there be light" and there was light. As you would find in the succeeding verses, this light was not light from the sun or the moon. In fact, the light does not refer to light as we know it. The light here means that the rebellion instigated by Lucifer had passed and God was restoring things again. In essence, God brought back light, where there had been darkness.

Some theologians postulate that the earth is about 6,000 years old, but that cannot be correct unless they are talking about the restored earth. The original creation dates to millions of years.

Also when scientists talk about how the earth was formed from a "Big Bang," I believe that they are talking about the angelic warfare that occurred at the time of Lucifer's rebellion. But they do not know what it is, and besides the devil lies to them because he does not want them to know the truth about his first defeat.

> "And there was war in heaven: Michael and his angels fought against the dragon, and the dragon fought and his angels, And prevailed not; neither was their place found any more in heaven. And the great dragon was cast out, that old serpent, called the Devil, and Satan, which deceiveth the whole world: he was cast out into the earth, and his angels were cast out with him" (**Revelation 12:7-8**).

We have so far obtained substantial revelations from these passages about Lucifer, the devil or Satan. We know that he was not created with evil; he was created a beautiful angel. His name was Lucifer, the son of the morning. God invested so much in him, but he disappointed God because he started looking at himself. You may be wondering, couldn't God have anticipated that Lucifer would do this? He is Almighty. He is all-knowing so that He would know, yet He did not prevent it; He chose not to.

Does that make God responsible for the rebellion of Lucifer? No - just like you and I cannot claim that the devil is responsible for our actions, even though he tempts us. God never wants us to be automated, motorized dummies that He programs to do stuff without a will of our own. He gives us the free will to love Him or choose not to. Lucifer decided to love himself. Self-love, by the way, is still the basis of all destructions today. It is the major reason why many relationships do not work. People love themselves so much they become inconsiderate of others.

So, in summary, Lucifer loved himself and got flattered by his beauty, wisdom, and insight – which were all given to him by God. He thought he could do anything; so he went ahead to push those ideas on others, corrupted himself and rebelled against God. Eventually, this one-time most beautiful, most powerful creature of God became transformed into a hideous enemy. His final place, of course, is the lake of fire.

THE CAREER OF THE DEVIL

In John 10:10, Jesus says, "The thief cometh not, but for to steal, and to kill, and to destroy: I am come that they might have life, and that they might have it more abundantly."

First and foremost, I want you to see that Lucifer had crafted an opposite kingdom for himself called the kingdom of darkness.

This kingdom has an order, hierarchy, and a governmental structure.

Apostle Paul tells us, by divine inspiration, in Ephesians 6:10-12: *"Finally, my brethren, be strong in the Lord, and in the power of his might. Put on the whole armor of God that ye may be able to stand against the wiles of the devil. For we wrestle not against flesh and blood, but against principalities, against powers, against the rulers of the darkness of this world, against spiritual wickedness in high places."*

Principalities rule over territories. Powers are high-ranking former archangels in the service of God who bought into the lie of Lucifer and so fell with him. They willingly serve his doomed purposes today. Rulers of darkness are a level of angelic order that controls the secret things behind the scene. They manipulate and control governance, commerce, religion, finance and the sex industry from behind the scene.

The Bible speaks of a host of wicked spirits in high places causing violence in the earth, doing damage upon the earth. We are ranged against them for mortal combat. There are millions, perhaps billions, of fallen angelic beings and demonic powers. Demons are of lower ranks, but they serve the purpose of Lucifer. There are angelic authorities at various levels under the command of Lucifer. They all do his will. They are all enemies of God and enemies of man.

THE CAREER OF THE DEVIL TODAY

The various hierarchies of satanic angels and messengers constitute the kingdom of darkness. Their sole purpose is to hinder the plan of God. Lucifer goes up and down supervising them. We see this in Job 1:6-7: *"Now there was a day when the sons of God came to present themselves before the Lord, and Satan came also among them. And the Lord said unto Satan, Whence comest thou? Then Satan answered the Lord, and said, from going to and fro in the earth, and from walking up and down in it."*

The sons of God came to present themselves, and Satan came among them. He was not meant to be there. When God asked him where he was coming from, he responded that he was going to and fro the earth, walking up and down in it. He has a ministry of walking up and down, going to and from all over the earth. Doing what? He is supervising his evil works and giving oversight to the assignments he has given to his fellow fallen angels and demons. They have partitioned the earth and the planetary system amongst themselves in order to effectively carry out evil plans upon mankind in the earthly realm; to oppose the things of God, and to attempt to hinder the work of God. This is the focus of their assignment.

Satanic forces control the politics of nations from behind the scene. They control the financial industry, the entertainment industry, sex industry, and they also control violent crimes, murders, and wars from behind the scene. They control drug abuse, misuse, and trafficking from behind the scene. They control commerce and industry from behind and even control the religious systems of every nation.

Satan's purpose is to seize upon the inheritance of God on the earth that was originally pledged to Adam in Genesis1when God created man. Man was created to take over the earth. God created man from a lower material (dust) and breathed upon him the breath of life (divine essence). He put him in charge and gave him governmental authority. He blessed man and charged man to multiply, replenish the earth and fill the earth with their kind. He gave man dominion to have control of the birds of the air and other living beings. He gave man control and authority over the planetary system. Man had control over every beast and creeping thing upon the earth. He had control over the fishes and every creature that passes through the path of the sea.

God was very strategic in giving man authority and control over these three realms. If the devil and his angels are going to function, they will do so from these realms, so God gave man control. God, Himself is in charge of the heavens of heavens, but He gave man control of the earth.

If man were to grow into his inheritance, and exercise governmental power, where would Satan be? Satan had only one option, hell. So Satan had to devise a plan, a smart move to seize the inheritance of man and possibly to seize that man and bring him to his side. That was where the temptation happened in the Garden of Eden, and man totally failed, disconnected himself from God and put himself at the disposal of the enemy. But God had a plan of redemption in place.

Satan is reacting to what he can see. He believes himself to be smart, that he has it together and knows how to defeat God; so he reacts to what he can see. But what about the hidden things in the heart of God? That, he cannot see. On the apparent level, he thought he could bring that man to his side, and so he went after Adam and Eve, presenting his manifesto. God stayed aside and allowed man to fail. Once the man had disappointed and failed God, He withdrew that God-kind of life and man became a dead spirit inside a body that would die within a thousand years.

Satan began to jubilate with his angels. But God did something to protect man from eternal doom – he sealed off the tree of life. Man would die, but his spirit had to go somewhere. The first man that was given dominion over the earth is just the copy of the real man that was to come. He was not the full potential man. That was just a picture of the real man. The real man was to come thousands of years later. The Bible calls Him the Son of Man and also the Son of God, who is the quickening Spirit, the life-giving Spirit.

You have to understand this to be able to function even in your status as a new creation man. What God did is that, in Adam, He gave man a human body and authority over the earth, born of the flesh; but in Christ He gave man a spirit body, giving him authority in the realm of the spirit. This is the real complete man that God is creating, and that complete man is a terror to the devil with dual citizenship – both earthly and heavenly citizenship in the Spirit realm.

Satan has strategically and politically partitioned the earth and the planetary system among his angels and demons for the purpose of rulership. Remember his original desire: he wants to rule and be worshiped. He is still seeking that today. He is stealing the worship of people by offering them flattering positions and lying to them. They bow down to him, and he gives them influence, and they then go ahead to influence other people. He works within the hierarchy of evil powers. Take religion, for instance; he is far more successful in religion than other areas.

What is the ultimate goal in the career of the devil? Why is he going up and down over the earth? Why does he partition the earth among his demonic hierarchies? What is his ultimate purpose? *"The thief cometh not, but for to steal, and to kill, and to destroy"* **(John 10:10)**. This is the career of the devil – to steal. To steal from man and cheat him out of his original inheritance. The earth belongs to man. The silver, the gold, everything here belongs to man. The great-grandfather of men sold out; so Satan stole what belongs to man and is still using that today to destroy man. He is offering man perverted versions of the original blessings that God gave to him. To destroy means to render people incapable of their original purpose.

What is the original purpose? *"Let us make man in our own image, after our likeness, and let them have dominion"* **(Genesis 1:26)**. Identity and rulership were God's original purpose for man. Now Satan is corrupting and perverting man. Jesus came to give His life in order to give us two basic things – abundance of grace and the gift of righteousness **(Romans 5:17)**. With these two things, we will be able to reign and dominate in life. That was God's original purpose for man. He made man in the image and likeness of Himself and gave him dominion. You need the image of God, and you need your identity in Christ to be in dominion.

What is the purpose of the enemy? To steal man's inheritance and to destroy him, render him incapable of functioning in God's original design and ultimately kill him. *"To kill"* is not just to attack the body but to separate man permanently from God so that he enters eternal death.

Anything the devil is pushing or promoting is what originally belonged to man. Satan has perverted these things and pushes them on to man so that man is lured away from pursuing his original destiny, his original identity, and by living on those perverted versions of the original, his soul and his potential are destroyed, and ultimately he enters into eternal doom. Satan is busy at it. That is why there is capitalism, communism, and all *"isms."* That is why there is religion of every type. He works through them to destroy man.

It is very difficult these days to separate between what is religion and what is Christianity. Christianity was not intended by God to be a religion. Christianity is divinity coming to man so that man can take his original place of inheritance and rulership.

THE RESTORATION PLANS OF GOD AND THE DEFEAT OF THE DEVIL

The Holy Spirit is upon the earth today to restore man back to his original glory, back to the original intention of God. Jesus came to restore man by giving man a dual citizenship – legal on the earth and legal in the heavens. Jesus says, *"I am the door: by me, if any man enters in, he shall be saved and shall go in and out, and find pasture"* **(John 10:9)**. The door to what? You might ask. It is the door to the supernatural nature and power of God – Divinity. He said when we enter in through Him, we shall be saved.

The word '*saved*' encompasses deliverance from sin, the power of sin, and future fear of punishment for sin. It encompasses provision, protection, and preservation. However, after being saved, He says you shall go in and out, and find pasture. This speaks of spiritual adventure. He is simply saying, "Do not be lazy. Do not stick to the flesh. Go in and out of the spirit realm and do business or ministry with what you are anointed with, the gift you have been given." When you do what God has called you to do, you will continue to increase and not diminish in the mighty name of Jesus Christ.

The mandate of the church's five-fold leadership today is to bring out mature manhood in the church, a new creation, properly credentialed on the earth and in the heavens. We are not dealing with mere men; we are dealing with wicked powers that have distributed themselves illegally and are dictating to the earth. We are to dictate to them and unseat them from territories, from families, from governments, from nations, and minister the healing power of God all over the earth.

Picture a militant church robed in the power and glory of God, moving forth with great authority, that have Satan firmly under their feet, who are lovers of and worshippers of God, who carry authority, fulfilling the original mandate of "*Let us make man in our image after our likeness and let them have dominion over the beasts and the creeping things of the earth, and over the fishes and whatsoever passes through the path of the sea"* **(Genesis 1:26).** This is the original mandate that Jesus came to fulfill. That is why He gave His life, and that job will be done. There are two opposing kingdoms that are fighting. Jesus said, I will build my church, and the gates of hell shall not prevail against it **(Matthew 16:18).**

When Jesus carried out His ministry, His objective was to reveal to people that there were two kingdoms at war. *"Then was brought unto him one possessed with a devil, blind, and dumb: and he healed him, insomuch that the blind and dumb both spake and saw. And all the people were amazed, and said, Is not this the son of David? But when the Pharisees heard it, they said, This fellow doth not cast out devils, but by Beelzebub, the prince of the devils. And Jesus knew their thoughts and said unto them, Every kingdom divided against itself is brought to desolation; and every city or house divided against itself shall not stand: And if Satan cast out Satan, he is divided against himself; how shall then his kingdom stand? And if I by Beelzebub cast out devils, by whom do your children cast them out? Therefore they shall be your judges. But if I cast out devils by the Spirit of God, then the kingdom of God is come unto you. Or else how can one enter into a strong man's house, and spoil his goods, except he first bind the strong man? and then he will spoil his house. He that is not with me is against me; and he that gathereth not with me scattereth abroad" (Matthew 12:22-30).*

What are we to infer from this? Satan is organized into kingdoms. There are rulers over nations, over cities, over families. There are satanic agents with lieutenants, enforcing the will of the devil. But you are the new sheriff in town, and you have come to take over. You are the new sheriff in town! In your family, you are the one who changes the game, and God will help us all to consecrate and pay the price.

Satan has a kingdom – the opposing kingdom, the kingdom of darkness. What Jesus is saying is that He (Jesus) is the Stronger Man. Before Jesus came, there had been a strongman called Satan who was ruling over the earth. Now a Stronger Man has come and has bound him and spoilt his goods. Now He is taking Satan's spoils. That is what the people saw in the form of blind eyes seeing, the lame walking, the dumb speaking – all of these were a sign that the strongman that was in town has been reduced, fired, and a new sheriff has come to town, and His name is Jesus Christ, the Son of the Living God. *"Forasmuch then as the children are partakers of flesh and blood, he also himself likewise took part of the same; that through death he might destroy him that had the power of death, that is, the devil; And deliver them who through fear of death were all their lifetime subject to bondage"* **(Hebrews 2:14-15).**

Because men are flesh and blood and Satan is spirit, and he uses that to take advantage of them, Jesus came to do something. He covered Himself with flesh to pass through the gates of death. By covering himself with flesh, He was able to pass through the gates of death because God cannot die, but flesh can die. Satan was the king of death because he was the first to be dead, cut off from the Source of Life. Jesus moved in to withdraw that authority from Satan. By dying, He moved into the realm of the dead, became a member of the dead that He might destroy him and deliver man, and become the King of the dead. When the Father raised Him from the dead, Christ became the First Begotten of the dead, the first to have life from the dead. Satan is still in the dead. He has no divine life. That is only available through Jesus Christ the Son of the living God. 1John 5:12 - He that hath the Son hath life; and he that hath not the Son of God hath not life.

THE RESURRECTED GLORIOUS SON OF GOD IS OUR PATTERN

John saw Jesus after He was resurrected and he was shaken. "*I was in the Spirit on the Lord's day, and heard behind me a great voice, as of a trumpet, Saying, I am Alpha and Omega, the first and the last:... And when I saw him, I fell at his feet as dead. And he laid his right hand upon me, saying unto me, Fear not; I am the first and the last: I am he that liveth, and was dead; and, behold, I am alive for evermore, Amen; and have the keys of hell and of death.*"

(Revelation 1:11-12; 17-18).

This is how Christ took the key from Satan. Jesus said, "I am the Almighty God. I was dead, and now I am alive forevermore and have the keys of hell and death. Satan no longer has them." *The "keys of hell and death"* means the authority over hell and death. Satan used to have the authority of hell and death but no longer has them. Jesus has them. Jesus defeated him and has given you and me the authority of His name.

> *"Let this mind be in you, which was also in Christ Jesus: Who, being in the form of God, thought it not robbery to be equal with God: But made himself of no reputation, and took upon him the form of a servant, and was made in the likeness of men: And being found in fashion as a man, he humbled himself, and became obedient unto death, even the death of the cross. Wherefore God also hath highly exalted him, and given him a name which is above every name: That at the name of Jesus every knee should bow, of things in heaven, and things in earth, and things under the earth; And that every tongue should confess that Jesus Christ is Lord, to the glory of God the Father"* **(Philippians 2:5-11).**

Do you see all of this? Jesus is Lord in heaven; He is Lord on earth; He is Lord under the earth. *So, where is Satan lord?* **No**

place! That is why he is illegal everywhere. Anywhere Satan asserts authority; he is illegal. You are here as a delegate of Jesus Christ to remind Satan of this reality and to enforce the law of God on him.

Jesus has given you dual citizenship; citizenship of the earth from being born by your father and mother, which is the only legal way to gain citizenship on the earth as well as citizenship in the heavens by being born again of the Spirit of God, which is the only legal way to assert authority in the heavens. You have both, so you are Satan's worst nightmare - but he tries to devalue you by making you to think you are less than what you are. When we lose our sense of identity, he can cause us to play his game of defeat and condemnation.

Living in the presence of God is vital. Otherwise you would be fighting from below up, which is frustrating. But when you live in His presence, you dictate downwards; **so always seek His presence.** It is the only way to go. *"And you, being dead in your sins and the uncircumcision of your flesh, hath he quickened together with him, having forgiven you all trespasses; Blotting out the handwriting of ordinances that was against us, which was contrary to us, and took it out of the way, nailing it to his cross; And having spoiled principalities and powers, he made a shew of them openly, triumphing over them in it"* **(Colossians 2:13-15).**

Yes, we were dead in our sins through our uncircumcised flesh. We were responding to the passions and promptings of the devil. Now, Christ has given us supernatural life together with Him to get out of the grave of this death and corruption called this world. In Christ Jesus, God defeated the devil and made a parade of him before all his hosts of angels. They witnessed Jesus stripping the devil of all authority, taking away the keys of hell and death from him, and him shaking like a leaf. So any time you and I agree in the name of Jesus, Satan has no option.

There are three levels of death: the first is spiritual death. You and I were in the realm of the first level of death. As soon as we are born into this world, "we are dead on arrival spiritually". The second level is physical death. If you go through the second level without having a spiritual life, you enter into the third level of death, eternal death. Satan abides in eternal death. Jesus entered eternal death for us and came back out. That's why He said, *"For thou wilt not leave my soul in hell; neither wilt thou suffer thine Holy One to see corruption."* **(Psalm 16:10)**.

You and I must know we have authority. Declare: **"I have the authority and every devil is subject to me through the name of the Lord Jesus Christ!"**

BREAKTHROUGH PROPHETIC DELIVERANCE PRAYERS

1. Every demonic corruption in my character be exposed now and destroyed in the name of Jesus. I decree that as I have borne the image of the first Adam; so shall I now bear in my mortal body the branding of the Lord Jesus Christ.

2. Heavenly Father, cleanse, heal and set me free from any compulsive and addictive behavior in the mighty name of the Lord Jesus Christ.

3. In the mighty name of Jesus Christ, I decree that any channel, connection to and flow of evil into my life be disrupted now, cut off and permanently destroyed.

4. Sovereign Lord, I submit myself for a deep work of the cross in my life. Let every corruption in my flesh and exaggerated aspects of my character due to demonic undercurrents be corrected, reclaimed and harmonized with your divine nature in the mighty name of Jesus.

CHAPTER 8

Three Sources of Demonic Trouble

How do demons gain access into people's lives to cause trouble and inflict harm? What loopholes do they exploit? There are vast amount of literature; therefore my emphasis will be on the major areas of concern.

1. The Congregation of the Dead

"The man that wandereth out of the way of understanding shall remain in the congregation of the dead." (Proverbs 21:16).

Membership of what the Bible calls the "congregation of the dead" is an automatic ticket for demonic infiltration, infestation, manifestation, and oppression. The Amplified Bible renders the above verse thus: "**a man who wanders out of the way of understanding shall abide in the congregation of the spirits of the dead**" while The Message Bible says "**Whosoever wanders off the straight and narrow ends up in

the congregation of ghosts." In other words, if you are not planted in Christ Jesus and growing in His knowledge and grace, then you will automatically remain in the congregation of the dead.

To understand what I mean by the congregation of the dead, you need to understand what the congregation of life is. The head of the congregation of life is the Living God. Any member of the congregation of life has his or her name maintained in the record of the Lamb's Book of Life. This is after you have given your life to Christ.

To put it simply, any man or woman born into this world is dead on arrival. "Dead," here, means spiritually disconnected from the Living God, and as the Bible puts it, **"cut off from the commonwealth of Israel"** (Ephesians 2:12); that is, not enlisted in God's covenant or inheritance.

Every man arrives on earth dead spiritually. Any person who is not in Christ remains among the congregation of the dead with their names in the Book of the Dead. The head of the dead is Lucifer.

So, how does the congregation of the dead function? First, there is membership. As I said, Lucifer is the head; and for membership, he has the principalities and powers, the rulers of darkness, and the hosts of spiritual wickedness in high places, plus men and women, who consciously enlist in and serve the purpose of the devil. They all constitute the congregation of the dead.

The congregation of the dead is territorially cut off from the life of God. The Almighty God is at once Light, Love, and Life (Eternal life or Zoe). He that has the Son has life (1 John 5:12). Since the Fall of Lucifer and the subsequent Fall of Man, territories in the vast known and unknown parts of the universe, besides the third heaven - the Throne of God - have been invaded by Lucifer and his demons.

> *"Membership of what the Bible calls the "congregation of the dead" is an automatic ticket for demonic infiltration, infestation, manifestation, and oppression... if you are not planted in Christ Jesus and growing in His knowledge and grace, then you will automatically remain in the congregation of the dead."*

There are satanic princes, the rulers of darkness, who are behind the secret things of this world and are in charge of the different nations. Adam sold out his lease on the earth to the devil. For that matter, every nation has a ruler, a demonic prince, which controls its affairs. Every state, city, community or family has a spiritual ruler.

A typical nuclear family, for instance, consists of father, mother, and the children; but that is not all. There is also a spiritual component. The father and the mother have the spiritual authority over the family structure and, of course, the spiritual dimension is controlled by the demon spirits or fallen angels, if such a family is not in a covenant relationship with the Almighty God.

Usually, in most traditional societies, cosmological orientation presupposes an existing symbiotic relationship between the spiritual and the physical. In the physical, people see themselves as representatives and extensions of their ancestors who are still somewhere in the spiritual realm and actively participating in the everyday life of the family or community. Their ancestors who died and passed on are regarded as having transited to a higher plain of life (spirit realm) but are still seen as valid members of the family. For this reason, in most traditional societies, various sacrifices, libations, and oblations are done as an act of worship or appeasement by representatives of those who have passed on to the spirit realm to enlist the help of the dead.

However, the Bible says it is appointed unto a man once to die and after that the judgment (Hebrews 9:27). In other words, earthly life ends the state of man's control over his family. Once you are dead, you face judgment. If your life was not lived in Christ Jesus, you are heading straight to hell.

There is no such thing as some ancestors being able to intercede for the living. The concept of engaging the help of forefathers or the worship of dead saints or ancestors is Satan's ploy to infiltrate the destiny of the misinformed, thereby perpetuating himself in the generations of a family, holding them in captivity, and transferring destruction from one generation to another.

Typically, therefore, when we offer worship to our forefathers, there is a demonic prince in the family acting as the ancestral spirit, receiving worship, limiting that family, and implementing the prescribed destruction of Lucifer. But it doesn't end there. Every child coming into that family is assigned a demon spirit, and that demon spirit is a familiar of such a child in the spiritual realm. It is an angel of Satan delegated to monitor and mold the life of that child according to the program of Lucifer. That is why the Bible says, you and I were dead in trespasses and sins when we were in the womb or the grave of sin.

Here is the exact quote: "**And you hath he quickened, who were dead in trespasses and sins; Wherein in time past ye walked according to the course of this world, according to the prince of the power of the air, the spirit that now worketh in the children of disobedience: Among whom also we all had our conversation in times past in the lusts of our flesh, fulfilling the desires of the flesh and of the mind; and were** by nature the children of wrath, even as others" (Ephesians 2:1-3).

It declares, right from the beginning, that we used to be among the congregation of the dead. We have, however, been quickened. 'Quickened' means being raised to life and having been forgiven of all our sins and trespasses. It goes further to say that when we were in the grave, we conducted our lives according to the dictates of the program of the prince of the power of the air, which is the devil, among whom we once had our lifestyles the same spirit that controls the children of disobedience to this day.

Typically, the spiritual dimension of an unsaved family is coordinated by Satan's representative of that family, the ancestral spirit, who delegates demons to the family members. At times, some people might see their fathers or mothers or relatives in their dreams, but it may just be demonic manipulation. It may simply be the demonic familiars of such relatives masquerading in the dreams to confuse and depress those who are not spiritually informed about such matters. If you are saved and believe in dreams, you still need to exercise discernment to avoid demonic manipulations.

This can be a real source of trouble for some people undergoing deliverance, especially if they are individuals from families where there were types of inherent occult abilities. There is a level of common cross-border bondage that, even if one of the family members becomes born-again, Satan would want to start to channel the flow of evil from other members of the family.

Simply put, when you give your life to Christ, the devil immediately regards you as a rebel against the family authority. That is why, for a born-again person, while it is necessary that you honor your father and your mother, you must be answerable to only God's Holy Spirit. If your parents continue to control your life, then that spiritual authority that works in them will hold sway in your life.

> *"...when you give your life to Christ, the devil immediately regards you as a rebel against the family authority"*

This is often the biggest area of trouble for many because when you are looking at major sources of demonic trouble, the biggest of it all is through the door of inheritance. Inherited curses and generational curses derive from the generations of struggle, pain, and demonic involvement of the family which continues to hold sway. By the Law of God, the things that a father does could have influence or effect for at least four generations. If your fathers, up to 400 years ago, were worshippers of idols, were involved in the occult, or were involved in witchcraft, those things still have spiritual relevance in your very life until you address them. You can do that through personal deliverance and aggressive, sustained, ongoing warfare to disconnect yourself from the flow of evil; and also to help other members of your family to be free from the evil effect of such satanic covenants.

One of the biggest issues in deliverance is generational curses. The delegated family spirit maintains a file on the life of individuals in the family and trains each child according to the program of the devil. Naturally, most people will not acknowledge this. They prefer to think that they are living their own lives, but the life they are living outside of Christ is a dictate of the devil.

The Apostle Paul, by the Holy Spirit, made some crucial observations in 1 Corinthians 12 concerning spiritual gifts. However, when you consider the lifestyle of the Corinthian church, you find an anomaly. Despite being so blessed with spiritual gifts, they had embarrassingly low morals - getting drunk during Communion (1 Corinthians 11:20-21) and having a man boasting of sleeping with his father's wife (1 Corinthians 5). Thus, as Paul began to intercede for them, God revealed some things to him, which led to his remarks in the twelfth chapter:

"...brethren, I would not have you ignorant. Ye know that ye were Gentiles, carried away unto these dumb idols, even as ye were led." In other words, there were certain things that characterized the lives of the Corinthians, which were not of their own making. They had been hijacked from the path of destiny that God had prepared for them. Sad to say, the destinies of many great lives, families, churches and whole nations are often hijacked by vicious spiritual powers and hardly anyone is speaking of it. God's servants, please raise up a war cry!

God said something to Jeremiah in Jeremiah 1:5, which could also be applied to every other person on earth. **"Before I formed thee in the belly I knew thee, and before thou camest forth out of the womb I sanctified thee, and I ordained thee a prophet unto the nations."**

Yes, God has a program; He had a purpose for you before you were conceived but this can also be affected by the roots of your family. This is where Christians who have had two or three generations of ministers in their family line before they arrived will have things a little easier. And by the way, even if your father and mother are born-again, every battle they did not succeed in fighting will be passed on to you.

The Christian life is a serious business; IT IS WAR! The moment you give your life to Christ, you have declared war. Once you are born-again, you are disconnected and removed from the congregation of the dead, and the devil fights you desperately.

THREE SOURCES OF DEMONIC TROUBLE

Something very interesting is recorded in John 11:38-44. Jesus had come to the tomb of Lazarus, His friend, who had been dead and He (Jesus) was to raise him from the dead. People, including the sisters of Lazarus, did not believe that this could happen. Anyway, Jesus went to the tomb and raised Lazarus from the dead.

The Bible has some striking observations about that encounter. As Jesus prayed a simple prayer, calling Lazarus out of the grave, we notice that Lazarus came out in response to Jesus, but there were certain conditions that continued to persist that needed to be dealt with. "**And he that was dead came forth, bound hand and foot with graveclothes: and his face was bound about with a napkin. Jesus saith unto them, 'Loose him, and let him go'**" (v. 44).

Please take note. Jesus had called Lazarus out of the grave. But there were some grave conditions, which still identified him as a member of the congregation of the dead, although he had been brought out of it. He had life; he was not dead anymore. However, the Bible says that when he came forth, he was still bound hand and feet. If you are bound in your hand, you cannot accomplish goals. If you are bound at your feet, your movement (meaning progress) is restrained. Grave clothes are a personal identification with the grave; which means demons will follow you as long as you have on those clothes.

Moreover, Lazarus' face was bound about, which means that he couldn't see. He had no vision. These are very serious realities in the life of people, and, as I said, it is most often one's family of origin and the things they had indulged in that will present the greatest source of trouble. If the father of the family, even to the third or fourth generation, was an occult member, everybody in that family line is enlisted spiritually in that occult system. That is why some people may never directly participate in some occult things, but they will have occult experiences. They will have difficulties getting ahead in life because of occult bondages.

Jesus said that those of a man's household shall be his worst enemies (Matthew 10:36), which means that your greatest source of trouble is not the person you meet on the job or the difficulties you think you have - it is often from your roots. That is where your greatest battles and warfare will originate. It is not the only source but the greatest and the fiercest. WHY? Because you were a member of a certain structure called the congregation of the dead. While you were there, you were a common inheritor of satanic debts and liabilities, and demons who are part of that covenant will want to collect from you throughout your entire life until you apply the Blood, break the curse, and stand up in warfare on your behalf and behalf of your other family members.

Understanding the demonic bondage, occult bondage, ancestral spirits, and common inherited curses on the family line will help you to take decisive steps in seeking deliverance to get yourself loose and to get your family members loose, including your children. As I earlier noted, this trend has a generational side. The enemy wants to perpetuate the constraints, pains, and oppression from generation to generation. You, the born-again Spirit-filled believer, are the curse-breaker of the family!

2. Territorial Demonic Pollutions

Another source of demonic trouble is what I will call territorial bondage, territorial exposure or territorial infestation. How does territorial bondage occur? I mentioned before that there are ruling powers in various territories. These ruling powers are behind the scenes, orchestrating conditions in communities. Certain communities behave in a certain way; certain nations dwell upon certain things that make them anti-God and anti-Christ. Certain cultures and popular trends are mere manifestations of the identity of the ruling principality in that locality.

So, if you are born in a particular locality, most of the things you are participating in are generated and controlled by that ruling principality, and they will have inroads into your life. If you attend a school in a particular locality, most of the things that are going on socially or culturally are demonically controlled from behind the scene. So when you just look at the attractions and seeming benefits, and you jump on board, what you do not know is that you are opening your destiny to the control of those demons.

The point here is that certain things become part of your life just by you being born, raised or educated in a particular territory. And even if you are born-again but do not know how to consecrate yourself, these forces will bring you under what I call containment by introducing some of their popular cultures to your life. This is why born-again Christians have to be people who can be discerning and decisive on what they permit into their lives. We are responsible to God for what we permit in our lives.

Territorial pollutions could also come through participation in religious activities that are anti-Gospel. Mind you, some of such activities occur even in churches! There are churches with serious occult foundations. If one of these is your family church and you are a part of it, doing all the things they do in that kind of setting, you are going to have a fight. If you do not know, the much you do not know will make you much more vulnerable and exploitable.

I will give you a personal example. I was born into idolatry, and as I grew up, for survival purposes, my mother enlisted in a church which we thought was a remarkable one because the people had the ability to see visions and revelations. The prophets could tell you almost anything about your life. What we did not realize at that time was that those seemingly prophetic abilities were not from the Holy Spirit but were manifestations of occult abilities.

Because I used to be a member of such a church, I feel free in my heart to mention it specifically in the event any person is reading this, they will be better informed ahead. I was a member of the Celestial Church of Christ for eight years before I met and gave my life to Christ. The Celestial Church of Christ is not a proper Gospel church; it is an occult-based church. There are many such occult-based churches. They are syncretic, having a pretentious appearance of serving God. Many members are innocent and, I should say, deceived so that they may fall into the category of deceived deceivers.

When I was a member of this church, we (the so-called prophets and I) frequently fought over the women. Sometimes a prophet and I would be dating the same woman. One of the distinguishing heritages of occult-based churches and prophets is promiscuity. People truly seeking God may go to such churches, but they will end up opening their lives to more demons just by being in the environment and

"... born-again Christians really have to be people who are discerning and decisive on what they permit into their lives."

participating in the activities.

If you have been a member one of these churches, when, by the mercy of God, you later come to the knowledge of Christ, you will have some battles because those forces will try to take advantage of you and sneak into your new experience to destroy you. You have to discern what they are properly, neutralize the Covenants, and you have to be taken through deliverance and then grow in the knowledge of the Scriptures.
I must also mention here that a few years ago, God gave me seven points for Pentecostal churches. He said if Pentecostal churches do not pay attention to these seven points, they will become semi-occult churches. I am amazed at how many Pentecostal churches have been invaded by occult practices. Some of them pretend to be prophetic churches, but they are not. You can read about those seven points towards the end of this book. But the point I was making is that your territory includes where you were born, where you grew up, where you were educated, and whether you were involved in any religion other than authentic Bible Christianity. All of these will open you up, just by being in that environment.

3. Personal Involvement or Flirtation with the Devil
A third source of demonic trouble is personal involvement in things that are demonically controlled. For instance, we join certain pseudo-social clubs which appear to have humanitarian orientations but are rooted in occultism.

THREE SOURCES OF DEMONIC TROUBLE

Participation in such activities as New Age directly opens people up to demonic infestation. Visiting false prophets or occult people, such as palm readers, is a doorway to demonic influences in the life of an individual. Tarot card reading and séances will also open the doorway to the occult realm. Believing in or reading horoscopes will open the doorway. These are things that people do on their own that create problems for them.

Moreover, there are types of music and works of art that are inspired from the demonic realm for the purpose of binding the souls of men. Many of the popular artists you see today have a covenant with the devil, and their record labels and releases have curses on them. When you dwell on them, then you open yourself up. These are self-inflicted demonic conditions. When you begin to expose yourself to cartoons and pictures that are vile and corrupt or those with occult undertones, they constitute a doorway that could open you up to demonic pollution and manifestation.

One of the biggest doors also is a sexual violation, and for that purpose, the enemy always pushes it. In fact, for many young people, from the age of five to seven, the enemy will make every effort to access them sexually, and when they are so

"Any sexual relationship outside of marriage is an open doorway to demonic infestation, pollution, and ultimately, oppression.

violated, he puts demons of immorality and rebellion in them. When they get to their teenage years, those things will show up.

Any sexual relationship outside of marriage is an open doorway to demonic infestation, pollution, and ultimately, oppression. There are some that are very serious in nature. There are some people male and female - who are agents of Satan, and they go about pushing for sex. When you engage in sex with such people, your destiny is taken, and you are no longer the same. Many people get into trouble this way without realizing it.

There are some very terrible cases I have seen in this regard. There was a young girl of twelve years who lived with her sister. The sister's boyfriend came one day, took the girl away to the Bush, violated her, and wiped her off. In adulthood, she found out that her menses did not flow. This was treated medically, but it was not a medical condition; it was demonic.

There are many cases of people who are seeking occult powers for money-making, and they look for young girls or young men to sleep with, and after that collect their body fluids for money-making rituals. Someone may enter into a sexual relationship willingly or unwillingly, and when they get out of it, their destiny may become totally destroyed. It takes the grace and the mercy of God to recover from these conditions; but with

God, all things are possible.

BREAKTHROUGH PROPHETIC DELIVERANCE PRAYERS

1. I repent and receive your forgiveness for wandering away from instruction and refusing wise counsel. Lord restore all my vandalized virtues due to past ignorance and stubbornness.

2. Every doorway into the congregation of the dead, I shut you now in the mighty name of Jesus. Every influence of dead and the grave in my life and destiny be liquidated now in the name of Jesus.

3. Every covenant with untimely death, Death of aspirations, opportunities, dreams and visions, be revoked and nullified now in Jesus' name.

4. Let the Blood of Jesus, fumigate and purify all aspects of my life from the smell of death and the grave and release an irresistible flavor of divine favor in my life. I cancel every appointment with death made on my behalf.

5. I resign my membership from the congregation of the dead; I declare I am offline with decay, corruption and stagnation in Jesus' mighty name.

6. I disconnect myself from the flow of evil from my family and all previous associations in Jesus' name. I command all generational evil inheritance to catch fire now in Jesus' name.

7. Every slaughter I have been experiencing because of the iniquity of my fathers has come to an end today in Jesus' name. I command the avenger of blood on ancestral altars to burn with the altars to ashes in Jesus Name.

8. I declare a new door to a new life opened unto me this day in Jesus' name.

    PSALM 16:9-11. Therefore my heart is glad, and my glory rejoiceth: my flesh also shall rest in hope.

    For thou wilt not leave my soul in hell; neither wilt thou suffer thine Holy One to see corruption.

    Thou wilt shew me the path of life: in thy presence is fulness of joy; at thy right hand there are pleasures for evermore.

9. Rejoice and give God praise.

CHAPTER 9

Some Signs of Demonic Oppression

Watch out carefully for these signs, as they are, more often than not, telltale indications of demonic oppression or influence.

1. Exaggerated patterns of human behavior

When an individual exhibits excessive, obsessive, and compulsive traits, there is usually an underlying demonic current fueling such behaviors. An overwhelming sense of helplessness in certain aspects of a person's character may be as a result binding demonic influence.

2. Addiction to chemical substances

The repeated use of alcohol and psychotropic substances will attract demonic spirits to move in and create scars and altars in the human soul, whereby the human will-power is eroded, the emotions disrupted, and a crippling sense of helplessness is generated. Most addictions will fit into this pattern.

3. Mysterious illnesses

Certain types of sickness that defy medical diagnosis may simply be a manifestation of demonic oppression. Sometimes people feel certain symptoms, but the conditions cannot be detected by x-rays, ultrasound or CAT scan. This is usually because the demons precipitating the conditions can hide away from x-ray pictures and so forth. This can also be true incertain types of missed diagnoses. The missed diagnosis is simply as a result of demonic manipulations to complicate the process and further the affliction.

In 2007, towards the end of a forty-day fasting and prayer period in my life, my younger daughter came down with a severe pain and for a couple of days was really sick. I hesitated to rush into prayer over her, so my wife advised to take her to the hospital. The CAT scan revealed ovarian cyst, and she was barely thirteen years at the time. I monitored things closely and concluded it was demonic, so I refused to panic. On the last day of my fast, we were in a church service, deep in worship, when I suddenly felt nudged by the Lord to call for those needing deliverance and healing. My daughter stepped forward, and the glory of God fell upon her, and the demon of ovarian cyst and all the symptoms vanished forever. Hallelujah! Blessed be the name of the Lord forevermore.

SOME SIGNS OF DEMONIC OPPRESSION

4. Across-the-board horizontal family reverses
You might notice a similar pattern of struggle in the life of all or most family members. Some families tend to experience the pain of untimely death among family members. This could be due to hidden covenants and curses which need to be located and neutralized. For other families, it might be repeat patterns of failed or late marriages. Yet others might be dealing with cycles of debilitating generational sicknesses where mother or father dealt with it, and now the children are also dealing with it.

5. Living below potentials
In John 11, the Lord Jesus raised Lazarus from the dead, but he emerged from the tomb having his hands and feet bound. Jesus said to others who could further help him to lose him and let him go. There are wonderful individuals with great potential, but demonic shackles and constraints effectively limit or altogether neutralize their ability to actualize dreams or goals.

6. Unexplainable delays
This occurs when nearly everything you do is a victim of unreasonable delays. We all can sometimes experience uncomfortable delays in life and such seasons can prove to be times of great learning or growth in character, but other times even the simplest of tasks like just processing a passport seems to take on a life of its own in protracted delay. When this

pattern of delays is common in almost anything you do in life, it may be indicative of the presence of a resisting evil power. Witchcraft spirits and ancestral powers specialize in delay and abort tactics.

7. Failure at the edge of success

This is another form of a delay tactic of the enemy, but it is mostly administered by the delegated ancestral power of the family. It is a high ranking power, and unlike the other scavenger spirits, this one mainly targets the appointed season of lifting or promotions in the life of the saints. This spirit, if not detected early and neutralized, can deliver punishing blows by repeatedly aborting your appointed seasons which can lead to barrenness in life.

8. Unidentified moving objects

Feeling of crawling and unseen moving objects through parts of the body may indicate demonic presence. In extreme cases, people report somebody pulling their hair and this can sometimes lead to actual depletion of the hair. Sometimes the feeling of movements can be both external and internal. Simply put, unidentified moving objects in the body are demon spirits.

9. Mood swings

Exaggerated or extreme mood swings - from being happy one moment to being depressed and even suicidal the next – is a sign that must not be ignored. Internal emotional disturbances, torments, turmoil, self-hate and in some cases cutting; extreme or overriding feelings of anger, revenge, murder, loneliness, isolation, fear, guilt, and rejection indicate demonic undercurrents.

10. Unbridled religiosity

Sense of religious superiority (holier-than-thou attitude), exalting visions and revelations above the written Word of God, critical and religious gossips, fear of man rather than fear of God (group loyalty including over-veneration of the ministers of God),denominationalism (putting your church above the Body of Christ),doctrines of demons, tolerance of immorality while claiming spirituality (spirit of lawlessness or iniquity) all indicate troubled waters of demonic activity.

11. Haunted homes and cursed items

When you move into certain homes, business places or bring cursed items into your home, the home and the surrounding environment are immediately greeted with oppression. In some cases, this could result in sudden reverse in fortunes. Poltergeist activities might commence, whereby things move around and noises are heard without human involvement. Other times, people might move into a new home and be greeted with unexplainable quarrels among family members and general lack of peace. This is normally the effect of witchcraft or voodoo involvements by previous occupants of the home or business.

12. Hearing voices, seeing or being followed by people visible to you and not others

This can be a fairly difficult situation, requiring warfare prayer, intercession, and judgment of a mature counselor to handle successfully. I find that in most cases of this nature, there is usually a background of what I call inherent or latent occult abilities. This can be as a result of mediumistic activity whereby somebody in the ancestral line was a medium and so remnant of residual occult ability continues down the line but potentially latent in the succeeding generations. When people from this type of background come to Christ and start to participate in spiritual exercises like fasting and spiritual warfare, the latent ability is triggered, and confusion and a state of semi-psychosis is generated. The veil between the physical and spiritual is illegally activated and the occult demon unleashes confusing conditions that can be potentially lethal to the mental stability of the victim. Like I said, cases like this require real skill, insight, judgment of mature counsel, and medical support may be enlisted alongside deliverance ministry. **The victim must be counseled to focus on the written Word of God as the basis for immediate and ongoing reality.** This requires real skill.

13. The dream state

The dream state is a spiritual gateway into the spirit realm. Once your body is rested and asleep, your spirit functions and interacts with what you are in touch with. There are three types of dreams that can come to you:

(1)   Dreams that come from God – called divine revelations;
(2)   Dreams that come from yourself – manifestations of your state; and
(3)   Dreams that come from the devil – manipulations.

The last two can reveal valuable information about conditions requiring deliverance in your life. Some examples include being pursued and shot at; sexual activities with persons known and unknown including, sometimes with animals/creatures; eating food (meal offerings), and waking up to find spiritual exercises a drag. I must here emphasize that all dreams do not necessarily indicate demonic activity; we must rely on The Holy Spirit who will give us necessary insight.

However, there can be an even deeper reality in a spiritual state that manifests in dreams. These can be indicative of an area of need. Particularly, this can happen in seasons of consecration when you are seeking God or seek to be closer to God, and something just shows up in your dream characteristically that throws confusion in your mind. By dreaming of wearing your teenage school uniform or your elementary school uniform, going to school like you used to go some thirty to forty years ago, and in the dream, you have no consciousness of your adulthood; you are just blending in; something is wrong there. Some have dreams of oppression, whereby someone known or unknown comes and has sexual intercourse with them with all the associated feelings, something is wrong there. Some have dreams of being naked; it is indicative of an area of trouble where you need help.

BREAKTHROUGH PROPHETIC DELIVERANCE PRAYERS

1. Today in the mighty name of Jesus, I ---- take my proper place in life and Destiny; I take my place before God, in my family as a priest and curse breaker, in society as a community builder and in the Church of God as a Kingdom builder. I take my appoint places in destiny and declare I am God's shining light in my generation!

2. I here and now repent for and renounce every demonic opened door in my life and family. Today, I fire every satanic power operating these doors and slam them shut permanently in the mighty name of Jesus Christ. Heavenly Father, I invite you to come through these doors yourself and because you have come through them today, they are hallowed and no satanic power is permitted to operate them again forever in the mighty name of Jesus.

SOME SIGNS OF DEMONIC OPPRESSION

3. I declare my total freedom from the unfruitful works of darkness today. The son of perdition has no common grounds with me. I declare my life a no safe zone for demonic activity. I am the light of Jesus Christ in my generation and as such, I fully embrace my responsibility to so shine, repel darkness and glorify my Father in Heaven. Thank you JESUS, I love you!!!

4. Declare aloud: Heavenly Father, I give You praise for the new covenant with You. I renounce the devil and all his demons in every area of my life. From today I will live my life for Jesus. I receive the life of Christ; I shall not die but live. With my whole life, I will serve You forever and be an instrument of deliverance to others in Jesus' name. Amen

5. Lord God, I repent and renounce every connection and exposures that channel the flow of evil into my life. From today, cleanse, sanctify and season every part of my life by fire in the mighty name of Jesus Christ.

CHAPTER 10

Other Demonic Doorways

He that diggeth a pit shall fall into it; and whoso breaketh an hedge, a serpent shall bite him" (**Ecclesiastes 10:8**)

There are no limits to our lives, but there are boundaries that have been clearly set by God. Boundaries exist to protect us. If you look at the Levitical priesthood, there were so many restrictions. Most of these are not necessary for salvation today, but they are very helpful in living a good life, whether it is in the area of dieting, in the area of social relationships, or our economic and financial lives. That is why, if you look at the days of Jesus, anytime anyone felt threatened with being thrown out of the synagogue, they were very careful because everything was regulated around the spiritual. If someone was cast out of the synagogue in those days, it was as if their entire life was taken from them; so they were always very careful.

OTHER DEMONIC DOORWAYS

That said, the important point is that there are boundaries. Under the Levitical law, a father must not see his daughter's nakedness. One must not uncover his father's nakedness, or his mother-in-law's, etc. There are moral codes that are meant to keep us from demonic openings. Satan will seek to open grounds in our lives in order for him to come in. He cannot readily jump on you, or anybody else for that matter. The door somehow, somewhere, must be open to him, and then he will work. That is why the Bible says *"He that diggeth a pit..."* **(Ecclesiastes 10:8).** Digging a pit is a way of creating avenues for the enemy. It further says that if you break a wall; (a wall is for protection) then the serpent will bite.

Let us identify some doorways through which demons find entrance:

1. Through the religious activities of your parents
Whatever your parents were into religion-wise has generational values. God was very particular in His restrictions. He said no worshipping of things that were made whether in heaven, in the earth, or beneath the earth or any likeness of anything. Why? Idolatry is a huge doorway that has generational curses.

> *"Idolatry is a huge doorway that has generational curses."*

This is one big problem with many of us from Africa and also other areas of the world. Our parents were not always believers in Jesus Christ; and others, even when they practiced some form of Christianity, did not practice it the correct way. When we talk about religion, we mean all forms of religion, whether Islam, Buddhism, Shintoism and even some pseudo-Christian professions that are not based on Bible standards for salvation.

There are Christian churches, denominational churches, not based on Bible standards of New Testament Christianity. They are religious, so when you get into those areas, demonic openings result from them. Anything outside of the Scripture, even if it is practiced within the church, constitutes a broken hedge. You have gone past the boundary. The Scripture is God's regulated code for behavior. Anything that you cannot find in the Scripture that you practice, even if it is in the church, is not covered, and it opens the doorway to the enemy.

> *"Anything outside of the Scripture, even if it is practiced within the church, constitutes a broken hedge."*

It is important to mention this because religion is very pervasive in all of the society in one way or the other. It is man's original attempt to get to God since the fall, and it comes in various forms, and the enemy uses it more than anything else.

2. From the womb

How can a child who is not even born, who is still in the womb, be demonically exposed? It is through the involvement of the parents. Whatever the parent does exposes the child. I know, for instance, that from my experience, my mother was a very ardent participant of a marine religion. She served marine spirits, had relationships with marine spirits and used marine power to protect her children and to fight for the fortunes of her children. Even when my elder brother became fantastically rich in those days, and I gave my life to the Lord and began to fight against the marine spirit, she told me that she was from marine and everything that we had come from that source. It was for this reason, among others, that I was rebellious against the family's wealth as it produced a lot of ungodliness.

Right through my deliverance, and even after my deliverance, one of the battles I fought in my life was with the marine spirit because of the way it functions. If a mother has it in her life while giving birth to her children, that demon spirit continues to regard the children as its children. So you might be seeing your mother in dreams but it may not be your mother, it might be the marine spirit. Even during my deliverance, it was the most difficult area on which to gain a handle. I would see myself wandering all over in my dreams with my mom hand in hand, walking and talking. I would wake up and know that it was not my mother it was the marine spirit.

At last, I finally just cried unto God and said: "can you just help me so that when I am in my dream moving about with this spirit, I will know it is not my mother." Then, one day, we were hand in hand moving all over the place I just heard what seemed like a phone call inside me. "You are in a dream state, and you are with the marine spirit. This is not your mother." I looked at it; she had that mischievous smile. I said, "You are not my mother, you are marine. The Blood of Jesus! The Blood of Jesus!" She vanished.

Another day, I was in the same dream state again, I recognized her again, and I said, "You are not my mother." My mother was semi-literate and could not speak the Queen's English, but this spirit would speak fluent English. So I knew. I started to plead the Blood, and she said, "It will not work for you this time around." I plead the Blood, and nothing happened. I said, "Lord, what is happening?" He said, "Because you are living in unforgiveness and malice with your roommate, you cannot claim the promise of God and violate the Word." That is why I say to people that my battles with the devil taught me godliness and in a lot of ways taught me the Word of God. That is why deliverance for me is not just theory or book matter it is something **very real.** I learned some things by Satan's constant attack on me.

I have also seen pregnant women taking their pregnancies to the coven. On the flip side, I have also seen women who are born again, filled with the Holy Ghost, whose babies in the womb would fight with them in warfare, because such babies are spirit beings. Remember that John the Baptist was filled with the Holy Ghost in his mother's womb. Children are spirits. So, depending on what the parent is in touch with or receiving help from, the child can become exposed while in the womb.

3. Parental disobedience to God has implications on children

You will readily remember Achan in the Book of Joshua. God instructed His people that they should not touch any of the spoils of Jericho. But Achan lusted after a Babylonian garment and a wedge of gold and brought defeat to Israel's camp. When the judgment was to fall for that sin, it did not only affect him but his wife and children also. So as parents, we carry a heavy responsibility.

The thing you do as a father has impact over four generations. The choices you make as a father will continue to have an impact. I think if we know the implications of these things, we would not be anxious about bringing children into the world. When you are younger, you are so excited about having children, especially if you are African. Children are awesome, but there is a huge spiritual responsibility that comes with them.

What did Jesus say concerning Judas? He said, "*The Son of man goeth as it is written of him: but woe unto that man by whom the Son of man is betrayed! It had been good for that man if he had not been born*" (Matthew 26:24). So, while it is good to have children, we must always be mindful that it is such a responsibility spiritually. This awareness will shake us up a little bit. Training and upbringing of children must be taken seriously.

4. Occult involvement

Any form of occult involvement, whether inherent occult ability or formal occult enlistment, is a demonic doorway. What do I mean by inherent occult ability? If your grandparents were involved in the occult, first and foremost, you are a member. When people get involved in the occult, they do not only swear their allegiance; they hand over their children and their children's children as well. Your parent's involvement means you are already a member, even without any willingness or contribution on your part. That is why you sometimes marvel when you see yourself in certain dream situations - you have become implicated in things you never formally engage in.

But there are other formal occult involvements, where you can enlist as a member and start receiving materials and instructions; in fact, some will contact you. Since my wife and I have been in the United States, we have been contacted. We once received a letter saying, "We are sorry to say that we have investigated you, and have seen your spiritual potential and with your agreement by signing this letter, we are sending this material to you free of cost." The senders even went as far as to tell us how expensive the material was and to furnish us with a list of names of people who had been members all the way from presidents down. I replied one to say, "the Blood of Jesus!" and seized the opportunity to preach the gospel message. For others, I just ripped up their letters.

So, the occult certainly does contact people. Now when you get involved and start reading their materials and patronizing them, that is a doorway. Satan is a spiritual prostitute who wants to pollute all and sundry. There are some occult involvements that don't seem so serious, but they create some form of a soul tie. For instance, I was in a coffee shop to get coffee. While there, I saw so many wonderful Hispanic people, all lined up, carrying their cups. I imagined they were going on a trip. But I later discovered that there was a man there, a medium, with a snake spirit, and they were all lined up to receive divination from him. By doing that, they were exposing themselves and their children's children.

Have you seen people reading the stars? Or those preparing or consulting horoscope which they claim can make predictions about your life? Don't be deceived - stargazing or star-reading is exposing yourself to witchcraft. It is a very dangerous practice to be reading stars. Once you do that, you are exposing your destiny to demonic investigations which you think is just about receiving information and nothing is done to you. They will modulate, reprogram and steal your destiny. Star-reading is a medium of exposure to demonic infiltration.

5. Demonic Material possession

A lot of the time we travel to different cultures and acquire pieces of art work. In December 1994, I attended a function in Thailand. Besides the business side, there was a tourism side to my trip, and Thailand makes big revenue from tourism. Some of the ladies that were in the same hotel as we went out and visited Buddha temples in the name of sight-seeing. One of the ladies during the visit tied a red ribbon to her wrist. What do you think that was? That was occult initiation straight away! They were not aware, but it had entered their lives and would have consequences and problems until maybe when that person gives her life to Jesus Christ.

6. Demonic transference from other people

Demons can transfer from one person to the other by close association. A more common type is sexual relationship outside of marriage.

I remember the story of this wonderful woman who used to love the Lord and was very dedicated to His service for some fifteen years as a single woman. Later, for some reasons, she left her church and severed her relationship with her pastor. A report came back later that this wonderful sister had started

OTHER DEMONIC DOORWAYS

dating and sleeping with a man who was a high priest of the devil, whom she said she hoped to convert. Unknown to her, immediately she started sleeping with that man, the exchange of body fluid is an offering on the devil's altar already. Demons are immediately transferred.

However, it doesn't even have to be an association as deep as this for demons to be transferred. That is why in church, you have to be aware. I talk a lot about my wife. She is popular anywhere I go. I remember when I was in Atlanta, and she was in Africa, there was this lady who told me that when my wife returned, she wanted her to be her prayer partner. I thought that was wonderful. I was anxious to tell my wife because that was one of my friends. I told my wife, and she said, "I will pray about it." I was mad at her because the lady was really reaching out to her. But my wife kept saying she would pray about it. However, shortly before we left Atlanta, my eyes were opened to the fact that this "*woman of God*" was very deadly spiritually. Can you imagine someone like that becoming your prayer partner killing you while praying with you?

The church is meant to be about fellowship, not mere relationship. When you and I are close, it is a type of fellowship. Fellowship means sharing. Sharing means I am taking a part of you and you are taking a part of me. The person you are close to, sometimes even while you are reading a book, you can hear their voice if you are sensitive to the spirit.

If they have been giving you spiritual advice, helping you, you will see them in your dreams sometimes when the Lord wants to talk to you. It is because you are sharing. That is why the Bible says if any believer is a fornicator, a railer, or an extortioner, do not eat with them. It says have nothing to do with them. If someone who is not a believer is fornicating, you can define your relationship level; but the one who is a believer, who is practicing these things and you are yoked together with them, a transfer takes place.

In other words, when you are close to people, let your light shine out, and let their light shine out and there will be fellowship. If it is not light to light, the demonic transfer can occur. This especially concerns your close friends. Watch out for gossip. Do not allow gossip between you and another Christian. That is spiritual carelessness. Let the basis of your relationship with your brothers and your sisters be the Lord Himself.

There are people who like to exchange clothing items. This can pose a risk of demonic intrusion. When you wear someone's clothes, there is a spiritual transfer. Look at it from a positive light too. Sometimes God wants me to impart my anointing, especially on the field, when I am under the power of God, and the Holy Spirit would lead me to put my cloth on an individual as a form of impartation to that person with what God has given me. Your clothing carries your essence. That is why the

Bible says that aprons and handkerchiefs were taken from the body of Paul and were taken to the sick, and many of the sick were healed, and demons departed from the afflicted **(Acts 19:11-12)**. Why? The anointing from him passed over the items. When Elisha cried to Elijah, *"My father, my father, the chariot of Israel, and the horsemen thereof"* **(2Kings 2:12)** what happened? The mantle of Elijah fell. Elisha immediately ripped his clothes and wore Elijah's mantle. From then on, the anointing of Elijah came upon him in a double measure.

If you are walking in the glory of God and given to prayer and fasting, your clothing will begin to carry the presence and the power of God. On the contrary, someone who is godless has the aura of evil around him. Can you imagine your daughter or your son exchanging trousers (pants) with a fornicator who is sleeping around? Demons from such person will be transferred to the child. Not too long, that child will be struggling with the demons and may begin to fornicate.

7. Sexual immorality

Sex is the easiest and most common demonic doorway because sex constitutes a blood covenant. Sex is not just an act; it is an impartation. When two people get together in sexual intimacy, they breathe into each other, and that becomes a soul exchange. Spirit is breath. It is the quickest, easiest way for spirits to be transferred. That is why the most dangerous bomb on the earth is not an atomic bomb; it is a prostitute. Her ability to move things around for the enemy is powerful. That is why the devil uses the doorway of sex like no other.

I can guarantee that between the ages of five and seven, he will work hard to open that door in the life of a child, either through some relative an aunty, an uncle, or through some other individual. With such violation, he tries one way or another to open the door and slots his demons there. That demon will produce rebellion, rejection, and sexual promiscuity later as the child enters into teenage years.

Of course, any sex that is not covered by God is a demonic opening. What do I mean by *not covered by God*? Sex outside of marriage is not covered by God. The only place for sex before God is within the context of marriage. Remember that the Bible says that when Adam and his wife were naked and were not ashamed. Why? God covered them with his glory. When they sinned, that covering was broken, and that was why they were looking for fig leaves and accusing one another. Outside of marriage, which is God's purpose, sex is a huge doorway for demons. It is a blood covenant. The exchange of fluid is blood covenant. The breathing on one another is soul impartation. The exchange of fluids and the exchange of breath mean that demons flow back and forth. But, in itself, sex as a covenant means you are swearing (covenanting):*Whatever I am, whatever I will become, whatever I will ever have I give to you,* and that person says the same thing to you. The covenant is then sealed by the exchange of body fluids and blood which seals the covenant.

When, for instance, a born again child of God lies with someone to whom they are not married, it is a curse; plus, imagine if that person were to be demonic. The devastation that comes through it is just endless pain. One time in the year 2000, I was preaching at a crusade in Lagos. Every night, after the crusade, the organizers would drive me back to where I was staying. On the way, I would see this beautiful, gorgeous, fair-complexioned lady sitting by the wayside. I knew that she was hunting for men; so, on one occasion, I asked the driver to stop the car. She moved to the car, and I noticed one of her legs was slightly disabled. I said, "How are you, sweetie?" She smiled at me. I started preaching the gospel to her, and she got angry. I said, "Well you heard me already. You need to repent and turn your life over to the Lord. Repent or perish." Then, I left.

When I got to where I was staying, as I began to change out of my clothes, there she was! In the spirit, I saw her. I said, "The Blood of Jesus!" Then I asked the Lord, "What is happening?" He said, "You thought she was an ordinary girl. She is a Satanist hunting for the destiny of men". That means that any man who slept with her had his destiny vandalized.

Can you imagine people just running around the street picking stuff and not knowing who they are picking? This is why you have to be careful if you have an adulterous partner. Because you are one body, if your partner is committing adultery you will feel it because it is your body out there performing. You have to know the ground you are standing on. That is why one of the sins that God gives as a ground on which He permits divorce is sexual immorality. It is right there in the Word and available if you cannot forgive and get past it. But if you have forgiven it and you are still with the partner, you have to know the Scripture to stand on before you get intimate with your partner again.

The Bible says,*"For the unbelieving husband is sanctified by the wife, and the unbelieving wife is sanctified by the husband"* **(1 Corinthians 7:14).** Take an authoritative stand and invoke that Scripture to bind the demons and declare that "my bed is holy, he (or she) is wayward, but I am standing holy for God, so you demons do not touch me!" This helps so that when you get intimate with them, they're not transferring demons to you. Sex is the devil's biggest doorway.

8. Misguided deliverance

Deliverance is by the power of the Holy Spirit. So, when you are spiritually naked, you cannot conduct deliverance. You can become careless and spiritually naked not just by open sin, but through careless living. If you are not maintaining an intimate relationship with the Lord but merely living like an ordinary person, you can become exposed. If you constantly neglect prayer and you do not fast, you can be spiritually naked but still carry the title of a minister of God. When somebody who is an agent of the enemy comes for deliverance after seeing your spiritual state, if you go ahead to minister the deliverance, you may get attacked by demons of lust, for example. And if you do not know your stand you will get in trouble.

There have been deliverance ministers who had gone to minister and ended up sleeping with the person they were supposed to be helping. Those were not accidents. They were attacked, and because they were open and naked, it happened to them. I remember, in 1987, there was this young lady in the church. Her parents would send her to me on Saturdays to assist her with her studies. I was still a bachelor, young and nice looking. I was teaching her one day, and she started to attack my genitals with a snake. You do not know these things if you do not have discernment of spirit and you do not live in the Spirit, but I knew.

A man of God without discernment would have begun to react. But I knew what she was doing. I felt the snake hitting my genitals. So I said to her, "Do you want to sleep with your pastor? She said, "Yes." I said, "When I am preaching, do you see the power of God?" She said, "Sure, I do." I said, "Ok, do you think that for thirty minutes of sexual gratification with you I would like to sell the power of God in my life?" She kept quiet. I said, "You need to repent. Take your Bible, go home. See you next week." That ended our Saturday studies.

There are agents of the devil who are out there. Not long ago, God kept saying to my wife and me consistently that there was someone who was going to come and say she needed deliverance, but she would not be truly seeking deliverance; she was an agent of darkness. I would share with my wife, and we would talk about it over and again. When the person eventually came, I did not know immediately that it was her. We did deliverance for her, and I embraced her but did not know.

During my wedding anniversary, our daughter decided to pay for a night for my wife and me to stay at a hotel. We went to the hotel and slept all night. The following day, after being well rested, God opened my eyes. It was as if I was watching TV. I said, "Oh my God, this particular sister is an agent. I saw her right there attacking people in the church". I was already trying to do so much to help her grow in God, but she had no intention of growing. This was not someone you would look at physically and think anything is wrong. From then, I started watching her a little bit more closely. I wouldn't send her away until she figured out that I knew who she was and moved herself away. Until she did, I struggled with the thought of whether to call her and warn her, or just let her go.

I say to people; the devil is joining us in the church. The church is not a refuge; it is a battlefront. We are here for one purpose to get souls saved and delivered. That is why we come, not to eat and drink coffee.

9. Soul ties

What are soul ties? There are positive soul ties, and there are negative soul ties. A soul tie is when two souls are intermingled, usually through the gate of love. God instituted soul ties for His purposes. The devil also implements soul ties for his destructive purposes. God will give you covenant friends. That is His investment to making sure His purpose comes to pass in your life. They will love you and give you a commitment that is beyond normal.

If you are not a spiritually mature person, God can put the love of someone in your heart, and you will be wondering am I lusting after this person? (if it is someone of opposite gender). If it is a Godly soul tie, there is no need to be scared. It is a measure of His purpose within you and the individual. God put that love there. When you pray for them in your prayer time, you will find peace and definition, but on a few occasions you might begin to wonder, *am I losing it? Am I going out of boundary?*

"Divine love... will never dishonor God."

It is not that it is not from God. God can give you that extra bit of love for somebody because there is a measure of His plan and purpose that He is positioning you to carry out in this person's life. This is a positive soul tie.

A classic Biblical example is Jonathan and David. As David came to Saul, Jonathan saw him and loved him. He removed his belt, his girdle, his sword and handed it over to him. That is divine opening, a supernatural love. Over the course of time, they became very close. His father wanted David dead so that Jonathan could be king. He protected David and said, *"When you become king, remember me."*

Now the devil has his perverted form of soul ties. It is on the reverse. Where two people are in a lustful relationship, where they cannot part from each other, the two souls have mingled and, because of that, even though things are wrong, they will still stay in that relationship. Through such negative soul ties, demonic flow is easily activated. How do you know that a negative soul tie has occurred between two people? Divine love is a platform for honoring God and fulfilling purpose. It will never dishonor God. When a negative soul tie is enacted between two people, they will dishonor God, and they will not mind. But real love will never dishonor God, for love is of God.

10. Demonic laying on of hands

One of the things that the enemy does is to quickly push his agents into churches. Can you imagine if God did not give me discernment? I could have fallen victim in so many cases. We started a ministry in a particular city, and I met a lady whom I received readily. I remember when she was given the microphone to pray, I thought, "This is a powerful woman; we can just groom her to lead the women's ministry."

She looked like a minister to me. Until we started having a revival and I had the opportunity to take a good look at her. She was wearing snakes. I was shocked. I looked at her, and I thought, maybe she only needed deliverance; maybe she was not an agent. But I noticed something else. When I gave her a hug, her hair touched my forehead, and I felt some sensations and vibes. Snakes! They tried to stir sensuality in me. I tell you, things happen in the Kingdom. Thank God for Jesus!

Again in her case, two months before she came, the Lord had told my wife that she would be coming and gave a complete description. But this is the funny part; when she came, we did not know right away. But I think it is proper in that way because you do not want to start scanning everyone who comes your way. That is not discernment. That is living in bondage and suspicion. You have to allow everyone to be free and God will inform you at the right moment this is what I was talking about.

Now, imagine that such an agent sneaked into the church. Pastors are constantly looking for helpers and workers. And the thing is, these agents are often very zealous and seemingly ready to render service. You may be thanking God for finally answering your prayers by sending you a responsible worker not knowing it's a snake you got! Before you know it you are saying, "Let us ordain him a deacon; let us ordain her a deaconess." That is Satan's way of promoting such people over others. From then on, they will start attacking the prayer life of the church; they will start attacking the members so that they become sluggish spiritually. They wouldn't know what hit them.

Supposing you are having a revival and you invite such agents to be laying hands with you. What do you think they will be doing? Transferring demons to people!

Fallen Generals
Demonic laying on of hands can also be from people I call *fallen generals*. I met a popular man of God in Atlanta and, immediately, the Holy Spirit showed me one or two things. He wanted to come and minister in my church. He asked when I held Bible studies and I told him on Fridays. He said, "OK, I will be there."

The man came and spoke powerfully. The following day, I allowed him, and he spoke powerfully. I even gave him some good money from the church. We, however, noticed that while the message was going on, he was openly flirting with somebody in the service. I play a lot, but there is a difference between playing and flirtation. The following day, Monday, I was driving around with my daughter and one other person in my car. I said to them, "Mommy and I do not have time to eat now; we will just drop you off at the restaurant, and you eat."

My daughter and that other person told us later that when they entered the restaurant, they were shocked that the lady the so-called minister was openly flirting with during ministration, and the man of God were in the restaurant having dinner. I was shocked. *Somebody he just met in my church the previous day for the first time?* I called the sister and said, "How is it that this man, while he was preaching, was flirting with you and on Monday you are having dinner with him?" She said, "Well, he took my number and called me to say he wants to marry me. I am sorry I went out of the way, but I wanted to know who this guy is. He was sitting there proposing marriage to me, but I told him you just saw me three days ago for the first time in your life."

I decided to take a closer look; so I began to investigate him on the Internet. I found enough. I called the pastor who introduced us, and I said, "When I meet people through you, I want to know that they are exactly like you. This man is not like you." She apologized and said she met him through a great international man of God. But he was not who he claimed to be. He had great knowledge of the Word of God. He could recite the entire Bible by heart. Listening to him, you would know that this was no ordinary man, but someone who should be far up there. A mighty general for God. But he was nowhere. Now, it is one thing for someone to make a mistake and be heartbroken and say, "God, I am sorry." But it is quite another thing to be living a double life deliberately, knowingly. That is the kind of person that demons will flow through. As he lays hands, he starts imparting the mess that is in him to others.

11. Inherited family curses
There are certain families in which you can see a curse operating. How do you know when there is a curse operating? It is usually the same kind of sickness striking different members of the family. This one dies of cancer, the other one is dying of cancer, and another one has died of cancer. There is an existing curse. Or it could be that the family members reach a particular place of prosperity and everything begins to go down. You can see the repeated experiences in each of them. That is an indication of a hidden curse. Or across the board, marriages do not work. This could simply be an existing curse that needs to be broken for the members of the family to be free.

What are the root causes of inherited family curses that can bring this dimension of oppression? Idol worship or idolatry; demonic worship or involvement in demonic rituals and satanic programs; curses pronounced on the family by a person with a demonic authority; as well as cultures and cultural practices that flow from demonic origins and sources, among others.

BREAKTHROUGH PROPHETIC DELIVERANCE PRAYERS

1. I decree and declare that I am a blood bought child of the living God and the Blood of the Everlasting Covenant is active in my life. Every operation of the Kingdom of darkness against me is illegal and therefore it shall not stand nor come to pass in the mighty name of Jesus.

2. I command all evil altars of sin, affliction, captivity, and bondage in my life to burn to ashes right now in Jesus' name.

3. I plead the Blood of Jesus upon me and upon every part of my body and every area of my life.

   Let the Blood of Jesus, cleanse me now from every contamination with evil in Jesus' name. Holy Spirit of the living God, I invite you afresh to take your rightful place my life. Holy Spirit, deliver me. Purify my soul and sanctify me in Jesus' name.

4. I declare that I am holy for I am the righteousness of God in Christ.

5. I command my stolen opportunities and possessions to locate me from today. Whatever I lost in my time of bondage and captivity, I recover all now in the mighty name of Jesus Christ. Give God thanks and quality praise.

6. Every blood or fluid covenant I entered into unknowingly, I revoke it in Jesus' name. With the fire of God I set ablaze every object taken out of my body in Jesus' name.

7. Today, I decree that my body parts or my clothing in the hands of the wicked will no longer answer to evil covenants and altars in Jesus' name.

8. Every evil load I am carrying because of evil sexual intercourse, I offload you now in Jesus' name. Through the Blood of Jesus, I am free at last, for whom the Son sets free is free indeed.

CHAPTER 11

Can A Christian be Demon-possessed?

This is a very sensitive issue and one that has been mostly controversial. It tends to put people off the benefits of deliverance ministry.

Now, when people say a Christian cannot be demon-possessed, they are correct, in a certain scriptural sense. Getting a demon out of a Christian does not mean that such a believer in Jesus Christ is or was demon-possessed. Very often, when the power of God's Holy Spirit is present and moving to dislodge demons in the oppressed, unenlightened Church members recoil, thinking those receiving help are not true Christians. Nothing could be further from the truth.

Ignorance about deliverance and cleansing is what predisposes well-meaning individuals to despise those who are seeking help and reject deliverance ministration, thinking those receiving help must not be true people of God to have been hosting demons. A born again child of God cannot be demon possessed; however, a born-again, spirit-filled, God-fearing, God-honoring child of God can host or have a demon or several, hundreds, even thousands of demons in their lives oppressing them.

God wants His people delivered and free indeed. Where the power of God typically initiates the process of deliverance and, depending on the severity of each case, you will have manifestations. Manifestations include visible shaking, foaming at the mouth, yawning, or rolling on the ground. All these indicate something positive. First, it indicates that the Spirit of God wants to bring about deliverance because, according to His wisdom, deliverance is possible. But the issues have to be worked out for effective deliverance to take place.

Now to stay on track, what does it mean to be demon-possessed? To be demon-possessed means that a particular demon is within the spirit of an individual and therefore has a claim of ownership over that person. It is a term that is very difficult to properly apply to any human being, much less a Christian. However, for somebody who has not received Jesus Christ, his spirit automatically belongs to the devil. Man is made of spirit, soul, and body, in that order - the spirit being the most important because it is the dwelling home of God.

The soul of man is his personality, comprising the mind for reasoning, the will for decisions and the emotions for affection. The mind further consists of imaginations and thought processes for seeing within the eye-gate of the mind in the course of reasoning, making decisions and processing of information.

Man also has a body. A body simply houses the man as long as he lives on the earth. The body has five senses – taste, sight, smell, hearing and touch, which enable him to communicate with his immediate environment. When somebody has not yet received Jesus Christ, the total man – spirit, soul, and body - is under darkness, due to the fall of Adam and because man is conceived in iniquity. This is when the devil can effectively possess and control the person

David said, *"Behold, I was shapen in iniquity; and in sin did my mother conceive me"* (Psalm 51:5). Every person who comes into this world is spiritually dead on arrival, and this has been so from the time of the fall of Adam. But when they come to Christ, they are passed from death to life. The Lord Jesus said in John 5:24: *"Verily, verily, I say unto you, He that heareth my word, and believeth on him that sent me, hath everlasting life, and shall not come into condemnation; but is passed from death unto life."*

When somebody is dead in sin and trespasses, not having come to the Lord, the motions of sin, the power of the grave, and the forces of darkness that are distributed throughout the earth maintain a major ancestral and territorial control over the individual. As I said before, an individual can be opened to direct demonic activity through the work of the parents or through the things the parents believed and participated in. I have found that even children who are still in the womb can be exposed to demonic infestation. From when they are born and as they grow up, depending on their environment, they can become further exposed to demonic infestation.

A DEMON CANNOT POSSESS A TRUE CHRISTIAN

However, when somebody acknowledges and receives Jesus Christ, demons cannot live in his spirit because eternal life has come into the spirit of that man. That eternal life is superior to the highest power of the enemy which is death. Resurrection life comes into that spirit, and darkness is dispelled, and the light of God is maintained by the Holy Spirit in the heart of the individual. That is why the Bible says that if a man has not the spirit of Christ he is not of Jesus Christ (Romans 8:9). In other words, if you have received Christ Jesus, if you know Him as your Lord and Savior, the Spirit of Christ comes to indwell your spirit. But He does not just indwell -He first regenerates; that is, gives life, the God-kind of life, to your human spirit, and then dwells in your human spirit. Then, neither Lucifer, nor death, nor hell, nor any other power can reside in the spirit of that man. That man belongs to Christ completely – spirit, soul, and body and cannot be said to be demon-possessed.

However, depending on what the individual had been exposed to previously, and depending on whether they had received appropriate help as they integrated into Christianity, that person can still host thousands of demon spirits in their body and aspects of the soul already violated and scarred. In other words, the demons do not possess that believer, but aspects of that believer's life have been demonized. This is what has to be addressed through deliverance ministry; through counseling and training in the Word of God, to reclaim aspects of human personality and behavior, which have been corrupted by evil powers that were there prior to coming to the Lord. That is what we address in deliverance, and to that extent, we cannot say that a believer is demon-possessed; rather it is a form of oppression being outside of the spirit of man.

> *"A demon cannot possibly own a Christian because a Christian already belongs to the Lord Jesus."*

I once ran a church in a certain neighborhood on the penthouse floor of an eight-story building. It was a lovely chapel. We enjoyed it, until one day, we found, to our amazement, that we were invaded by fast-moving, smart little mice. It was big trouble most especially for the sisters. You can just imagine a sister coming to the office, and this little mouse shows up, bumps us, and runs around. Some would scream, some would jump on the chairs. It was quite interesting, to say the least. Would you, therefore, say, at this point, that my church was owned by the mice? This is what it implies when someone says possession suggests ownership.

A demon cannot possibly own a Christian because a Christian already belongs to the Lord Jesus. The mice were in the church, moving around, and we had to deal with them. The mice did not possess the church. The church, at that particular time, possessed some mice because the church was housing some mice. That is the proper word. A Christian can be "housing" demon spirits, of which they may not be aware immediately. Because those demons are able to stay undercover, they can gradually destroy the benefits and the peace of that individual believer. However, the purpose of deliverance is to locate the demons, either by the anointing or by the gift of the Spirit, called discerning of spirits, or even by mature counseling and observation. When we see certain types of behaviors which do not subscribe to the Word of God on a pronounced basis – I call them exaggerated behavior due to demonic corruption - we can then bring those people into counseling and get the demons to leave.

ONLY BELIEVERS CAN RECEIVE DELIVERANCE

Another way to answer this question is to inquire: Can you cast a demon out of somebody who is not a believer? The answer will be no. You cannot cast out a demon from somebody who is not a believer because Jesus already indicated that when an unclean spirit is gone out of a person, he walks about in dry places seeking rest and finds none (Matthew 12). This means that demons are spirits without bodies that try to find homes in any individual they can invade and then manifest their evil nature. When you get rid of them, they become tormented and wander around like homeless people. Then these demons decide to return to their original abode with stronger assistants. They record easy success if the place is found empty, and the last stage of the person becomes worse than the first.

This indicates that, for an individual who is not willing to be submitted to the lordship of Jesus Christ and become His disciple, it is useless to try to get demons out of them because we will complicate their already bad conditions. This is why I often say that you cannot deliver anybody who is not already delivered. In other words, what we call deliverance - which I will more appropriately call cleansing - is cleaning out demons from an individual. That cleansing is only applicable to people who have made a profession of faith and are ready to be disciples of the Lord. These are the people you can cast demons out of. Your casting demons out of them simply mean you are enforcing the law over these demons because as soon as people receive the Lord Jesus Christ, they are His property and any demon that remains in that individual is in violation or committing spiritual territorial trespassing. Any child of God who is conscious of the authority of Christ that has been delegated to them can cast out that devil and get rid of it.

A Christian cannot be demon-possessed, and deliverance cannot be done on the unbeliever. That being the case, we can conclude that deliverance is the bread of children. There is a case of the Syrophoenician woman in Matthew 15, who was not in the Abrahamic covenant, but who, during the ministry of Jesus went after Him, desiring deliverance for her daughter who was demon tormented. The Bible says the Lord would not answer her and she followed hard after Him. When her persistence became unbearable, the disciples complained to the Lord. He replied, *"I am not sent but unto the lost sheep of the house of Israel."*

In other words, in His first coming, His ministry was primarily to the house of Israel. But the woman pressed on in faith. So, Jesus turned to her and said, *"It is not meet to take the children's bread, and to cast it to dogs."* Remarkably, the woman answered in faith; she didn't feel insulted having just been called a dog by the Lord Jesus. She said, *"Truth, Lord: yet the dogs eat of the crumbs which fall from their masters' table."* She was simply saying, *"I am not asking for real bread, just give me the crumbs. Whether bread or crumbs it still has enough power to cast out the devil."*

Here, we see that deliverance is called the children's bread. Of course, Jesus was impressed by the woman's faith and said, *"O woman, great is thy faith: be it unto thee even as thou wilt."* From that hour, the demon left. The most important point here is that deliverance is called the bread of children. So we can conclude that deliverance is for God's children. The unsaved person cannot rightly benefit from deliverance.

As I have explained before, the Bible says that we have been translated into the Kingdom of God's dear Son, having obtained redemption through His Blood, the forgiveness of sins (Colossians 1:14). There are four classes of spiritual realities from which created beings can function. The lowest level is the man who is in sin and does not know the Lord Jesus Christ. Such a person runs around with a dead spirit. Immediately above that is the kingdom of darkness where we have Lucifer, the leader of that gang of rebels, the other fallen angels (in the categories of principalities, powers, rulers of darkness, and hosts of spiritual wickedness in high places). Then there are men, who are vested with satanic authority, also functioning at the level of the rebellious one being alienated from the life of God. The third category of spirits are the angels that have not rebelled but are still with God who are in a superior position now and have authority over the kingdom of darkness. They serve God, God's Family, and God's Kingdom. Finally, we have the highest class of spirit beings, Father, Son, and Holy Spirit. Every person who is born again is a part of this Family of God. That is the superior class.

BELIEVERS CARRY GOD'S DNA

I say superior because every born-again person carries God's DNA; they carry the divine nature and have escaped corruption by becoming partakers of the divine nature. It puts us even in a superior class to the angels. This is not to be disrespectful to the phenomenal work that the angels of God do, but that is the truth. The angels are God's servants (Hebrews 1:7). They are sent forth to minister for the heirs of salvation (Hebrews1:14). If you are born again, you are an heir of salvation, a joint heir with Christ; you are in a family relationship with The Almighty God - God is your Father, and His DNA resides in you.

What I wish to emphasize with the above explanation is that demon-possession is far from Christians. However, Christians who are born again and made partakers of the divine nature, filled with the Holy Spirit and walking in the will of God, can also, in fact, have thousands of demons in various aspects of their lives, depending on what they had been exposed. At the point they become Christians, those things ought to be cleaned out so that they can serve the Lord meaningfully.

BELIEVERS CAN HAVE DEMONS

We see a very parallel example in the Bible in the deliverance of the demon-oppressed man of Gadara in Luke 8:26-39. Gadara is a part of Israel. When Israel came out of Egypt, two and a half tribes inherited the Amorite kings and possessed the first set of inheritance before everybody crossed over Jordan to possess the Land of Canaan. These two and a half tribes always seemed to be having trouble aligning spiritually and theologically with the other nine and a half tribes. At a point in time, their spiritual condition deteriorated. Until even the time of the ministry of Jesus, they were openly raising swine and thriving in the swine business which was forbidden to the Jewish people.

Here, in Luke 8, we find a man who was possessed by a legion of demons. A legion is at least 6,800 demons. This possessed man was a son of Abraham, within the Abrahamic covenant; yet he was possessed to such a level with that many demons in him. What did Jesus do? In fact, the man initiated the actions, because this man who was carrying close to 7000 demons or more, had enough sense to run to Jesus and worship Him. His tormented soul could still recognize his Maker, and he worshiped the Lord Jesus - whereas many religious, self-righteous people were in the temple, persecuting the Lord throughout His ministry. It was in such scenario that Jesus challenged the demons to get out of the man, and with His command and glorious presence, He cleaned out the entire haul of demons from this man.

Can you imagine what would have happened if Jesus had not addressed those demons but just accepted the worship, and the man became His follower? It would have happened that some days the man would demonstrate sanity, but on other days, he would act insanely.

There are many in Christianity who have dual characters: bipolar characters. One day, they are good Christians; at another time, you find them behaving strangely. One day, they are very good parents; another day, they are just pure evil. This is a sign that something is tormenting and working there to tear down their Christian profession and to torment them and those who are close to them. Often, when we discover people like that in the church, we just counsel them. We do not pray or fast to discern what is producing this type of behavior and to get to the root of it.

I remember some years ago there was this wonderful individual who was so kind to us. However, at some point, I realized that this wonderful child of God who was so good to us, walking in holiness and devoted to God, had some demonic undercurrents which were undermining her effectiveness and had substantially destroyed some of her blessings. I requested her to join me on a seven-day fast, where we could pray for eliminating what I thought I saw. We embarked on the fast, and at the end, when I wanted to pray, the demon surfaced and tried to feed my pride by shouting that I was too tough for it; that it had cleverly concealed its behavior hiding itself all this time, and now I had come to expose it. I answered that I was not the tough one; it was the Lord Jesus who had the stronger power.

Demons can be very clever and subtle. They can be in a Christian and carefully dodge the fire. What will happen is that these Christians will be very zealous and will work very hard for God; but every time that the demon knows that they will be face-to-face with fire, it manipulates their circumstances so that they are not in those meetings. This can go on for years. What the demon is doing is simply protecting itself from the line of fire. But if by some divine intervention the individual is exposed to the firepower of the Holy Spirit in an atmosphere that is charged, what happens is that the demon is forced to appear and flee.

It is a very embarrassing situation for the devil because his well-conceived agenda of destruction is brought to the open and his weakness is exposed as his demons bow out under the superior firepower of the Holy Spirit and the Almighty name of the Lord Jesus Christ.

I will say conclusively that, according to the Word of God, a born-again Christian cannot be demon-possessed. That is the final word. But a Christian can be oppressed; he can be suppressed, he can be obsessed, he can be depressed. These are demonic conditions. They are abnormal, and they are to be addressed by the Word of God.

BREAKTHROUGH PROPHETIC DELIVERANCE PRAYERS

"Shake thyself from the dust; arise, and sit down, O Jerusalem: loose thyself from the bands of thy neck, O captive daughter of Zion" **(Isaiah 52:2).**

1. I shake myself from every dust of my past failures and defeat; I break the grip of every satanic limitation and restriction in the mighty name of Jesus' Amen

2. I release the fire of the Holy Spirit to destroy every fire that is keeping me down and bound; I set ablaze every anti-progress spells of the enemy in my life and command divine supernatural acceleration in all my life endeavors in the mighty name of Jesus'

3. I command every power scattering/wasting my resources/opportunities to expire in Jesus' name. Amen

4. I hereby decree that I shall no longer serve sin and my oppressors in Jesus' name. Amen.

5. Every power suppressing my divine elevation, be destroyed now; I embrace my moment in the limelight in Jesus' name.

CHAPTER 12

Practical Deliverance Sessions

There is a compelling need to conduct deliberate and effective deliverance sessions at the earliest possible opportunity for people coming to faith in the Lord Jesus Christ. Such an early start in this important direction will help to eliminate grounds for recurrent demonic activity and spare God's people years of delay, pain, and needless frustration in their journey of faith. God's people will be empowered to walk in the liberty that the Lord Jesus Christ purchased for us through His atoning death, burial and resurrection.

There are four levels at which this may be done.

1. Group Deliverance Services

Group deliverance service is a somewhat more general form of deliverance. It is like a church service or a crusade service where the issues of demonic bondage are highlighted and people are generally taught or counseled by the Word of God. This might be followed by questions and answers, after which the deliverance minister leads the congregation in a session of warfare prayers - breaking covenants and hidden curses, and applying the Blood of Jesus. And in that corporate anointed atmosphere, the power of God is released.

This kind of general deliverance session has its own advantage in that many people can be helped under that corporate anointing. Chains get broken, yokes are removed, and healings flow freely. Such sessions, however, can be way more effective if there are deliverance team members within a given anointed structure, who have received training on how to handle people, so that when that corporate anointing is moving, people then can be assisted generally to come into liberty, and the demonic issues are cleaned up properly and thoroughly.

2. Faith Clinics

A Faith Clinic is another form of group deliverance but it is group deliverance "par excellence." This is the method often employed by specialized deliverance ministries and groups. Just as the name implies, this type of group operates like a hospital or clinic. It combines a unique blend of deliverance emphases with an interdisciplinary pool of other ministry gifts or specializations to address the multifaceted needs of different case scenarios that otherwise might prove difficult if they were handled in the more general type of anointed atmosphere.

Typically, you would have a pool of skilled spiritual counselors, word teachers, prayer warriors, prophetic hands, seers, and support staff, all working together in a team to secure the thorough release, cleansing, and healing of the oppressed and afflicted person.

How is this done?
The leadership of the deliverance team or ministry decides on a given date to schedule a deliverance clinic. Groundwork before the date will include preparation of advertorials and questionnaires for collecting data in the counseling sessions. There should also be statements of release from legal prosecution, duly signed by those benefitting from deliverance ministrations. Such statements should be prepared by a qualified legal practitioner. Spiritual preparation includes a time of fasting, prayer, and seeking the Lord for direction and the release of His anointing of might in the coming event.

On the given date, the ministry team is broken into smaller units to give emphasis to specific areas, including the following:
(a) The registration desk, to properly log in those appearing for help. This is a good time to fill out the deliverance forms, as well as the legal release forms.

(b) There should be a general area where worship, teachings, and questions and answers are provided nonstop by the teaching unit.

(c) While this is going on, seekers are quietly picked out and assigned to skilled spiritual counselors in the counseling unit who then counsel and make notes on the deliverance forms earlier filled out by seekers.

(d) This is passed on to the prayer warrior team, among them prophets and seers, who pray through and make their own recommendations based on revelation from the Lord.

(e) By now, those casting out devils or implementing cleansing are fully ready to clear out the demon spirits and minister healing.

Keep in mind here that I am suggesting an ideal situation where you have a large pool of dedicated and trained warriors upon which to draw. This is the best case scenario and deliverance works seamlessly. However, the Lord can always find a way to do His work where people love and desire to do His will, no matter the limitations.

3. Individual Counseling Sessions
This refers to one-on-one ministry encounters between the deliverance minister and the individual seeker. In this

scenario, the minister has more room because he is the one scheduling the people for ministration, and he is able to schedule one or two sessions to really counsel an individual in detail. The essence is to probe into the personal life of the average seeker, to hear their stories of struggles, to invite the searchlight of the Holy Spirit to take an introspective journey into the individual's life, and to locate underlying reasons for demonic oppression and struggles.

It is important to always remember that the Lord, the Holy Spirit, is the actual Deliverer so as to deliberately allow Him to lead and guide the process. If we allow Him, we can quickly get to the root cause of the oppression.

In the course of conducting deliverances through the years, I have found that individual counseling sessions actually offer a very unique opportunity to teach the person who is being delivered about the details of what is involved, what they are to expect, and what their responses may be for them to meaningfully participate in the process. Also, I have found that it is useful in many cases to ask the individual to go into some kind of fasting so that the Holy Spirit can show them things that they do not know but are very important as part of the strategy for their liberty.

You will get to know firsthand, as the Holy Spirit begins to unravel details of their lives and bring it to their awareness, things they did not even know or perhaps did not reckon were important to their deliverance. These things can come to us by way of divinely inspired dreams, visions, and revelations. This will make the deliverance session more direct and to the point. The individual who is receiving deliverance in this process comes to find out that the Holy Spirit is far more involved in their deliverance than the deliverance minister who is providing the help. Then they can be appropriately motivated to continue the deliverance issues on an ongoing basis with the Person of the Holy Spirit who is actually the Deliverer. The individual counseling sessions or ministry can be the most effective.

4. Self-Deliverance

Self-Deliverance, as the name suggests, means to conduct deliverance on yourself: set yourself free and cast out the devil, using your God-given authority in the mighty name of the Lord Jesus Christ! Self-Deliverance refers to when an individual who is in some kind of demonic struggle realizes what is going on and has a measure of understanding or revelation in the Word of God, particularly in relation to our authority in Christ. The believer has authority over every devil through Jesus Christ. Even before the atoning

> *"Dealing with the devil outside of our authority in Christ puts the believer in a disadvantageous position to the enemy and you can bring yourself into cheap bondage to the enemy."*

death of our Lord Jesus Christ, He delegated this authority to his disciples to go out and preach the Gospel and to cast out devils. The Bible says that they returned again with joy, saying, "Lord, even the devils are subject unto us through thy name" (Luke 10:17-20).

Believers who have an understanding of their God-given authority in Christ Jesus can exercise that authority in self-ministrations, break demonic covenants, apply the Blood, and command the demons to be flushed out. The advantage of self-deliverance is that you are handling your deliverance between you and the Holy Spirit and things are facilitated quickly. Besides, you are able to quickly learn how to use your God-given authority to control the devil.

Actually, the only meaningful way a Christian can relate to the devil is to use his authority in Christ Jesus to control the enemy. Dealing with the devil outside of our authority in Christ puts the believer in a disadvantageous position to the enemy and you can bring yourself into bondage to the enemy. Self-deliverance actually enhances growth in that authority but a basic understanding of your authority, to begin with, is very necessary, especially realizing that the devil is subject to you in the name of Jesus. When I say the devil, I mean any category of evil spirits, from Lucifer to the smallest demon, is subject to the believer in Christ Jesus through the name of Jesus. Self-deliverance will enhance growth in the development of a believer's authority.

The flip side of self-deliverance is that if you do not have that much knowledge about your authority in Christ Jesus, or if the level of bondage is slightly on the stronger side and manifestations begin, you probably will not be able to handle it correctly. In such cases, it is good to get some help by approaching your minister or a trusted hand that is anointed and walking in God's authority to walk you through at least up to a certain extent.

ISSUES ADDRESSED IN A PRACTICAL DELIVERANCE SESSION

1. Repentance

Repentance means godly sorrow over sin, a change of mind and position regarding sins which then re-aligns us in total agreement with God. Repentance can be both direct (for personal sins) and also through identification with the misdeeds of past generations. This forms the foundation or bedrock for securing divine attention and intervention.

The person seeking deliverance must first become properly informed about the issues and doorways, both personal and generational. Repentance here means coming into agreements with the Word of God about sin, evil covenants, and demonic worship. This includes personal identification with the faulty foundation our ancestors stood upon to incur the wrath of God. We can humble ourselves in brokenness, acknowledge our sins, and accept God's offer of mercy.

Genuine repentance invites God's mercy and intervention. In Psalm 51:17, the Bible says, "The sacrifices of God are a broken spirit: a broken and a contrite heart, O God, thou wilt not despise." Repentance is like issuing an eviction notice to the devil. The Blood of Jesus is the legal ground for deliverance, but repentance is a way of telling the binding evil powers that their time is up.

2. Breaking Evil Covenants
(Renunciation, Denunciation and Revocation of Evil Covenants- applying the blood of Jesus to the root causes of demonic bondage)

Why is this necessary? The enemy, as I said earlier, really cannot bind anyone without some kind of covenant, which results from interacting with things that are controlled or engineered by the wicked. The Blood of Jesus, however, is the legal ground for liberty; so applying the Blood of Jesus to break every hidden curse or satanic covenant, is a firm starting point.

"Repentance is like issuing an eviction notice to the devil.... repentance is a way of telling the binding evil powers that their time is up."

Such covenants might be blood covenants, meal covenants, covenants enacted through sex, through dreams, through participation in occult activities, or covenants through ancestral exposures where they might have sought the help of the enemy. These and others are what the enemy uses as breeding grounds for oppression. They must be renounced and broken by the application of the Blood of Jesus.

It is important to reckon with the standing of the Blood. The Blood is the same as the very life of Jesus, the being of Jesus, the essence of Jesus. The entirety of who He is and what He has done is represented in His Blood. The Blood of Jesus is the highest investment on the face of the universe, as far as God's grace and power are concerned. Jesus is the Lamb of God slain from the foundation of this world. From the foundation, the Blood is already there. The Bible calls it the Blood of the Everlasting Covenant (Hebrews 13:20).

So, through the operation of the Blood of Jesus, no matter how far or how deep or how wide satanic bondage may pretend to be, it will be broken. Even if you had dined or gone to bed with the devil, as soon as you realize that it was wrong and decide that you do not want to continue that relationship with the devil but want to serve the Living God, be set free, and walk in the liberties of the sons of God, the Blood of Jesus can be brought into that situation and the curse simply broken.

This is where Satan is really weak because even though he likes to keep people in bondage forever, he quite simply does not have the means to do so because the Blood of Jesus has broken the curse. Colossians 2:14-15 says: "**Blotting out the handwriting of ordinances that was against us, which was contrary to us, and took it out of the way, nailing it to his cross; And having spoiled principalities and powers, he made a shew of them openly, triumphing over them in it.**"

The Amplified Bible (Classic Edition) puts it this way: "**Having cancelled and blotted out and wiped away the handwriting of the note (bond) with its legal decrees and demands which was in force and stood against us (hostile to us). This [note with its regulations, decrees, and demands] He set aside and cleared completely out of our way by nailing it to [His] cross. [God] disarmed the principalities and powers that were ranged against us and made a bold display and public example of them, in triumphing over them in Him and in it [the cross].**"

So through the Cross of the Lord Jesus Christ, every curse has been broken and Satan has been disarmed. His lethal weapon, his poison, which was introduced into our system, can all be cleared out by the application of the Blood.

3. Authoritative Warfare

This involves aggressive warfare and forceful confrontation of binding powers. Having eliminated the legal grounds for demonic oppression by breaking evil covenants and denouncing hidden curses, it is now time to take the battle to the evil one in warfare prayers. This is a vital step, whether in group deliverance, in individual counseling sessions, or in self-deliverance.

In aggressive warfare, we demolish the strongholds of the enemy and close the doors that may have validated the devil's illegal activity. I cannot overemphasize the fact that in this session, the Holy Spirit must be allowed to guide us. We therefore must open ourselves up to Him in worship and adoration. And, as we worship God, we move into that place of authority and begin to break the powers through the application of the Blood and warfare prayers.

Let me emphasize, one more time, that the Blood of Jesus provides the legal grounds to liquidate any liability that the enemy may be acting upon to perpetuate a situation of bondage. Prayer warfare allows us to confront the "higher ranking powers" in their demonic enclaves, base or cities and dismantle the chains at the root levels.

4. The Holy Spirit Power and House Cleaning

House cleaning involves flushing out residual demonic elements. The ground has been made ready and it is now time for the power of the Holy Spirit to move through the deliverance ministers and through the deliverance team to eliminate and cast out demons from the house. This is the part most folks are anxious to reach, but care must be taken to carefully follow the first three points above.

I want to state here that as deliverance ministers, we are to be very patient and tolerant, methodical, and deliberate. We should not come into deliverance session if we are tired and worn-out. We should come in prepared, relying on the Holy Spirit to work through us, so that the demons do not manipulate us and continue on, while we think that they are gone. We should also not be distracted by the manifestations but carefully move with the Holy Spirit to ensure a thorough clean out.

House cleaning involves flushing out residual demonic elements.

Flushing demons out of an individual is only one side of the coin but the final objective of Deliverance is discipleship. The work of deliverance does not stop in the deliverance session rather, it's only the beginning of an important but ongoing process. This brings us to the critical point that the work of deliverance is really not the work of a deliverance minister. It is the work of the Holy Spirit. God's Holy Spirit takes over from this point, particularly as the individual is taught to pay attention to His work in their own lives. Here, the person who has just received ministration must maintain fellowship with the Holy Spirit of the Living God, within the community of believers, and other pastoral authority so that the process will be effectively and thoroughly monitored to its logical conclusion.

What do you expect after the conclusion of a deliverance session? A deep work of cleansing commences.

5. Deep inner Cleansing

Let us examine the Scriptures to understand exactly what I mean by the work of deep cleansing. The Book of 2 Corinthians 7:1 says, **"Having therefore these promises dearly beloved, let us cleanse ourselves from all filthiness of the flesh and of the spirit perfecting holiness in the fear of God."**

What promises is the writer talking about? In the preceding chapter, we are exhorted to come out from uncleanness, filthiness, and demonic pollutions, and be separated, so that God can dwell or tabernacle in us. In other words, God's promise to the believer is that He will be a mobile ark, a mobile vehicle for carrying around the very presence of God, the Divinity and Person of God. So, we are God-carriers.

This was God's original purpose for man. He made us in His image and likeness in the beginning - male and female - so that we can have dominion and exercise that dominion over His creation. That remains His purpose. What is the enemy's purpose? To reverse that order.

> *"Any compulsive behavior that we have acquired over time that makes us feel helpless to control our desires is because of demonic corruption that has taken over our human personality."*

The enemy's purpose is to dominate man, bind him, and seize his authority over all creation. In order to do this, the demons open an individual up to gain access. Thereafter, they begin to reproduce their evil nature in the person. This individual grows up thinking that the evil nature of the demon is their own personality.

Just imagine how many people think that they were born to be homosexuals simply because they feel that way! God does not create anyone to be a homosexual; it is the demonic infiltration of man that creates such conditions. And once you start accepting and validating it, by claiming 'that's the way you are,' you become what you say you are because the demon is then able to completely take you over.

This goes for all things that are contrary to sound doctrine that people embrace - whether it is fornication, lying, stealing, or adultery. Any compulsive behavior that we have acquired over time that makes us feel helpless to control our desires is because of demonic corruption that has taken over our human personality. Demons enter to reproduce their evil natures. An individual may look at certain aspects of their character and say "I am out of control, completely helpless." These are demonic issues. What the Lord wants to do is to effect the work of deep inner cleansing and reconfiguration.

> *"The Word of God recaptures grounds that the enemy has stolen in our soul realm and begins to reconfigure them."*

6. The Word of God and Cleansing

There is a work of the Holy Spirit that ensues from the initial deliverance session. He goes to work and arranges every circumstance and begins to apply the Word of the Living God. This is why teaching and discipleship in the Word of God is a major issue of concern to me. If you and I are going to walk in liberty, we do not have an alternative to the Word of God. The Word of God will clean us up. The Bible says, "How can a young man cleanse his way? By taking heed according to your word" (Psalm 119:9).

The Word of God cleanses. How does this happen? The Word of God recaptures grounds that the enemy has stolen in our soul realm and begins to reconfigure them. The Bible refers to this as renewal or reprogramming. The Word of the Living

God reprograms us. Why do we need to be reprogrammed? So that we can be harmonized with Divinity. Demonic pollution, possession, and infestation have one objective, and that is to configure us into the devil's image. If you are reconfigured in the devil's image, you automatically belong to him, and he does not only take residence in you, he works hard to make sure you end up in hell with him in eternity.

Why was the Word of God given to us? To reconfigure us, so that our nature becomes harmonized with Divinity, and we become like God in character and in nature. The more we become like God, the more demons will actually fear, hate, and flee from us. That is why as soon as a believer starts walking in the image of God, the devil will start to blackmail them, persecute them, and generally fight them; but if we stay in the Word, fellowship, and accountability, the Word continues to work from deep within us.

Most of the compulsive behaviors and attitudes that people cannot seem to control, whether it be emotions of anger or perverted emotions of love (that function and fester as

> *"Demonic pollution, possession, and infestation have one objective, and that is to configure us into the devil's image. If you are configured in the devil's image, you automatically belong to him, and he does not only take residence in you, he works hard to make sure you end up in hell in eternity with him."*

uncontrollable, lustful desires for things or people) or some lewd or unnatural desires and vile affections, have been programmed by the enemy through the years. The Word of God can go to the root of these behaviors and begin to work a cleansing, a restructuring, a reprogramming from within, and with time, people will come into real liberty.

This is how to achieve meaningful deliverance. This is why Jesus said to those who believed on Him: **"If ye continue in My Word, then are ye My disciples indeed; And ye shall know the truth, and the truth shall make you free"** (John 8:30-32).

The Word of God will restructure, revamp, and reconfigure areas in the human soul or character that have been demonized, bound or corrupted, so that this person will achieve total wholeness. Inner healing and wholeness is the final objective of cleansing. The more we look at the Word, the more we become the Word. We become a marvel to ourselves and to others. This is true deliverance.

Let me make this point very clear. The desire to just experience temporary freedom from constraints without a corresponding commitment to walk the path of discipleship is recycled bondage, not deliverance. It is wrong for deliverance ministers to make the process more confusing by emphasizing only the material benefits that come from deliverance. The benefits are real, but excessive emphasis on them cheapens the whole objective of deliverance; and those who are participating in the deliverance soon find out that they are in endless cycles.

I would suggest to anyone seeking deliverance that you go to a deliverance ministry and get some help (if necessary), but stay in a local church that focuses on the Word of God. I say this with a sense of responsibility. People who congregate in what is called "deliverance ministries" cannot grow because most deliverance ministries are not equipped to truly disciple people to become strong in the Word of God. The reason is this: the anointing of deliverance is an aspect of the working of miracles. Working of miracles is in the realm of the ministry of an evangelist. The gift of faith, the gift of healing, and the working of miracles are all in the realm of the ministry of an evangelist. So, even if it is an apostolic evangelist that is equipped to start a church and start mobilizing masses of people, those people cannot be established in the grace of God without the Word of God.

> *"The desire to just experience temporary freedom from constraints without a corresponding commitment to walk the path of discipleship is recycled bondage, not deliverance."*

FIND A TEACHING MINISTRY AND CONNECT

A teaching ministry will do far more good particularly for people who have gone through demonic circumstances. I will go even further to say a teaching ministry, with emphasis on faith, will help you even faster, and especially if you had been in an occult background or occult church but have now come into deliverance. If you decide to stay in a deliverance ministry forever, you will not go beyond the basics. Very quickly, the enemy can move in on you and begin to cripple your life. And that is why you find that people can be in "deliverance ministries' for years and their lives are not moving anywhere.

You cannot get people together and continue to teach about witchcraft endlessly. People cannot be strong in faith by that type of knowledge. The just shall live by faith! Faith in the Word of God is the ticket for daily living. And this is why faith teachers must not lose their bite. New creation teachers must not lose their bite because the people of God need the Word of God.

> *"Inner healing and wholeness is the final objective of cleansing. The more we look at the Word of God, the more we become the Word."*

The Flip Side

On the flip side, however, faith teachers and new creation teachers oftentimes presume a lot about deliverance ministry. They believe that in Christ you are already delivered. Actually, this is true, in a way. In Christ, you are delivered, but there is something called deliverance or cleansing from demonic infestations. There is something called deep bondage that merely responding to an altar call doesn't resolve. The Word of God is the major instrument of deliverance. Everything hangs on it. Everything stands on and falls on the Word of God. All creation, the whole universe, is hanging on the Word of God. Even the devil himself does not have a reality outside of the Word of God; so he is subject to the Word of God. That said, we still counsel people and do some warfare for many to enjoy real liberty.

I really do not know how much I can emphasize this truth. There is no deliverance without the Word of God. And, if I may say this also, if people obey the Word, no matter what the kind of bondage may be there at the beginning, if they continue to obey the Word of God, that bondage will break; it will snap. The deliverance anointing is an extra layer of help that God has brought to the end-time church to promote cleansing, wholeness and reclaiming of lost inheritances, so that the church can come into the full blessing and do the work of ministry.

7. The Fear of the Lord and Cleansing

Another important consideration in effecting deep cleansing is knowledge of and correct response to the fear of the Lord. The Bible says, **"Having therefore these promises, dearly beloved, let us cleanse ourselves from all filthiness of the flesh and spirit, perfecting holiness in the fear of God"** (2 Corinthians 7:1). Two things are outlined here. First is cleansing ourselves of pollutions of the spirit and the flesh (these are the two levels of pollution). The second thing is to mature in holiness or completeness out of reverence for God.

Remember, when the Bible talks about deliverance in the Book of Obadiah, it says, **"But upon Mount Zion shall be deliverance, and there shall be holiness; and the house of Jacob shall possess their possessions"** (1:17). Holiness, as I said earlier, is wholeness, completeness. God is holy because He is absolutely complete lacking in nothing. So, holiness is not only in the sense of moral purity, but it is also in terms of completeness in all that we are meant to be, so that we can do all what we are called to do. God is completely whole, so He can meet any need. That is why He said **"upon Mount Zion shall be holiness and the sons of Jacob shall possess their possession."** Deliverance is connected to your inheritance.

How the Fear of the Lord helps us

How, practically speaking here, does the fear of the Lord help us? Let me explain it to you this way. When demons live in somebody, they reproduce their evil nature, particularly in things that are addictive. Anything that has an addictive element is fastened by demonic forces in the mind. Here is an example. I once worked among drug addicts in Nigeria and noticed that addiction has two levels. The first level is the psychological, or the mind. The second level deals with the physical side, the body.

Take for instance, an addict who is using a particular drug of choice which he enjoys. When he takes that drug, sensations in the central nervous system are triggered and feelings of pleasure are generated, but they are short-lived. What causes addiction therefore is the desire to repeat those initial pleasurable experiences. The addicted person wants to feel euphoria, so he takes the drug again but finds out that he needs increasing doses of the same drug to get the high. So he keeps doing that, but while he is at it, another level of bondage is occurring. Besides the mind being captured, the physical body is also becoming adjusted, or tolerant to the drug to the point that, after sometime, the body becomes chemically dependent on that drug and cannot function without it.

Now, there are two problems the person's mind is captured he wants to repeat the feeling; and the body is adjusted, or addicted, or dependent on the chemical and he cannot function without the chemical. If he withdraws the chemical, he goes into painful withdrawal symptoms. Now, the addicted person has two motivations. He wants the feeling but also fears the pain that withdrawal can bring on; therefore he is in hot pursuit of the drug.

Demons hide their evil intentions
Behind attractive images

The devil works exactly the same way. He might trigger some behavior or behavioral malady by first encouraging someone to engage in some type of illicit pleasurable behavior. While they are doing that, he captures the mind. And, after a while, he enters their body and adjusts the body and begins to reproduce the conditions.

So, the devil is not only in the mind, he is also in the body. When you cast him out through a deliverance session, the job would have just started because the devil is going to continue to trigger certain pictures in the mind of the individual. As he triggers those pictures in the mind, the body starts to react. If people are not trained in the Word of God, after enduring those hallucinations and haunting pictures, feelings are going to be triggered in their body to move and their wills will be broken. And that is why some people are in a trap. To break the power of the enemy, you have to deal with that image.

A character in a Chinese movie I watched some time ago said something quite instructive. He said that the enemy hides its intentions behind images. To break the power of the enemy, you have to find the image and break it. What is the image? The pleasure you are seeking to have; that thing you cannot do without. The enemy hides behind it. So, if you cast out a demon from someone, it is just relief. The image is still there, and it is only the Word of God and the fear of God that can correct it.

Where does the fear of God come in? When you have just gone through a deliverance session, the demons are cleaned out of you. However, because your body system had over time adjusted to the behaviors triggered by the demons, the Word of God takes you through a process of reclaiming and revamping. For this process to succeed, you have to have a level of respect for God.

When you are alone in a place and nobody is watching you, you will be tempted to do certain things. You will be tempted to go to certain places. It takes only the fear or respect you have for God to prevent you from doing these things. This is why the Psalmist says "the fear of the Lord is clean, enduring forever" (Psalm 19:9). The fear of the Lord is a spiritual antiseptic that will clean your life from contamination with evil. If you do not have the fear of the Lord and a commitment to discipleship in the Word of God, deliverance is a nonstarter. Think of it this way. How comfortable would you be as a believer, who is going through a deliverance process, if most of the things you agree to do when no one is watching were to be played on public television? Well, you may consider this as a mere hypothetical allusion, but the fact is that the things you engage in are all on the monitors of heaven. And if these activities are ungodly and immoral, the angels are being embarrassed, and God is forced to look at these things, which is a great dishonor to Him.

So, the fear in 2 Corinthians 7:1 actually refers to a deep personal reverence for your Father in heaven. If you respect God, you will not subject Him to the harrowing experience of looking at you down here once again giving yourself, your body, to work wickedness. Why would you engage anymore in immoral behavior? Because nobody is watching you, or you think God will understand? Well, God understood enough to put His Son on the Cross in order to save us from a burning hell so, why not obey the Word of God?

> *"The fear of the Lord is a spiritual antiseptic that will clean your life from contamination with evil."*

People need a little respect for God particularly in this perverted and crooked generation where the preachers of the Gospel of love are making people lose their sense of responsibility and accountability. You have to make a choice. The fear of the Lord comes by choice. It is something you choose. If you choose to fear the Lord, then His fear will be in you, and His fear will protect, defend, and keep you clean from contamination with evil. God says in His Word, **"A son honoureth his father, and a servant his master: if then I be a father, where is mine honor? And if I be a master, where is my fear? saith the LORD of hosts unto you, O priests, that despise my name. And ye say, wherein have we despised thy name?" (Malachi 1:6).**

You and I have to make that choice. It is by choice we love our Father and show appreciation for the great work of salvation, the tremendous privilege of deliverance, cleansing, and wholeness. But we certainly do not intend to continue to cohabit with the devil so that grace will abound more and more. No, we are a delivered people and we are a determined people also. We are an accountable people who are committed to walk the Word of God and leave no room for Satan's bondage.

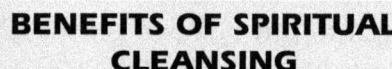

BENEFITS OF SPIRITUAL CLEANSING

What is the benefit of this level of spiritual cleansing?

1. Freedom

Firstly, it is very rewarding to be free indeed! Just to be able to look at Satan's addictive behavior that once held you bound and robbed you of personal dignity; just to be able to look at it in the face and say, *I am not there anymore. I was once a fornicator but I'm not anymore. I was a cheat but I'm not anymore. I was a compulsive liar but I am not anymore. I was a slave to some demons who could ride me at will, but I am not anymore.* It is so liberating! Praise the Living God!

2. A Definite Promise

Secondly, God made a promise. **"Wherefore come out from among them, and be ye separate, saith the Lord, and touch not the unclean thing; and I will receive you, And will be a Father unto you, and ye shall be my sons and daughters, saith the Lord Almighty" (2 Corinthians 6:17-18).** Think of it! As the enemy is kept out of our lives, room is made for God to fill us. When I carry God, when I carry His love, His nature when I carry His authority, I will go out there and begin to victimize the same devil that once victimized me before.

3. Regain your Inheritance

Thirdly, the Bible says when we are delivered and embrace the Holy Spirit, we are empowered to receive our possessions or our inheritance. Many of God's children are groaning under bondage; the enemy wants to keep them shackled because they represent the hope of their families. There are certain levels of blessings and increase that God wants to give His people, and if we allow God to transmit this inheritance to us, we will become the showcase of our generation, the hope of our families and the hope of the church.

In other words, if God is given the opportunity by you and me to really bring us into His full glory and the full measure of blessings He has for us, then we automatically become blessings. Consequently, when we appear on the scene, poverty bows out; when we appear on the scene, sickness bows out; when we appear on the scene, family dignity is restored and enhanced. As our families gather around the light that we now have from God, they will receive help; our children and our parents will be blessed; and our generation will smile because we are here. All of these the enemy is working hard to prevent by trying to bind and ridicule us. But bless the Lord that the Holy Spirit is helping the church this day!

4. Live out your Destiny

Another benefit of accepting God's help and true deliverance is that you would truly have embraced your destiny. The Bible says that we are going to be the repairer of many generations and be called the priests of our God (Isaiah 61:4). Instead of laboring under a generational curse, you are actually unleashing and perpetuating generational blessings. You are the curse-breaker in the family; you bring an end to the pain and the shame, and you unleash generational blessings so that those coming after you will not have to struggle under the yoke. You make a difference, a positive difference.

WHEN DEMONS ARE EXPELLED

I want to mention some things you might see in the process of cleansing. As the initial process of cleansing commences, there may be manifestations or there may not be. When I say manifestations, I mean strong manifestations during prayers like falling, foaming at the mouth, phlegm being coughed up, and so on, when the power of God hits and the enemy is coming out.

For some people, during the cleansing process, continuous flow of sputum might set in lasting several days or more. If this happens, do not be embarrassed; just go through it. For others, as they are reading the Bible, they may constantly yawn or tear up. These are cleansing processes and the person should not be embarrassed. And for some others, depending on the severity of what they were involved in, this period of cleansing and breaking covenant can open up bizarre dream experiences. Those who go through this level of reaction should seek close monitoring from experienced and trained deliverance counselors.

Dreaming is an important gateway into the spirit realm. In your dream state, depending on how or where you were before, or even the nature of your family background, you might have all kinds of experiences. The first line of defense for you is to read the Word of God. I call it Word Therapy.

Saturate your mind with the Word, because your mind is a gateway into your spirit. If the Word of God is not guarding your mind, then deliverance becomes a total failure and your spirit becomes an open expressway to all kinds of demonic influences and manipulations.

> *"If the Word of God is not guarding your mind, then deliverance becomes a total failure and your spirit becomes an open expressway to all kinds of demonic influences and manipulations."*

So, the first line of defense is just doing Word Therapy. Word Therapy means that you are not necessarily studying but you are just reading several chapters to bombard your mind with the Word of God. That cleanses your mind and reprograms your mind and resets your mind so that the enemy's manipulative strategies become ineffective to a great extent.

Secondly, you should, if possible, seek close monitoring or mentoring from an experienced deliverance counselor, more especially one that has a prophetic vein and can interpret dreams and is able to decode the source of dreams, because not all dreams come from God.

I explained a lot about dreams in my book, *"Prophetic Gateways,"* but let me mention here that there are three types of

dreams that can come to you:
(1) Dreams that come from God called divine revelations;
(2) dreams that come from yourself manifestations of your state; and
(3) dreams that come from the devil manipulations. This third category of dreams is the one to most watch out for when you have gone through deliverance prayers.

Manipulation is the enemy swinging on the other extreme. There are two ways the enemy functions:
(1) He wants people to think that he does not exist; this way, he can destroy quietly without being detected.

(2) He wants people to know that he exists but passes himself off as being so relevant or powerful that nothing can be done about him, which of course, is a lie. He is a creature, and a fallen one at that. He has lost his original position with God, so he cannot even maintain the originality of his power. He is a fading power, which is another topic as to how the devil is able to maintain his power on the earth. Suffice it is to say that he is a bloody creature, which is why he triggers a lot of violence on the earth to generate blood to sustain his demonic activities.

What is the sign that you are being manipulated by dreams? Hopelessness! Any time you are being manipulated in your dream, you feel hopeless. Anything that makes you feel hopeless is not from God. It is an antichrist spirit. Even when God is rebuking His children, He will generate faith and hope. Anything that neutralizes your faith and removes your hope is demonic. Fear, hopelessness, and faithlessness are the hallmarks to indicate that there is demonic manipulation going on.

 **PEOPLE COMING OUT OF AN OCCULT BACKGROUND**

I have a special message for those coming from an occult environment, particularly occult-based "churches." I say occult-based churches because there are so-called churches that are not founded on the Word of God. They are syncretic with a mixture of the Word and occult practices. These are churches that are founded by people who had an encounter with Christianity but were not really born-again and cleansed from an existing demonic or occult background. Thus, the enemy manipulates them into thinking they are hearing from God and they go on to start churches and organizations that are syncretic.

Syncretism results from a mixture of the previous occult foundation through visions, illusions, manipulations of the enemy and then trying to teach the Bible. This constitutes two opposites coming together. If people come from that kind of church environment, where there is usually much emphasis on visions and dreams, the enemy will seek to perpetuate that when you come to faith.

The just shall live by faith (Hebrews 10:38). This was why I emphasized earlier on that the faith teachers of our day and age would do the church of Jesus Christ an injustice if they do not teach the faith message. The faith message is critical. Why? The Bible says the just shall live by faith. And as we are entering the end zone of the end time, there is a much more upsurge of occult phenomena trying to penetrate authentic Christianity. If the faith message is lost, we will be in trouble.

And as I would say to every person who is reading these lines, invest in materials that teach on faith. For example, the writings of the late Kenneth Hagin on faith will help you. Get hold of faith-building materials and build up your faith. Faith in the Word of God is an important foundation. The Bible does not say the just shall live by dreams or by visions or by prophecies. I stand in the prophetic office but I will say to you, you cannot live by prophets. You only live by the Word of God. There are so many people who congregate in meetings, wanting a prophet to prophesy to them. Even though I operate in the prophetic office, I do not like this because I know that commitment to prophets, visions, and revelations often neutralizes the faith of the people. Faith is to be in the Living Word of God. Read that Word. Get some faith materials, build your faith. In your daily fight against the devil, you need your faith.

It takes faith in the Word of God to function in the required authority. With God, you relate with faith and submission. With man, you relate with conscience. But with the devil, you need your authority. If anything affects your authority, you become beggarly. That is why faith is so important. The just shall live by faith, not by dreams!

BREAKTHROUGH PROPHETIC DELIVERANCE PRAYERS

1. Precious Holy Spirit my Deliverer and Counselor, unveil every hidden satanic undercurrents and enabling character deficiency in my life; and like a mighty River, visit me and mobilize a new standard in me that the evil one cannot handle.

2. Lord God, I invite you to correct every area of contradiction in my character due to demonic corruption and implement a deep work of cleansing within me in the Mighty Name of the Lord Jesus Christ.

3. I reverently submit myself to the working and washing of your Word. Let your Holy Word work within me and abide in me until I become one with your Word. Reconcile and harmonize any violated parts of my soul to yourself in the mighty Name Jesus Christ.

4. I confess and declare here and now that I am the righteousness of God in Christ Jesus and that every devil is subject to me in the Mighty Name of my Lord and Savior Jesus Christ.

5. Lord God of glory, I this day commit to honor you in my life and personally chose your Fear over the fear of evil. I reverently submit myself to you and commit to shun every evil way and instead keep myself in your love. I will abide in your love forever my God in the mighty Name of Jesus Christ.

CHAPTER 13

Three Days of Deliverance Prayer With Fasting

There is spiritual significance to three days. In the Old Testament, God would often command His people to consecrate themselves for three days before His visitation and blessing.

Exodus 19:10-11, for example, says: **"And the LORD said unto Moses, Go unto the people, and sanctify them today and tomorrow, and let them wash their clothes, And be ready against the third day: for the third day the LORD will come down in the sight of all the people upon Mount Sinai."**

The Lord Jesus defeated eternal death and brought immortality to life in three days. There is something very special when we wait upon the Lord in a three-day fasting and prayer retreat for deliverance. This can also be a seven, fourteen or even twenty-one-day deliverance fast, but a three-day fast can effectively unleash resurrection glory and allow the Lord the opportunity to get to the root of binding powers and dislodge them.

I have a lot of personal testimonies in my life and the lives of others resulting from a three-day shut in with the Lord for personal release and blessing.

PREPARATION TO START A THREE-DAY SHUT IN

1. Before you are due to start fasting, begin to make a faith presentation of yourself to God for grace to rest upon you in the fast (Romans 12:1-2). Present or commit your fast ahead to Him before you begin to receive even more grace to complete the fast.

2. While preparing to start, continue in counseling with your deliverance minister and write all dreams and revelations you might have along the way.

3. It is time to agree on the set date and location with your minister. Once the date is set, have a determination to follow through as the devil will fight hard to distract and stop the deliverance session from happening; he is merely making a play for survival. You should have an iron-clad determination to follow through even if you fall sick in the process. If you stay on the plan, God's grace will kick in. Remember, the Lord Himself is watching and monitoring

the entire process.

4. Have a final counseling session to review observations, dreams, revelations, recollections and draw up a working list of items to address in prayer warfare for the three days.

DAY ONE

1. Avoid distractions
Arrive a night, preferably before, to minimize distractions. Turn off your phone and cut off the internet, television, and social media interactions.

2. Immerse yourself in worship
Don't be overwhelmed. You are in your Father's presence and will leave there changed. Start out with Thanksgiving and appreciate Him.

3. Repentance
Repentance means godly sorrow over sin and a change of mind and position regarding sins, which then re-aligns us in total agreement with God. Repentance can be both direct (for personal sins) and also through identification with the misdeeds of past generations. This type of repentance forms the foundation or bedrock for securing divine attention and intervention.

The person seeking deliverance must first become properly informed about the issues and doorways, both personal and generational. Repentance here means coming into agreement with the Word of God about sin, evil covenants, and demonic worship. This includes personal identification with the faulty foundation our ancestors stood upon to incur the wrath of God. We can humble ourselves in brokenness, acknowledge our sins, and accept God's offer of mercy.

Genuine repentance invites God's mercy and intervention. Psalm 51:17 (Amplified) says, "**My sacrifice acceptable to God is a broken spirit; a broken and a contrite heart (broken down with sorrow for sin and humbly and thoroughly penitent), such, O God, you will not despise.**" Repentance is like giving an eviction notice to the devil. The Blood of Jesus is the legal ground for deliverance, but repentance is telling the binding evil powers that their time is up.

4. Applying the Blood of Jesus (Renunciation, Denunciation, and Revocation of Evil Covenants)

Why is this necessary? The enemy, as I said earlier, really cannot bind anyone without some kind of covenant, which results from interacting with things that are controlled or engineered by the wicked. The Blood of Jesus, however, is the legal ground for liberty; so applying the Blood of Jesus to break every hidden curse and the satanic covenant is a firm starting point. Such covenants might be blood covenants, meal covenants, covenants enacted through sex, dreams, or participation in occult activities. They could be covenants through ancestral exposures where they might have sought the help of the enemy. These and others are what the enemy uses as breeding grounds for oppression and should be renounced and broken by the application of the Blood of Jesus. It is important to reckon with the standing of the Blood. The Blood is the same as the life – the very life of Jesus. The being of Jesus, the essence of Jesus, the entirety of who He is and what he has done is represented in His Blood. The Blood of Jesus is the highest investment on the face of the universe as far as God's grace and power are concerned. Jesus is the Lamb of God slain from the foundation of this world. From the foundation, the blood is already there. The Bible calls it the Blood of the Everlasting Covenant. So, through the operation of the Blood of Jesus, no matter how far, how deep, how wide satanic bondage may pretend to represent, the Blood of Jesus will break the curse.

Even if you died or went to bed with the devil, as soon as you realize that this is wrong and decide to discontinue your romance with the devil so as to serve the Living God and walk in the liberties of the sons of God, the Blood of Jesus can be brought into that situation and the curse will be broken. This is where Satan is really weak because even though he likes to keep people in bondage perpetually, he quite simply does not have the means to do so because the Blood of Jesus has broken the curse. Colossians 2:14-5 says:

"Blotting out the handwriting of ordinances that was against us, which was contrary to us, and took it out of the way, nailing it to his cross; And having spoiled principalities and powers, he made a shew of them openly, triumphing over them in it."

This is how the Amplified Version puts it:
> Having cancelled and blotted out, and wiped away the handwriting of note (bond) with its legal decrees and demands which was enforced and stood against us, that is hostile to us, this note with its regulations, decrees and demands he set aside and cleared completely out the way by nailing it to his cross. God thereby disarmed the principalities that were arranged against us and made a bold display and public example of them in triumphing over them in it and on the cross."

So through the Blood of the Lord Jesus Christ, every curse has been broken, and Satan has been disarmed. His lethal weapon, his poison, which was introduced into our system, can all be cleared out by the application of the Blood.

DAY TWO

Worship

1. Deep Worship

Worship purifies the heart of unidentified rebellions. It also brings you in complete alignment with your Victory in Christ. Remember there is absolutely no need to be tensed. You are in your Father's presence to be cleansed, empowered and blessed.

2. Authoritative Warfare

This involves the application of the Blood of Jesus to the root causes of bondage. Having eliminated the legal grounds for demonic oppression, by breaking evil covenants and denounced hidden curses, it is now time to take the battle to the evil one in warfare prayers. This is a vital step, whether in group deliverance, in individual counseling sessions, or in self-deliverance.

In aggressive warfare, we demolish the strongholds of the enemy and close the doors that may have validated the devil's illegal activity. I cannot over-emphasize the fact that in this session the Holy Spirit must be allowed to guide us. We, therefore, must open ourselves up to the Holy Spirit in worship and in adoration, and as we worship God, we move into that place of authority and begin to break the powers through the application of the Blood. Let me emphasize it one more time that the Blood of Jesus provides the legal grounds to liquidate any liability that the enemy may be acting upon to perpetuate a situation of bondage. Prayer warfare allows us to confront the stronger forces in their demonic enclaves, base or cities and dismantle the chains at the root levels.

DAY THREE

Time to Cast Them Out

1. Review your dreams and revelations. Make a note of them and utilize them in your prayers.

2. If you are implementing self-deliverance, command the demons to come out and leave. You are likely to sense some movement in your lower abdominal or throat areas; do not be alarmed. Keep commanding the demons to leave and breathe in and out. If you are receiving help directly from a deliverance worker or counselor, it could even speed things up; just follow instructions and do not be alarmed.

WHAT CAN HAPPEN WHEN DEMONS ARE EXITING

This will depend upon a number of factors, chief among them being where you are in your deliverance, meaning if you have done this before or not. I want to emphasize that regardless of where you are in your walk with God, you can still benefit to a large extent from deliverance exercises if you can humble yourself before the Lord without presuming that nothing can be wrong.

The following may be observed when demons are leaving:

a. *Coughing* - ranging from a dry cough to coughing up a lot of phlegm.

b. *Blowing air from your mouth or nostrils* (spirits are breath).

c. *Spitting or foaming at the mouth continuously.*

d. *Foul smells.* Some demons can generate a very foul smell when exiting. If they are as bad as they smell (which of course they are) then you want to get rid of them fast. The devils really stink!

e. *Falling and rolling.* The demons might try to knock you down; if this happens, control them, using the authority of the Name of Jesus. Remember always that the devil is subject to you through the name of the Lord Jesus Christ. If you have difficulty with this, get some help from an anointed believer or minister.

f. *Yawning and tearing.* You might be yawning and tearing up while undergoing deliverance as the demons leave. This happens to me from time to time just reading my Bible. Oh, the glory of His presence! I acknowledge His rich mercies and take everything He offers for my benefit with joy and appreciation. Thank you blessed Holy Spirit.

g. *The deliverance worker.* The deliverance worker should please be informed that the demons will try every trick in the book to try and survive the onslaught against them. As a last desperate measure, the types of demons you are about to cast out especially the ruling demon may try to attack you days before the deliverance session. This could actually be a giveaway to a discerning deliverance worker because you can know what you are dealing with in part, based on what is coming against you!

THE MUCH LONGER FAST

The much longer fast means that which could take up to seven, fourteen, twenty-one or forty days. It provides a great opportunity to put the flesh out of the way. This type of fast could be a partial one (which may involve skipping dinner, taking only liquid or vegetables, etc.) or it could be a complete one (in which only water is taken).

The same approach of the three-day fasting deliverance mentioned above are the effective areas to look out for in the longer fast. That said, the individual seeker will be able to draw heavily from revelation prayers peculiar to the longer fast. In the longer fast, the Holy Spirit unveils from day to day, the things that really need to be dealt with.

 **BREAKTHROUGH PROPHETIC DELIVERANCE PRAYERS**

Romans 12:1-2
Therefore, I urge you, brothers and sisters, in view of God's mercy, to offer your bodies as a living sacrifice, holy and pleasing to God—this is your true and proper worship. ²Do not conform to the pattern of this world, but be transformed by the renewing of your mind. Then you will be able to test and approve what God's will is—his good, pleasing and perfect will.

1. Eternal and Living God, I here and now present my spirit, soul and body to you as a living sacrifice. Sanctify me by fire. Cleanse, purify and use me.

2. Lead me on the path of total deliverance and cleansing from all contamination of spirit and the flesh. Write your name on every path of my being today in the mighty name of Jesus.

CHAPTER 14

Why Deliverance Cases Delay

POORLY IDENTIFIED BACKGROUND ISSUES

"And you hath he quickened, who were dead in trespasses and sins; Wherein in time past ye walked according to the course of this world, according to the prince of the power of the air, the spirit that now worketh in the children of disobedience: Among whom also we all had our conversation in times past in the lusts of our flesh, fulfilling the desires of the flesh and of the mind; and were by nature the children of wrath, even as others" (Ephesians 2:1-3).

There are many factors why some deliverance cases seem to go on without results. One of such factors is the failure to reckon with the history of the individual. People have a record, and sometimes, to one degree or other, the enemy is involved in their past. You cannot completely understand what is required for an individual case to succeed if you fail to reckon with the history of the person. Listed below are some important points to consider.

1. Previous Occult Involvement

Previous involvement with the devil, especially in the occult, can present real difficulties. This can occur if an individual had related with the devil directly and benefited from him. This may sound surprising, but it is, in fact, the case with many individuals who have come to Christ and needed deliverance. They had been involved with the devil, and the devil had benefited them before. Now that they have come to Christ, the enemy wants to take back what he once gave to them and begins to fight. Thus, a period of reverses may set in for them. This requires careful consideration and handling if success is to be achieved.

There are also people who have a background with the devil; that is to say, a family history through the generations that were servants of the devil. In other words, they carry satanic authority. He might have made them influential or had given them the power to do things for themselves and him. When such a person comes to Christ from that kind of background, the devil will fight and try to tag him on the former agreement. But with careful help and determination, God will bring them through.

Some persons have been deeply corrupted by the devil while they sojourned with him. Those seeds of corruption have to be identified and dealt with. I will be more specific and detailed with that when I start to look at points of contact. Moreover, in the course of using the devil's power to advance purposes for themselves or their family, some individuals might have been waiting next in line to carry on the program the devil had in place for their family; but before they can actually step into such program, the Lord comes across them and brings them to faith. Because of that program that the enemy had for them, he is going to fight to try to have his way. So, an understanding is required, plus determination. This is why I say that in deliverance cases, the individual really has to be well integrated into the community of faith.

Many people today have a shopping list for pastors but they themselves are not ready to endure the demands of true discipleship. Yet, in reality, pastoral authority, discipline, accountability, and of course, support is required in some of these types of cases to have a real sustained breakthrough.

2. Misunderstanding of the Deliverance Process

Another reason for a delay in some deliverance cases is a lack of understanding of the deliverance process. As I wrote in a previous chapter, there is a process whereby God delivers. To everything, there is a process. For instance, in farming, there is a process of planting the seed, and watching it die, grow, mature, and bring forth a harvest. Similarly, there is a process for having a baby – conception, pregnancy for nine months, in most cases, and during that time, the baby is adjusting to the mother, the mother is adjusting to the baby, and the family is preparing for the new arrival.

In the same way, there is nothing like drive-through deliverance. There is a process. You have to understand what that process entails and what is required for each segment of that process to succeed in order to really get the best from what God is doing. Read more about this from Chapter Two in my book, "Foundations for True and Complete Deliverance."

3. Impatience and Distractions

Impatience and distractions come up because the individual who is seeking deliverance is focusing majorly on the problems or the demonic oppression or affliction, instead of trying to find out what God is doing in his or her life regarding the problem so that he or she can meaningfully cooperate with Him.

If you do not pay attention to or find out what God is doing regarding your case, you are unlikely to be able to participate meaningfully in the process. The psalmist says, **I regard the work of your hand, the operations of your hand; therefore thou shalt build me up** (Psalms 8:3). This means there are people who do not regard or pay attention to the operation of the Hand of God.

The Lord, through the Holy Spirit (Hand of God), is doing something in you. If you do not find it out and cooperate with Him, you will become impatient and distracted, hopping around, thinking that your answers will come from men and women of God.

It is true that God uses men and women who are trained and consecrated to help us but those individuals are not the deliverers. The Deliverer is the Lord Jesus Christ, and the Lord Jesus Christ in your life is represented by the Lord, the Holy Spirit. If you give attention to the Holy Spirit, men and women of God will still play their role. They will encourage you, pray for you, and counsel you but you will mostly enjoy the activity of the Holy Spirit who will perfect your deliverance.

CASE OF A DIFFICULT PREGNANCY

At this point, I want to reference a case in Genesis 25, where a woman who has had a delay in childbearing for twenty-two years finally gets pregnant. But then, at a point in the pregnancy, she notices that there is a battle going on inside her womb. Think of it. She has had twenty-two years without a baby; now that she is pregnant, a battle constantly rages in her womb. So she goes to inquire of the Lord, and the prophet of God tells her, "Inside your womb are two manners of people.

One shall be stronger than the other and the elder shall serve the younger."

Now every time she feels the fighting, the rumbling in her stomach, she just smiles, and says, "Oh, these people are at it again." She is not troubled. But if she had not gotten that understanding, she would have been troubled and might have started going to all kinds of places. She might have even gone to some wrong places and have the pregnancy aborted.

This is what often happens to people because they lack an understanding of the deliverance process. They do not connect with the Holy Spirit. They just rely on different prophets and deliverance ministers; they hop-around and are not established anywhere. They are not under discipline, not under commitment, not under accountability, and not surprisingly for many of such people, the devil manages to keep certain kinds of sin in their lives through which he further reinforces himself.

Again, understanding the deliverance process and connecting with God will help to reduce the delay and give quicker results.

4. Failure to Reckon with the Three Stages of Deliverance

There are three stages in the deliverance process, each requiring a different approach: Stage One is when we come to

WHY DELIVERANCE CASES DELAY

Christ, become born-again, and then discover there are some demonic activities needing to be cleared from our lives. Curses can then be broken, while evil covenants are renounced through the prayer of deliverance and the initial cleansing is done. This is where people fall down, throw up, yawn, and spit, cough up phlegm, and other kinds of manifestations. As I said before, this is just the initial relief.

Following this is Stage Two of the deliverance process which involves warfare prayers. All these processes are important as part of God's strategies, all working together for our good. The second level is all warfare where you are taught how to pray. For good measure, there are many wonderful ministries that are teaching the Body of Christ today on spiritual warfare – how to take authority, and how to bind the enemy. This is crucial because at the initial stage we are dealing with demons in the individual. But the principalities do not really stay in a person's body; it is the lower classes of demons that seek embodiment and work in that direction.

During warfare, we are able to take the battle further to the demonic territory, to the demonic base, and as warfare prayer is going on, the power of God, the lightning of God, the arrow of God, and the sword of the Spirit, are going forth, cutting off things at the base level. Indeed, the greater the warfare, the greater the victory for the people of God.

However, this warfare also has some implications. When you begin to do warfare prayers, typically, you are hitting the demonic authorities at the control base. When this warfare intensifies, the principalities become affected, and so they want to find out, "*What's going on here? We had this person bound and controlled; we are going to take a closer look at you to devise strategies to contain your fire power, to neutralize your ability to damage the kingdom of darkness.*"

Remember, bondage, in most cases, is a shared experience. For instance, it may be observed in a family that, across the board, marriages do not last. The reason is that most bondage often happens at the familial or ancestral level. And that is why warfare prayers at Stage Two of the deliverance process are so critical. As you are doing warfare, you are not only affecting the individual's destiny, but you are actually affecting the destiny of the family also. It is a protracted warfare, and the devil will try to survive it. How does he do this? By trying to open your file and study what they may have on your character so that they can continue to attack your character flaws and cause you delays and frustrations.

> "*... Every person is born into an average family, and that family has a ruling principality detailed there by Lucifer to represent his interest in the family.*"

They can do this easily because every person is born into an average family, and that family has a ruling principality detailed there by Lucifer to represent his interest in the family. And for every child that is born into that family, there is a familiar spirit detailed to monitor that child. Most often, it is that familiar spirit that trains that child in certain types of habits which the child considers his own lifestyle.

That is what Ephesians 2:1-3 is talking about. I present the exact quote here:

"And you hath he quickened, who were dead in trespasses and sins; Wherein in time past ye walked according to the course of this world, according to the prince of the power of the air, the spirit that now worketh in the children of disobedience: Among whom also we all had our conversation in times past in the lusts of our flesh, fulfilling the desires of the flesh and the mind; and were by nature the children of wrath, even as others."

In the womb of sin, there were satanic powers and demon spirits that controlled us and dictated a program. That program was according to the plan and purpose of the

"When you fully yield yourself to and those elements of the flesh are crucified, a transformation takes place."

prince or power of the air, which is Satan himself, and through such programs, he was able to transplant certain characteristics in each one of us. Through those characteristics, he replicated himself – his evil nature - in each of us. When you became born-again and liberated from the grip of the demons that Satan has implanted in you to carry out his work, these evil forces will try to return to attack those elements or character traits that they had placed in you.

This is why the second stage of deliverance is very important. As you are doing warfare, you must realize that the Word of God is a double-edged sword. With one edge, you are judging satanic powers that are trying to frustrate your destiny and that of your family. But it doesn't stop there; you are also pointing the other edge of that sword on to yourself. Why? You have to deal with the satanic character in you.

Suppose you are binding the devil, but you have a problem with uncontrollable anger. What happens? Every time you try to achieve something significant, the enemy simply finds a way to trigger that spirit of anger and thereby robs you of that blessing that should have come into your life. This effectively brings you back into bondage.

Aspects of our character, which have been so corrupted by the activity of the demons that lived in us before now and which have now been eliminated, must be crucified by the Word of

God. When you fully yield yourself to God and those elements of the flesh are crucified, a transformation begins to take place. The nature of the enemy is broken, and the nature of God gradually replaces that. Warfare is what activates this. This is why when some persons begin to engage in warfare, the devil fights them back to throw them off track. I emphasize to people again and again: "there is no deliverance outside of the Word of God."

The Third Stage in deliverance is divine encounters for transformation. I mentioned earlier that the first stage is when you are having the demons cast out of you, and that in most cases such demons belong to the lower cadre of demons, not principalities. In the second stage, we are engaged in warfare. As you are warring, you are touching the power base of the enemy, and you are affecting the principalities.

Now, the principalities fight back by attacking your character. They have taken your entire lifetime to develop certain habits, replicating their evil nature through the demons that they put in your life, especially the work of the familiar spirit. Now, what they do, as you are growing in faith, doing warfare and increasing in anointing, they try to neutralize your faith by attacking your character weaknesses. We have to deal with this because this is where many tend to be entrapped their entire lives. Such people may have potentials and abilities, but they often do not enjoy the benefits. Why? Every time they try to make headway, the demons, having already known the character they placed in such people - whether it is lust, malice, anger, or pride - will attack their oncoming miracle and success through their character weaknesses. This is what results in the syndrome called 'failure at the edge of successes.'

WHY FAILURE AT THE EDGE OF SUCCESS?

For some people in the Body of Christ, something always seems to abort their efforts at the last minute, resulting in *failure at the edge of success*. Why at the edge of success? Because principalities can see people's seasons. And one of the most powerful strategies of the strongman is to target your seasons. When your season of lifting, promotion, and blessing is approaching, they see it, and they activate that faulty trait in your character. If you are caught, and you truly begin to misbehave, you may end up losing that season. This can lead to painful delays and fruitlessness in life and destiny.

Your seasons are your opportune times. I addressed this in greater detail in my book, *Prophetic Gateways* - where I talked about the cycles of God. There are divine cycles. There are prophetic cycles. And there is also an appointed season, which is the zone of your opportune time: the time that your gifting and your opportunities come together. It is the season for your lifting. That is the time demons love to come around you and abort your oncoming miracle.

As I already mentioned, church people are particularly prone to this syndrome. People may be very good in church. They may be committed to giving, loving, and serving. Then, suddenly, they start to misbehave. Those who are prone to gossiping start to gossip; those who are susceptible to lust start to lust; some others fall into malice, while others start to walk in pride. It is often in their season of promotion that the enemy comes to attack their character. Cheeringly, in the case of Jesus, He had a striking testimony to share: "The ruler of the world (Satan) is coming. And he has no claim on Me [no power over Me nor anything that he can use against Me]" (John 14:30, AMP). In other words, Satan could find no common ground or point of contact for him in the life of Jesus. The reason was that Jesus was fully committed to the will of God in all He did. This is the key to cutting off demonic points of contact from our lives.

I will explain more about **points of contacts** later, but for now, let's establish a few things. First, how do you overcome the strongman, the principalities, so to speak? The way to overcome them is to overcome yourself, or better put, let God overcome you.

Let me explain this with the life of Jacob. Jacob was a man who had been prone to usurpation, right from the womb. God had a prophetic destiny for him, which was profound. He had done nothing to merit this divine program; God simply chose to bless him. When he was leaving home, God met him again and reaffirmed the divine arrangement concerning his life. However, he had a nature through which the enemy could work. He, therefore, needed to be liberated from all that threatened to truncate his destiny.

Here is a summary of the stages of Jacob's deliverance. First, he was delivered from his brother who wanted to kill him. I will liken that to the first level of deliverance. In the second level of deliverance, he was with his uncle, a crafty strategist and callous taskmaster, who changed his salary ten times. Every time he tried to work against Jacob, God turned things around for his (Jacob's) good. That is the second level of deliverance – warfare. In warfare, you cannot run from the enemy; you confront him. To put it simply, in the first stage of deliverance, God delivers you *from*. In the second stage, He delivers you *in*. Hallelujah!

Interestingly, most people just want to be delivered *from*; they do not want to be delivered *in*. God did not deliver Daniel *from* the lion's den; He delivered him *in* the lion's den. You must understand that your deliverance process is intended to work out something good for you. If the devil had no purpose to fulfill in the believers' lives for our benefit, God would have taken him away completely – as it will eventually happen. But until his time is up and God takes us to heaven, we will still have to deal with him and be all the better for it.

When God delivers *from*, you are protected *from* evil. But when God delivers *in*, you are *in* the midst of the evil, you are confronting the evil, and that not only forces you to change, but also gives you authority. If God had delivered Daniel *from* the lions' den, he would not have had any authority over the lions. But by God delivering him *in* the lions' den, he confronted the lion and came out alive. The lion could not hurt him, so he came out of the lion's den as a man with authority over the lions. We can conveniently conclude that from that point in his life, the fear of lions would no longer bother him.

Jacob further underwent a third and most powerful level of deliverance, which I will discuss in the subheading below.

POWER OF DIVINE ENCOUNTERS AND TRANSFORMATION

The focus of the third level of deliverance is for God to grow our authority in the areas where we have been bruised, and firmly establish us in dominion and bring about total transformation in our lives. This is to ensure that the enemy completely loses his power over our lives. In the case of Jacob, we have seen how he was delivered *from* Esau, and later delivered *in* the house of Laban; but by the time God met him after he had left Laban, something happened to him.

That account is recorded in Genesis 32:24-30. The Bible says Jacob wrestled with "a man" (an angel) all night, and the man touched him. This supernatural man was actually the Lord Jesus in His spirit nature. He touched the hollow of Jacob's thigh and it went out of joint. So, technically, God disabled Jacob. Why? Because his seeming ability was his problem. He believed so much in his natural slyness, which made him to always do things on his own terms. And, as long as he continued to approach life this way, the enemy could easily program, predict, and contain him.

This is why many people, including believers, have issues. We do things in our own strength, not knowing that the enemy already has his program within us. If we do not allow God to have his way in our lives, the enemy can always predict and contain us by aborting our seasons. But the moment we accept transformation, which is the purpose of deliverance, we will outsmart the enemy. Why would God want to deliver us and bless us with material things if we would still continue to be like the devil and end up in hell? Evidently, therefore, the whole focus of deliverance is for us to become like God.

Still, on Jacob, the Bible says that as the heavenly being touched him, the hollow of his thigh went out of joint, and Jacob realized he was dealing with God. He consequently surrendered and asked to be blessed. God granted his request and told him that he would no longer be called Jacob but Israel. He was thus transformed from a cheat, liar, and con artist to become a prince of God. In other words, the nature of the demon that was placed in him was cleaned out and replaced by the nature of Christ.

The Bible further says that having been so transformed, Jacob "had power with God and with man", and thus prevailed. God disabled him so he was compelled to depend on God. God who disabled him would have to fight for him. When we lose our strength, we will lose our fight to God; and then, God takes over our fight. Without spiritual brokenness, we can never subdue the demonic prince that controls our family. That wicked power will continue to reproduce our forefathers' experiences in our lives. It is a generational thing.

We often have to deal with generational issues, but you cannot overcome generational issues by just praying. You also have to overcome generational characteristics that the ancestral spirit controlling the family has dictated from generation to generation. As we overcome that, our nature will become

> "... you cannot overcome generational issues just by praying. You also have to overcome generational characteristics that the ancestral spirit controlling the family has dictated from generation to generation."

transformed into the image of Christ, and the hold of the evil one will be broken.

The Bible says that when Jacob left Peniel, where he had met with God, he said, "I have seen God face to face, and my life is preserved" (verse 30). He was simply saying that he had gone through the gates of death, and now possessed a resurrected life. The devils cannot handle a resurrected life.

We are also told that the sun rose as Jacob departed. The sun rose upon Jacob. The Sun of Righteousness wants to rise upon us. If we wholeheartedly allow this process to happen, the spotlight of God's blessing and promotion will be upon us, and we will acquire spiritual authority to help others. This is the direction of authentic deliverance.

 BREAKTHROUGH PROPHETIC DELIVERANCE PRAYERS

1. Everlasting Father, you abound in mercies, longsuffering, forgiving iniquities and sins to a thousand generations of them that love and obey you. Today, I declare my everlasting love for you and your word. I ask your pardon for the occult involvement of my ancestors and the sin of rebellion against your will and order.

2. I invite the blood of the Everlasting Covenant (Hebrews 13.20) to invade the foundations / generations of

my family and erase all occult signs, marks, webs and destroy all forms of occult bondage from every member of my family.

3. Today, every inherit occult abilities corrupting and counterfeiting the glorious gift of God in my / our lives, catch fire and be reduced to ashes in the Mighty Name of Jesus.

4. Lord teach me how to correctly interact with your glorious Holy Spirit and grant me discernment on how to identify lying, seducing and counterfeit spirits. Keep me from error of the wicked in the mighty name of Jesus.

5. Lord God, I fully embrace your total deliverance in my life. Help me to stand strong in your love, unshaken by satanic distractions and external manipulations.

6. I take authority over the power of failure at the edge of success. Let the strategy of this spirit be exposed and destroyed in Jesus Name

CHAPTER 15

More Reasons for Delay in Deliverance Cases

1. NEED FOR A BIGGER VISION

I thank God for the deliverance and warfare transformation taking place in the Church today. Sadly, however, we are mostly reducing these happenings to the physical manifestations – with little or no emphasis on character building. Without character building, we cannot handle our inheritance in God. Of course, we can have miracles but can we handle our inheritance?

There is a vast difference between seeking after miracles and understanding our proper roles in destiny and then developing the mental capacity to embrace the bigger picture. Miracles, as good as they may seem, are merely God's way of responding to our crises through time; but His original design is to develop our moral stamina and build our mental capacity to function in our inheritance as heirs of God and joint-heirs with Christ.

It is time for the much needed mental shift from a mere preoccupation with miracles of survival to building an army of believers who can wield spiritual authority and break the curse over their families, communities, cities and nations. To walk in true power, we need to reposition the Church from being a place for seeking the blessing to a place where one becomes the curse-breaker of the generation.

God's people must be trained to embrace and exercise our inheritance; otherwise, we cannot be significantly used of God, and neither can we handle the devil effectively. Without this crucial reorientation, Satan will continue to seek to tamper with our firepower. We would be like the children of Israel whom Pharaoh told, *You can go, but only the men, the women, and children. Leave your flock and herd behind. Leave your stuff behind. Do not go very far* (Exodus 10:24). This is much like serving God on conditions dictated by the evil one, and we must never allow this.

> *"Yet, without character building we cannot handle our inheritance in God. Of course we can have miracles but can we handle our inheritance?"*

Moses and the children refused to yield to Pharaoh in Egypt; we also must boldly refuse to be compromised by the enemy. Thank God for Moses. He simply replied Pharaoh, *No, we will go with our wives; we will go with our children; we will go with our stuff; in fact, we are going with some of your stuff.* Eventually, the Israelites demanded of the Egyptians silver and gold and spoiled them.

Indeed, God is waiting for deliverers who will go all the way, so that He can entrust them with the inheritance and the riches of the world; so that they can do a great work for Him. You are one of those God wants to use. This is why you must take up the revelations and principles in this book and use them to take your inheritance. You must become that next great person in your family, in your nation, in your generation, and in the Church of Jesus Christ.

2. DEALING WITH POINTS OF CONTACT

Points of contact, in deliverance, are the loopholes that the enemy has established to reinforce or exert his authority over our lives. They constitute the legal grounds for him to keep meddling with our lives. Satan often manages to establish some legal basis in people's lives (in their time of ignorance) from where he can continue to maintain his evil relevance. We have to identify these points of contacts and dislodge them.

When Israel as a nation was going into the land of promise, God warned them about the issue of points of contact. He particularly warned them about the high places of the land of Canaan. The high places were hills where the Canaanite tribes served their false gods, and God knew that the tendency was there for the children of Israel to go up there, renovate those same places, and begin to defile themselves therein (which, in fact, they eventually did). Thus, God emphatically told them:

> "Ye shall utterly destroy all the places, wherein the nations which ye shall possess served their gods, upon the high mountains, and upon the hills, and under every green tree: And ye shall overthrow their altars, and break their pillars, and burn their groves with fire; and ye shall hew down the graven images of their gods, and destroy the names of them out of that place" (Deuteronomy 12:2-3).

CATEGORIES OF POINTS OF CONTACT

A. CURSED ITEMS

These are items that have been dedicated to the devil. They include items that were originally inspired by the enemy and then produced and released into the market. Most people who travel to different cultures have indiscriminately bought things in those cultures that they thought were mere works of art (items from occult temples, for instance) and brought them home – not realizing the spiritual implications. Some buy crafts and other works of art from places like Africa and Asia but do not realize that some of these artifacts are carved faces of demons or replicas of demonic idols. These collectors often consider such items beautiful but, alas, they are cursed items; and thus they invite demonic presence into their lives.

It was for this reason that when the Israelites were to pass through Jericho to enter into the land of Canaan, God told them not to touch anything in the city because the place was wholly given to idolatry and everything in it was polluted. Unfortunately, a devious and greedy man, named Achan, saw a beautiful Babylonian garment and a wedge of gold and took those things into his own home, bringing a curse upon the entire nation (Joshua 7).

Any item dedicated to the worship of idols or inspired by Satan - books, videotapes, cartoons or any similar thing - will invite the presence of the demons when you bring them into your home. And so, to get rid of those demons, you have to identify what those things are, and remove them from your home.

B. DEMONIC SYMBOLISMS

There are people, for instance, who have certain types of dreams, and once they have such dreams, they will experience certain types of occurrences. Such dreams become a point of contact. Why? The devil's vocabulary has been built into these people's belief system through such dreams from which they get the message as to what to expect when they have such dreams.

MORE REASONS FOR DELAY IN DELIVERANCE CASES

There are some people that at certain times when their hand is itching, they believe that this means they will receive monetary gifts, but this is occult-based thinking. It is a point of contact. Even though you may indeed get the money, it is the devil fulfilling his purpose of binding you in a much stronger way. There is no such thing as an itchy hand bringing money in the Bible. Anything that is not from the Word of God is a ground for satanic oppression and bondage.

Again, there are some who believe that if they feel a particular way in a certain part of their body, they will experience a misfortune. Unknown to them, this is actually a satanic code, which is a point of contact. I call it a satanic code because he has programmed such people to believe that system of control. It is the negative law of faith because when you see such things, you expect certain reactions, and your expectation gives the power or authorization to the enemy to fulfill them.

This is why you must learn to live by the Word of God only. If you used to have a pattern of these types of experiences before you came to Christ, now that you are in Christ, you must go through counseling, meet with your pastor, renounce the satanic belief system, believe the Word of God, and consciously think and act contrary to the expectations of Satan. The enemy's power will be broken over your life.

C. DUMB IDOLS OR DEMON SPIRITS

I will take the Word of God on this directly. **"Now concerning spiritual gifts, brethren, I would not have you ignorant. Ye know that ye were Gentiles, carried away unto these dumb idols, even as ye were led"** (1 Corinthians 12:1-2).

The Corinthians, before they came to Christ, had been possessed by Satan through dumb idols or demon spirits. Those demon spirits led them down a certain path that built certain character traits into their nature. I referenced this earlier when I was talking about the final stage in deliverance and the need for character transformation.

If there is a Luciferian spirit functioning in a family, members and descendants of such a family will be mostly arrogant and unteachable. That character trait is not of God, it is demonic, and the demons will use it even after an individual has come to Christ.

There are Abbadon spirits that bind certain families to immorality. The members wallow and revel in it. The Corinthian church provides a good case study here. Even though they had the nine gifts of the Spirit in operation, yet they would be drunk in Holy Communion services, and one of them could even be boasting of sleeping with his father's wife in the church – a supposedly born-again Christian!

Paul observed that the Corinthian city was bound by the Abaddon spirit (spirit of destruction). Abaddon, the principality in charge of immorality, had so much influence on the city that people would come to do business and then go to the temple where there were free women. This demonic lifestyle of free immoral sexual activity that had previously bound the believers in Corinth in their past life was carried into their Christian experience. This was why Paul had to address them severally on the issue of sexual immorality.

Now, apply this to yourself. What is there in your past life that is trying to transfer into your Christian experience? There are some people, mostly Africans, who used to go to traditional occult sources to look for visions. Usually, when people like that come to Christ, they are often looking for prophets to help them solve whatever challenges that confront them.

Don't get me wrong. There are genuine prophets. They can come to you during a prophetic meeting, and you get a word from the Lord, which is good. But when you start looking for prophets to prophesy to you before you can make decisions in your life, there is a serious problem somewhere. And it is this loophole that the devil will exploit to send some false prophets to bring confusion and crisis to your life.

If you want prophecy, open your Bible. That is the prophecy that can never fail. I am not saying this to despise prophesying or the office of prophets. I am saying this to emphasize that the prophetic ministry is one thing that has been so severely abused by the principality called Leviathan. He is corrupting it, and whole generations of people in the church are practicing witchcraft and self-hypnosis, not knowing that they are in occult bondage.

What I am saying here is this: certain habits that we acquired when we were without God were habits that the enemy wanted us to exhibit for life. He programmed them himself because they are part of his nature. If we do not deal with these habits, they become points of contact for recycled bondage. If you have anger, deal with it. The Bible says, **"Be ye angry, and sin not: let not the sun go down upon your wrath: Neither give place to the devil"** (Ephesians 4:26-27).

One of the hallmarks of witchcraft is malice and unforgiveness. People think that you can only be called a witch if you regularly go to the coven and eat human flesh. This is a myopic perception of witchcraft. There are witches in the church who never go to the coven. These are people who never forgive anybody. There are husbands who are witches without realizing it. They never forgive and never forget. What your wife did ten years ago is fresh in your memory, and you remember it as if it happened

> *"One of the things that witchcraft spirits do is that they maintain hurts in our minds."*

yesterday. That's witchcraft – un-forgiveness. It is there. It is latched into your system, and the devil uses it to hold you back from your destiny.

What does the Bible say about forgiveness? **"Be kind one to another, tenderhearted, forgiving one another, even as God for Christ sake has forgiven you"(Ephesians 4:32)**. If you are a believer who cannot forgive, it means you are hard-hearted. And since there can't be a hard-hearted believer, it means you are practicing witchcraft. You only go to church for show, and you don't even know it. This means that, apart from witchcraft, you also have the problem of ignorance. And where does ignorance lead? Destruction! God says, **"My people are destroyed for lack of knowledge…" (Hosea 4:6)**.

We cannot lie against the truth and pretend to be Christians. Tenderheartedness is a hallmark of Christianity. One of the things that witchcraft spirits do is that they maintain hurts in our minds. What was done to you years ago, they maintain a fresh hurt there. Why? They use your wound to keep you bound to your past, so you are not advancing. This is why we must learn to let go and let God heal us. When we are healed and made whole, the enemy can no longer use us.

3. JEWELRY, LITERATURE, VIDEO MATERIALS, AND MUSIC THAT ARE DEDICATED TO SATAN

Satan places curses upon anything dedicated to him. And when you place such, whether on your body, or in your car or your home, demonic presence will be invoked. You must do away with such things so that your deliverance will not be delayed.

God wants His people to be separated from anything that defiles either our spirit or body. We must allow the Word of God to do a complete work in our lives. We are to take authority and control our dwelling places. Your children would want to access occult-projecting channels or programs on your TV, and this could bring the whole house under occult oppression and bondage. This is why there is constant tension in some houses. The atmosphere is toxic. But go to other houses where people pray all the time, and you would find the atmosphere is so peaceful and inviting.

4. HIDDEN CURSES

Delay in deliverance could result from unidentified curses and covenants in the family which have not been broken. These types of curses will perpetuate problems in people's lives. For instance, during the conquest of Jericho, Joshua, the servant of God declared that whoever attempted to rebuild Jericho would set up the foundation with the death of his firstborn and he would set up the gates with the death of his last born. About

500 years down the line, a man by the name of Hiel the Bethelite, not knowing this curse, came and started rebuilding Jericho. As he laid the foundation of the city, his firstborn died, and while setting up the gates, his last born died (1 Kings 16:34). That was an example of a hidden existing curse which was still effective over 500 years later.

There are other types of hidden curses which may not be of long duration. Sometimes curses can come from the way we relate to persons of authority. If for instance, you do not relate well with your pastor, employer, or with your parents, you can incur curses. These hidden curses can hurt you. There are people who are in churches but do not understand these things. They trivialize the anointing of their pastor while honoring visiting ministers. Such people can incur curses on themselves.

In the home, the husband occupies the office of a husband, while the wife has her place. If couples do not relate properly, they can violate moral territorial laws and incur curses. In fact, I am finding out that one of the strongest areas where witchcraft powers are effective in checking the progress of families is in marriage. A marriage may be romantic, yet spiritually bankrupt. If you do not reverence your husband by Bible standards, you will violate things in the spirit realm. If the man does not nurture and show understanding and consideration for the wife according to Bible standards, he will rupture things in the spirit and open the family in spiritual nakedness to the devil. More on this in my book, *War Is Normal*.

One of the effective ways by which the enemy builds different points of contact is to set up unidentified altars in our lives. Altars can be built around habits and appetites that do not honor God. These violate the presence of God in the family. The enemy could work with such loopholes to checkmate the progress of the family for years. People can be in the same spot for years. Why? Because the enemy has set up altars of anger, insubordination, rebellion, gluttony and other obsessive behaviors that have not been submitted to God for cleansing. These will serve to impede the progress of the family.

So, if you want your deliverance to be quick and successful, you have to obviously identify those points of contact that the enemy uses in recycling bondage and perpetuating his presence and control over your life.

BREAKTHROUGH PROPHETIC DELIVERANCE PRAYERS

1. Lord, increase my mental capacity to fill the role you have assigned to my life and destiny. Increase my vision of all that I can be and do.

2. I come against every demonic point of contact in my beliefs, life, and around my dwelling in the Name of Jesus. Be located by fire and burn in Jesus Name.

3. Holy Spirit of the living God; reveal any cursed items or objects in my life and home in the Name of Jesus.

4. God of fire, locate by your Spirit, sources of hidden curses and personal attitudes promoting and reinforcing these patterns in my life and help me uproot them once and for all in the mighty Name of Jesus Christ.

CHAPTER 16

Other Reasons for Delay in Deliverance

HIDDEN ALTARS

An altar is a spiritual point of exchange. Under the Old Covenant, God told His people to consecrate hallowed places to serve as altars whereby His people could bring Him sacrifices. Those sacrifices represented points of submission and consecration to do and to live in the will of God. They were binding places of blessings. God would meet with His people at the altar, commune with them, and transmit His blessings to them while receiving their worship.

The enemy seeks to maintain an illegal hold over people by creating certain types of altars. There are, in some families, existing altars that are generational in nature. That is to say, the ancestors of a family could have raised up altars where they served and worshiped the devil. And even though those altars are no longer there in the physical, they are still there in the spiritual realm. Even after the next generations have come and moved on to modern family life, with some becoming Christians, the altars remain intact. They can only be demolished in spiritual warfare. This is why some unexplainable dream encounters happen where a born-again Christian finds himself in some bizarre situations in the dream life.

I remember when, some years ago, I was ministering in Europe and I ran into a wonderful servant of God. The Lord told me that he had a sentence of death upon him and I wanted to know more. The Lord told me that his lineage served as a priesthood to the devil but that that generation had gone. However, being in the line of the male generation, he was supposed to have continued the priesthood, but he came to know the Lord. He dedicated his life to the Lord and completely renounced the devil; but the Lord said to me: "Even though He is serving Me, he is represented on the altar of the enemy."

So, to break that power, the Lord gave me a prescription which was quite uncommon. The man was to be adopted by another servant of God who had a higher authority. This way, God no longer considers his genealogy after his fleshly heritage. There is some precedence of this in the Bible. In the case of Joseph, for instance, the children he had in Egypt before Jacob arrived were taken up by Jacob and placed directly under his

> *"Demonic altars lead to barrenness of the spirit – having potentials without success."*

own genealogy. They were reckoned like other sons of Jacob. So, Joseph as a father became like a brother to his own children. There are other types of demonic altars that Satan actively seeks to erect in the lives of the children of God. These could be in the form of habits – habits that people do not repent of, such as anger, lust, gluttony, pornography, etc. In the Book of Acts, the Bible talks about the Athenians having different types of altars to different gods and Paul said they even had an altar to the 'unknown god.' Our negative habits that we do not repent of can constitute a demonic altar – an altar to an unknown god that the devil can work through to attract our worship, neutralize our effectiveness, and abort our seasons. This can cause painful delays.

As a matter of fact, when I was studying about ancestral spirits, I found out that what they often do is to replicate the nature of the familiar spirit in the character of an individual. When the person begins to advance in the things of God, they repeatedly come visiting with the negative character trait that can hold him to a lifetime of bondage.

Altars of the enemy cause delay because once the enemy can repeatedly predict and abort our prophetic cycles and seasons of blessings, they can be aborted over and over again. It is as a woman who has been pregnant nine times and suffering miscarriage on each occasion. It means that over the course of those nine pregnancies, she had no baby to show for her efforts. Demonic altars lead to the barrenness of the spirit - having potentials without results.

This is why I often say deliverance must be taught through the Word of God so that people can understand those aspects of their character that are under demonic manipulations. This knowledge will help them to crucify and yield all aspects of their character to God. Thus, the profaned ground in the human soul and personality will be sanctified, hallowed, and reclaimed, and the power of the controlling spirit will be broken.

The Prey of the Terrible

> "Shall the prey be taken from the mighty or the lawful captive delivered? But thus saith the Lord, Even the captives of the mighty shall be taken away, and the prey of the terrible shall be delivered: for I will contend with him that contendeth with thee, and I will save thy children" (Isaiah 49:24-25).

What does 'the prey of the terrible' mean? It means that the spiritual power that is binding the individual is at such a severe level. This could be either because of the high level of authority of that demonic power- the enemy's power relative to the individual's helpless state, or because the bondage has been of a very long duration, and thus the enemy has successfully established a basis and system of control. It is rightly called 'the prey of the terrible' because it looks like this is a hopeless case; nothing can be done to salvage the prey. It is like trying to take a rat from the teeth of a hungry lion.

THE LAWFUL CAPTIVE

The Lawful Captive involves someone who has himself violated spiritual territory and is therefore legitimately, as it were, bound by the satanic power. Cheeringly, God's promise is that "Even the captives of the mighty shall be taken away, and the prey of the terrible shall be delivered: for I will contend…." This assures us that with God, there are no impossible cases.

There is also something we must consider here - the contending power of the Lord. Let me give you two examples of this in the ministry of the Lord Jesus Christ.

One day, Jesus was coming down from the mountain when He saw people gathered around His disciples. He queried why they were questioning His disciples. Someone spoke up – the father of a young man who had been bound by a demon. He said, "Master, I have brought unto thee, my son, which hath a dumb spirit; And wheresoever he taketh him, he teareth him: and he foameth, and gnasheth with his teeth, and pineth away: and I spake to thy disciples that they should cast him out, and they could not." Jesus said to him, "If thou canst believe, all things are possible to him that believeth." And the man said, "Lord, I believe; help thou mine unbelief."

At that point, the demons went into action and tried to distract Jesus, but Jesus was not about to be drawn into battle with the enemy. He does not fight on the enemy's terms or invitation. So, He asked the Father, "For how long has he been this way?" The father said, "From since he was a child. Often, it tries to throw him into the water, into the fire; it seeks to destroy him." Jesus rebuked the demon, and it left the child, and he looked like he was dead. Jesus took him by the hand and delivered him to the father (Mark 9:14-27).

This was a very severe case that required a certain level of authority to break. When cases like these are brought to the church, if the required authority is not there, the case will be prolonged. The disciples of Jesus later asked him, "Why could not we cast him out?" He said to them, "This kind can come forth by nothing, but by prayer and fasting." So we know that there are some cases that can be called "this kind..."

What is the role of prayer and fasting? To unearth the secrets. Also, Jesus queried to find out the nature and extent of demonic possession. He learned that the affliction had been there from childhood. That is a strongman demon there. Another way to know is straight from the Holy Spirit through discernment. Jesus discerned what was in operation, its duration, and all the relevant information. One of the reasons we encourage pre-deliverance sessions, fasting, and waiting on the Lord is to gather specific information that is relevant to the case so that it can be handled better. That information will release a level of authority that will break the resistance of the enemy.

The unfortunate thing is that, most often, we do not take the time to prepare. We just do haphazard work, and the oppressed continue to endure their pain. This fasting and prayer and pre-ministry intercession will be helpful in dislodging these types of cases.

Another example is that of the demoniac of Gadara (Mark 5). This man was in the tombs, crying day and night, cutting himself. He had often been bound with chains to restrain him, but he was so demonically possessed that he plucked the chains asunder. However, when Jesus came by, he fell down and worshiped Him. His soul obviously yearned for God, but the bondage was much. We know it was much because Jesus rebuked the unclean spirit, the demon that was in the spirit of the man. That was the spirit seeking sexual pleasure through cutting, which the man was practicing. However, that demon initially boasted, "My name is Legion, for we are many."

One legion is over 6000 soldiers, according to the Roman army. So the demons were over 6000. It is no wonder that when Jesus cast the demons out, and they ran into a herd of swine, the swine couldn't cope. They all ran into the river. So, here, we see another case. The Bible says that after Christ's intervention, the man who had been so mad, who had been so terrible, was cured instantly and came to his right mind.

I must emphasize that the degree of authority that Jesus exhibited here is at the glory level. There are levels of authority. There is an anointing of power, but there is also the glory level of anointing. At the glory level, the flesh is totally extinct. It is God and the devil. And, of course, when the glory of God collides with evil, evil bows instantly.

> *"The unfortunate thing is that, most times, we do not take time to prepare. We just do haphazard work and the oppressed continue to endure their pain."*

I remember in 1986; we were ministering deliverance to a wonderful young woman. I was in fact initially doing the deliverance from 7 p.m. to 10 p.m. and wasn't making any headway. One of the anointed vessels, a lady came by, uninvited, to help us. Immediately she arrived, the demons recognized her authority and were attempting to attack her. She commanded them to bow, and they bowed, and we began casting them out. After about 300 demons had left the sister, we had still not gone anywhere. I was tired, burnt out; so, I laid on my back.

Then, I had a vision. I saw a mountain that was full of darkness. In the middle of it, a flickering light began. That light grew stronger and stronger until it became brighter than the brightness of the noonday. Instantly, my hands were flung in the air as I exclaimed, "the glory of the Lord, the glory of the Lord, the glory of the Lord!" The atmosphere of the room changed. The demon-oppressed lady, under the active manifestation of the demon, looked terrified. She looked around and started screaming; the demons ran out of her instantly. When the glory of God shows up, it is a very wonderful thing to behold.

Demonic Cycles

There are demonic cycles, just as you have the cycles of God – comprising spiritual cycles, prophetic cycles, and appointed seasons (this you can read about in my book, *Prophetic Gateways*). Demonic cycles are cycles within which certain demons execute their evil programs in the life of an individual, a family or a nation.

At certain times in the course of the year, some people are sick. In some families, when people reach a particular age, they must suffer reverses. Some individuals, within specific months, in the course of the year, must suffer unexplainable, unaccountable reverses. Perhaps any of these illustrations relates to your personal life. What you need to do is to consecrate yourself to break the power of the demons that are behind the reverses, misfortunes, and afflictions in your life. You can actually mobilize other people, or other members of your family and target the base of those demonic powers, break them asunder, and force out a release of God's program in your life.

Understanding demonic cycles in your life are vital. The Holy Spirit will point this out to you because He will monitor you and will let you see the trend over time and know what to do.

Now, there are some cases that are so surreal that even the minister who is doing the deliverance has to apply wisdom because there is so much that the human nature or personality can take. Many years ago, I was ministering to a young woman. I do not know what happened to her when she was young, but it had so severely altered her personality that as we were ministering deliverance on her, tons of demons were eliminated; but we got to the point where we felt that inner restraint to stop because she could not take it anymore. If we had put in more pressure, it would have led to a breakdown, and that would have been counterproductive.

So, we had to stop and ask the Holy Spirit to take charge of her. We laid hands on her, blessed her, and ministered healing.

There were some intricate healings that needed to be worked at the soul level, and the Holy Spirit knew exactly what to do.

That is why, again, I will say, anointing is good, but skill is needed to go with the anointing. You develop skill by being called to pay special attention to a particular area of ministry, and through continuous practice in that area, skill is developed. Consequently, with anointing and skill, you can more appropriately respond to the Holy Spirit's strategy for achieving results.

One of the things that cause a delay in deliverance, which I mentioned previously under lawful captivity, is that there are people who want God and the devil at the same time. People want to give God a wedding suit and the devil a wedding gown and combine the best of both worlds. It does not work that way. The Bible says God cannot be tempted with evil, neither does He tempt any man with evil. If any man is tempted, he is being drawn away by his lust. This means we have to deal with our lusts. We cannot have one leg in the world and one leg in the Kingdom and expect things to work.

> *"People professing faith in God go about sleeping around and engaging in other forms of depravity that validate the enemy's presence in their lives."*

It's so painful to observe that much of modern-day practice of Christianity is a perversion by the wicked one. We are constantly being told about the God of love but not the God who calls us to accountability. People professing faith in God go about sleeping around and engaging in other forms of depravity that validate the enemy's presence in their lives. The Bible says that **"Whosoever is born of God doth not commit sin; for his seed remaineth in him: and he cannot sin because he is born of God" (1 John 3:9)**. It also says **such a person keeps himself and the evil one is not able to touch him (1 John 5:18)**. If you keep yourself in the love of God, then the enemy will not be able to bind or to touch you.

Illegal Collections

Another thing that can cause delay is ignorance. Ignorance can permit the enemy to perpetuate what I call illegal collections. Demonic spirits are like debt collectors. They claim that there are covenants or curses in place and so they move in to collect their "dues" by visiting the individual with affliction, sickness, reverses, struggle, oppression, suppression, depression, pain, and retrogression. However, the Word of God counters this deception of the enemy. The Bible says that every handwriting of ordinances that was against us or stood hostile and contrary to us, He Himself, the Lord Jesus, took it out of the way, blotted it out by His own blood, and nailed it to the Cross (Colossians 2:14).

So, if every negative handwriting, obligation or contract has been blotted out by the Blood of Christ, how come the enemy is still collecting on people? Through ignorance. Ignorance of the law limits your ability to enforce your rights. When you know what belongs to you, what your rights are, you can go to the devil, with that written Word of God and confront him.

Again, I must say that knowledge of the truth is not enough. Our faith is not a passive faith; it is an active, warring faith. In case you do not know, you are supposed to be fighting – fighting the good fight of faith. If you merely quote Scriptures while the enemy is fighting you, how will you be able to take advantage of your spiritual authority and break his aggression? We are to fight meaningfully and purposefully. That way, we can destroy the enemy's delay in our lives.

Ancestral Spirits
Finally, to sum it up, I will go again to the subject of ancestral spirits. I mentioned this when I began to talk about the congregation of the dead. What do I mean by ancestral spirit? I mean the controlling power of your family.

Let me use the African culture for instance. In African culture or cosmological composition, the family has two dimensions – the natural, physical dimension, and then the spiritual dimension. The natural dimension of the family is composed of father, mother, and the children; whereas in the spiritual dimension of the family, according to African cosmological orientation, the family also includes the ancestors or the fathers who have passed on. These dead entities are regarded as representing the family on the spiritual plane and having a valid contribution to make to the day-to-day well being of the physical or natural family.

For this reason, therefore, a number of sacrifices are done in certain seasons of the year to appeal for the continued support, guidance, and help of the ancestors. The truth of the matter is that this is just a satanic philosophy because the Bible says **it is appointed unto man once to die and after that the judgment (Hebrews 9:27).**

Once a person is dead, they no longer have any influence on the living. They have no power or control of any kind. Instead, they immediately face divine judgment – the outcome of which will depend on whether they lived for God (which will make them to be received by Him), or whether they lived for the devil (which makes them liable to a retribution consequent to their poor choices.) Either way, the point is that they no longer have any relevance on the living.

So, who fills the gap? Who comes through dreams to manifest as the departed one? It is that ancestral spirit, Satan's delegate that has controlled the family for generations, masquerading as their late forefathers, drawing worship from the family and assigning punishment to every member of the family.

The first level in Satan's use of ancestral spirits is to attach a familiar spirit to everyone born into a family. This familiar spirit is used to train a child and put habits in that child that will enable the Luciferian program for the family to be extended and manifested in the life of that child. This is how a familiar spirit busies itself as the child grows up, putting different types of habits into him. These habits gradually form a part of the individual's character, and he soon begins to think, *this is my life; I am living my life*. Sadly, he is not living his life; he is living according to the dictates of the devil through the ancestral spirit.

The Bible talks about the prince of the power of the air, the spirit that now works in the children of disobedience (Ephesians 2:2). This spirit that works in the children of disobedience seduces and implements the program of Lucifer for each member of a family. When someone born into such family eventually comes to Christ, he wants to enjoy the benefits of his relationship with Christ; he wants to exhibit spiritual power and authority – but what happens? The ancestral spirits simply call for his file according to the habits in which they had been grooming him over the years, and they begin to attack him through his character. If it is anger they had put in him, they nurture this anger and begin to work with that. Or it could be some other forms of lusts, perversions, and

OTHER REASONS FOR DELAY IN DELIVERANCE

addictions with which they choose to work. They begin to stir up those base instincts, using them to attack and abort his seasons. This is the greatest source of delay for a believer.

There is a power called the spirit of delay. It is Satan's most powerful weapon in ensuring that people are non-achievers in life. It delays and then aborts. Understanding your history, family line, and structure will give you the revelation and momentum you need to conquer this spirit.

I remember a wonderful sister I once ministered to in the course of my pastoral work years ago. When she came to see me, she was 36 years old at the time. She said, "Pastor, Please, I am 36 years old, I have been a faithful Christian and a virgin. For all these years, no man has ever proposed to me, not even to give me the opportunity to say no. What is wrong?" I said, "I do not know, but we can pray."

The Bible says **if the foundation is destroyed what can the righteous do? (Psalm 11:3)**. Well, the righteous can pray and rebuild the foundation. So I set for her three days of fasting and prayers so that we could pray together. On the first day of the fast, I brought myself to the Lord and was presenting her case before the Lord. Suddenly, I drifted away in the spirit, and I saw four huge, menacing, ferocious dogs walking towards me and asking me in a human voice, "Is it by power? Is it by power?" trying to knock me down. And I replied, "It is not by power, nor by might but by my spirit, says the Lord. I come against you by the power of the Living God."

I opened my eyes and asked God what the revelation meant. God told me those were the Abaddon spirits in charge of her family and that they were the ones that had held her in captivity. On the third day, the sister and I got together to pray. Other prophetic things came up belonging to another chapter of another book.

Suffice it to say that these powers can cause really heartbreaking delays. To break their stronghold, you have to know your family history and what incriminating traits are in your character. Otherwise, a man of God can labor, fast and pray, and nothing happens. You may even get some release, but that power can come back to attack your next season. His ability to attack your season is based on the character traits he has placed in you.

This is why you must identify the loopholes in your character and bring them into submission to the Word of God. Once the Word of God works on you, that area of your life is broken and cleaned out. From that point, the evil power will lose its hold on you, and you can then proceed to live a productive, fruitful life, to the glory of God.

BREAKTHROUGH PROPHETIC DELIVERANCE PRAYERS

1. Every hidden altar channeling evil into my life and family; catch fire and be destroyed in the name of Jesus.

2. I bring any opening in my life that furnishes the enemy legal rights against me under the redeeming blood of Jesus. I declare the curse broken and nullified by the superior claims of the blood of Jesus Christ.

3. All demonic cycles of pain, reverses and struggle; be now liquidated and deactivated.

4. I decree a speedy divine arrest for all illegal demonic collectors in my life, family, and ministry. I demand and receive double restoration for everything or lost opportunities I have suffered due to illegal collection activities in the Name of Jesus.

5. The ancestral spirit delegated to monitor and undermine the glory of God in my family; you are fired in Jesus Name. Jesus is the new sheriff in town.

CHAPTER 17

The Strongman of The House

"'"When the unclean spirit is gone out of a man, he walketh through dry places, seeking rest, and findeth none. Then he saith, I will return into my house from whence I came out; and when he comes, he findeth it empty, swept, and garnished. Then goeth he, and taketh with himself seven other spirits more wicked than himself, and they enter in and dwell there: and the last state of that man is worse than the first. Even so, shall it be also unto this wicked generation" (Matthew 12:43-45).

It is critical in deliverance to pray for discernment. Jesus clearly demonstrated what it means to have discernment. He was always very specific; and when it was necessary, He asked questions. I will reasonably assume that, if He did not ask questions, it is because it was not required for He already had insight given to Him by the Father about the particular demonic situation with which He was dealing. So, knowledge of what we are doing is necessary.

Revelation received (particularly discerning of spirits) is far more important when you have to dislodge demons from people as you move in the anointing of God. The presence and power of God may be available to deliver, but with limited knowledge and inability to benefit from the presence of the Holy Spirit at any given moment, we will run short of the kind of victory God wants us to have.

A remarkable encounter is recorded in Matthew 12. The Pharisees had heard about the glorious things that were being said about Jesus and His ministry, and they started castigating him out of envy and jealousy. **"But when the Pharisees heard it they said this fellow does not cast out devils but by Beelzebub, the prince of the devils" (v. 24).**

> *"Revelation received (particularly discerning of spirits) is far more important when you have to dislodge demons from people as you move in the anointing of God."*

I want you to see something here. Even though we know that the Pharisees spoke out of envy, there is something significant about it. These people saw that Jesus was active in casting out devils, so they said He was doing this through the power of

Beelzebub, the prince, or the chief of the devils.

Who is Beelzebub? He is, of course, the principality in charge of witchcraft - the Lord of the Flies. But what they were implying here is that Jesus had a link with the prince of the devils, so His actions were hardly surprising. If He had a relationship with the prince of the devils, then, of course, the other smaller demons would obey. The above position would apply, for instance, in the case of a false prophet who is in league with the devil and who is deceiving people. But in this particular rise, it was a malicious lie being told by the Pharisees against Jesus.

GOVERNMENTAL POWERS IN THE SPIRITUAL REALM

There is something else I want you to see in the verse above. Cadres and levels of authority exist in the realm of the spirit. This understanding is particularly important when you are doing deliverance against the strongman or the ruler of the house. Let's look at the Scriptures again to learn one or two things about this.

Jesus, in response to the accusation of the Pharisees, said, **"Every kingdom divided against itself is brought to desolation, and every city or house divided against itself shall not stand: And if I by Beelzebub cast out devils, by whom do your children cast them out? Therefore they shall** be your judges. **But if I cast out demons by the Spirit of God, then the kingdom of God is come unto you" (Matthew 12:25-28).**

Jesus simply told the detractors to wake up to the reality that through His demonstration of the omnipotent power of God, the Kingdom of God was in operation on the earth already. The Kingdom of God, the governmental authority of God, His presence, is here. In other words, every time demons are being dislodged and you see manifestations, it means that two kingdoms are in a clash. It implies that God's governmental authority is in action to compel obedience.

Beyond this, however, Jesus gives us a bigger clue: **How can one enter into the house of a strong man except he first binds the strong man and then spoil his goods and take his house, or dispossess him of his armor? (v. 29).** What is Jesus saying here? In many cases of demonic possession or oppression, to relieve the oppressed and dislodge the demons, you have to discern the strongman of the house and oust him. Once you overcome the strongman of the house, you will be able to liberate his captive.

Let me now refer to the house mentioned in the passage, and what is meant by the strongman. Earlier on, I noted that demons are disembodied spirits (spirits without bodies). In this same passage of Matthew 12, Jesus said something about the nature of these demon spirits. **He said when a demon is cast out of a man he goes about seeking rest but finding none. Then he says to himself, I will go back to my house, from where I came out (vv. 43-44).**

Notice that the demon said "my house." What is the demon claiming as his house? That same individual that he was occupying before. So when Jesus mentions the strongman of the house, he is referring to the gatekeeper, the doorkeeper, the one who first established his presence as the rightful owner, even though illegally, in that individual who is so oppressed or demonized.

I want you to pay proper attention to verses 44 and 45 of that passage. **"Then the demon saith, I will return into my house from whence I came out; and when he comes, he findeth it empty, swept, and garnished. Then goeth he, and taketh with himself seven other spirits more wicked than himself, and they enter in and dwell there: and the last state of that man is worse than the first Even so shall it also be unto this wicked generation."**

Jesus is saying something far-reaching here. Who is claiming ownership of the house? One particular spirit. And when that individual spirit is cast out, he roams about and finds no rest. This means that demons are disembodied spirits and are tormented when they have no house to inhabit. That *house* is a body. During winter, it is cold out there, but you go out because you have business to do; but then, at the end of the day, you return to the warmth and comfort of your house. That aside, as humans, we tend to have some degree of psychological and emotional attachment to where we live. You are, for instance, used to the way your bathroom and kitchen are. And once there's a disruption in these settings, you get uncomfortable, and you immediately try to fix the situation.

This also applies to demons. As I said before, they do not have a body. Thus, they have to seek out a human body to occupy. And as soon as they find one, they settle themselves in there, and it becomes uncomfortable for them to leave.

To be an effective deliverance minister, when you are scheduling somebody for ministry, you need to ask the Lord, "What is the strongman?" Also, in the course of counseling, you can determine what the strongman is, that is, the predominant spirit that first got hold of the person. That is the strongman. It doesn't necessarily mean it is the strongest demon as the above Scripture shows.

In the example cited by Jesus, the demon believed that he was cast out because he was not strong enough. He thought he needed to get seven other spirits more wicked than himself to come and occupy the man. Let us look further into the Scripture, and we will see how Jesus dealt with the strongman.

Here is the account in Mark 5 again:

> "And they came over unto the other side of the sea, into the country of the Gadarenes. And when he was come out of the ship, immediately there met him out of the tombs a man with an unclean spirit. Who had his dwelling among the tombs; and no man could bind him, no, not with chains: Because that he had often been bound with fetters and chains, and the chains had been plucked asunder by him, and the fetters broken in pieces: neither could any man tame him. And always, night and day, he was in the mountains, and in the tombs, crying, and cutting himself with stones" (Mark 5:1-4).

Here is something you must not overlook. What did this man have? An unclean spirit. How many is that? One. By the way, whenever the Bible talks about an unclean spirit, it has something to do with sexual perversion. Not only that, but the passage also says that no one could bind the man, which means that he was also fierce and wild indicating that this case was beyond that of an unclean spirit. There is a condition that is called masochism - which is the habit of deriving sexual pleasure from pain, including inflicting wounds on oneself. So, we know that this unclean spirit, however he gained entrance into this man, was tormenting him so badly that the man resorted to cutting himself. And I believe that with each cut, he derived some sexual pleasure, so he cut himself even more. People tried to help him, but how did they go about it? They went about it as regular religious people do. They put ropes and chains on him. But what the man needed was a real anointing. It is the anointing, not the chains, that will help a person like that.

Have you ever been to some weird places where in the name of deliverance the recipients are flogged so that the demons in them could go out? The truth, however, is that such behavior only entertains the devil. It is the anointing – not the chains or the whip – that works.

As for this demoniac, they put chains around him, and nothing worked. As a matter of fact, he broke the chains. Do you think that was natural? No. Rather, the demonic energy snapped the chains and the ropes. He moved to the mountains crying and cutting himself, seeking relief. The demons were indwelling him and sexually tormented him.

In the course of ministry in 1987, I had an encounter with a lady who had been attacked by sexual madness. I sometimes think when you see evil in its true nature, you will learn to fear God the more, be compelled to respect the Word of God, and you will appreciate the value of a relationship with God. By seeing evil in its rare manifestation, you will realize you want nothing to do with it. You will honor God the more.

Let us continue to explore this account in Mark 5.

> "But when he saw Jesus afar off, he ran and worshiped him, And cried with a loud voice, and said, What have I to do with thee, Jesus, thou Son of the most high God? I adjure thee by God that thou torment me not. For he said unto him, Come out of the man, thou unclean spirit. And he asked him, What is thy name? And he answered, saying, My name is Legion: for we are many." (vv. 6-9).

Can demons worship? Who worshiped here? The man. Even though he was carrying thousands of demons in him, when he saw his Creator, he worshiped. If you would stop for a moment and worship God with your problem, your problem will bow. The demonic bondage was heavy on this man; the real him longed for the freedom that comes from worshipping his Maker. He worshiped Jesus, and cried with a loud voice and said "What have I to do with thee, Jesus, thou Son of the highest God? I adjure thee by God that thou torment me not." Reader, please note that Jesus had already commanded the demon, saying, "Come out of the man, thou unclean spirit." Note that this was not the man responding to Jesus. It was the demon that had begun to claim his right.

In verse 9, Jesus asked the demon "what is thy name?" Why was it necessary for Jesus to ask for the name? Observe that

Jesus had just called him "thou unclean spirit;" yet he went further to ask for his specific name. It is important to note the sequence of events here. When Jesus first told the demon to come out of the man, his response was, "torment me not." He obviously didn't want to let go. Jesus knew that there was something more going on; this was why He asked for the name of the demon.

It is not in every deliverance case that we are required to ask "what is your name?" Jesus did not do that in every case. The thing is, there are no formulas in deliverance; there are simply principles. I made that mistake when I was young in deliverance work. I read books by the person whose team members delivered me, and whatever the book said to do I would do. Some of the things I followed and did to get people delivered were simply unrequired and certainly most controversial. I wanted to practice everything in the books until the Holy Spirit said, "I am the One you are to follow and not necessarily the formulas."

So, there is no formula; we just act as the Holy Spirit leads. There is no deliverance without the Holy Spirit. It is our responsibility to acknowledge Him, recognize Him, reverence Him, respect Him, and then He will take control. Once He takes over, the yoke has to go.

When Jesus asked, "what is thy name?" the demon answered, "my name is Legion for we are many." **"And he besought him much that he would not send them away out of the country. Now there was there nigh unto the mountains a great herd of swine feeding. And all the devils besought him, saying, Send us into the swine, that we may enter into them"** (vv. 10-12).

We already know that only one demon was speaking before. But after that demon had been addressed and the evil spirit showed reluctance, Jesus, through a release by the Holy Spirit, and also (I believe) for our learning, asked for his name. I think Jesus could have just said, "Get out!" but He wanted us to learn a principle of deliverance. Indeed, some of the miracles Jesus did were for teaching purposes.

So, the demon, in response to Jesus' question, said, "My name is Legion, for we are many." How many constitutes a legion? Over 6000! More than 6000 demons were living in this one person, but only one was possessing him. The others were there to back that one demon, to make sure he went nowhere. Who invited these other demons? The unclean spirit, the strongman.

Verse 12 says **"And all the devils besought him, saying, Send us into the swine, that we may enter into them."** Now, it's not just one demon that was begging Jesus; it was all of them.

They begged him to send them into the swine.

I want you to know that Jesus, at this point, was functioning in one of the gifts of the Spirit called discerning of spirits. So, the veil of the spirit was torn apart, and He could see all these thousands of demons, all of them pleading for Him to send them into the swine.

The unclean spirit that originally possessed this man was represented in his character. What were his habits? He liked to stay in the tombs and the mountains. However, we know he had more than just the unclean spirit because we saw other behaviors that he exhibited such as breaking chains. An unclean spirit would not entice him to be breaking chains; he was supported by the legion. Imagine having to be bound by over 6000 demons, when one is enough to handle a human being. Even 2000 swine could not cope with the legion.

Again, we read that this man would cry and cut himself. I want us to study that because there is a correlation between medicine if it is genuine science and the spiritual things of God. There is a condition, as I mentioned before, called masochism, which is the act of deriving sexual pleasure from inflicting pain on oneself, which I think factors into this. We know it is a demonic condition, just like we know same-sex relations is a demonic condition. People just do not know. You hear them say, "Well, this is my nature." No. It is not God's original design for your life. But as soon as you accept it, then you validate it. It is a demonic condition. It is the same thing as fornication, adultery, pornography, and masturbation. All kinds of uncleanness are under this category.

I want you to understand that man is a spirit being that has a soul and lives in the body. If a man is not born-again, what part of the person is possessed? It is his spirit. Only one demon can possess the spirit and distribute his personality through the man. But the body and soul of the man can be filled up with thousands of demons, depending on how much the person can carry. Flip it on the other side. You can carry the grace of God to such a level that you wouldn't even believe it.

So, now, we have a better understanding of how to correctly handle deliverance cases as Jesus says in Matthew 12:29, **"Or else how can one enter a strong man's house, and spoil his goods, except he first binds the strong man? And then he will spoil his house."** The key is knowing the strongman. Once you dislodge him, the others have to go. Think of it this way. Once you evict the real tenant on a lease, you do not need to know the names of those on sub-leases. You just need to have the name of the person on the lease correctly.

Now, let us return to the next incident in Mark 9:14. In doing so, I must ask you, deliverance student, how do you know when you are going to encounter "this kind"? In reality, you cannot tell. So, what do you do? Live a fasted life – that is, fast and often pray and be prepared to handle challenges as they arise.

Deliverance and plenty of food cannot go comfortably together. You have to live a fasted life to be effective in deliverance ministry. You can readily preach and teach, but if you are going to move in the deliverance anointing, you needed to be fasted up and prayed up. Those two areas are critical for you to be sensitive to the Spirit. This way, you become so yielded to the Holy Spirit that instead of the demons encountering you, they are encountering the glory.

There are degrees of manifestations of power – faith, anointing, and the glory. Each is a different level. We can minister by faith without the anointing being present. We simply rebuke demons and trust that God will work. However, when the anointing is present, you move in the energy of that anointing – this is another level. But, beyond the anointing, once the glory is present, the demons leave quickly. I have had instances of this in my life and ministry. The times when we function in the anointing are excellent. But sometimes the glory comes and takes it over the top.

God is indeed awesome! I pray that we as His body will have the hunger to seek Him. Spiritual hunger is what is needed at this time. It is true that we sometimes have challenges and difficulties in our lives, but these are mere strategies of the enemy to distract and wrongly engage us. He knows that the more we are preoccupied with trying to deal with the challenges, the more spiritually naked we become. Demons know how to handle delay and hinder us once we become spiritually naked. But once the glory comes on us, corruption cannot stand, and no demonic power can stand. Let us pray that we know our Father the more, that we love Him the more, and that we get drawn into His presence even more.

Now, in looking at the case in Mark 9, please note again that Jesus never followed a formula. He did not handle this case like the other one. Why? Because He always followed the leading of the Holy Spirit. He said it clearly that **"the Son can do nothing of himself, but what he seeth the Father do…" (John 5:19)**. He was so in God and followed the Holy Spirit so much that He looked at Nicodemus and said, "Except a man is born-again…" He looked at the woman at the well, and said, "Go and call your husband." He was always on point because He followed the Holy Spirit accurately.

In this case under consideration, He was coming off the mountain after having an encounter with the Father. He saw some of his disciples and a crowd was around them and the scribes were questioning them. He said, "Why are you questioning my disciples? "Then a man came forward,

… the devil does not choose for us when to fight.

saying, "**Master, I have brought unto thee my son, which hath a dumb spirit; And wheresoever he taketh him, he teareth him: and he foameth, and gnasheth with his teeth, and pineth away: and I spake to thy disciples that they should cast him out; and they could not.**" Jesus replied that the boy is brought to him, and as soon as the child was brought, the demon knocked him down, and he started wallowing and foaming at the mouth.

The demon was communicating something here. It was simply saying, "Okay, Jesus, we are on, let's start." But Jesus did not even look in his direction, which tells us that the devil does not choose for us when to fight. Our Commander-in-Chief, the Holy Spirit, chooses when and how we get to fight. We do not respond because we are faced with a battle and we need to react to it; if we do so, we can get sucked in. We respond only to our Head, our Master, who will then lead us in and tell us what to do.

Once the anointing of God comes upon you, there is the danger of getting distracted by manifestations. Church services are frequently disrupted this way. We can be having a deliverance conference, and before we know it, one person begins to react, and the man of God leaves the teaching, and the service becomes a circus. That is a distraction.

One time, I invited a prophet to minister, and he came with his assistant and the family of the assistant also attended. While he was ministering, the sister of the assistant began to manifest, and the prophet started to react. I turned to him and said, "No prophet, my ministers will take her to my office and go and deal with it there." The brother of the girl was so angry and openly disrespected me right in my church. I forgave him because it was ignorance.

And he came with his assistant and the family of the assistant also attended. While he was ministering, the sister of the assistant began to manifest, and the prophet started to react. I turned to him and said, "No prophet, my ministers will take her to my office and go and deal with it there." The brother of the girl was so angry and openly disrespected me right in my church. I forgave him because it was ignorance.

We did not need that prophet to cast out that devil; we had hundreds of other born-again Spirit-filled believers who could

We can emulate Jesus' example by deferring to the Holy Spirit

have simply taken that girl to my office and knocked the devil off of her, while we continued without being distracted. Jesus did not start reacting because the devil began to manifest. He seemed to be saying, "I will get to you when I am ready." What He did instead was to ask the father how long it had been since the affliction came upon the child. (Again, this was for your sake and mine). The father said it had been since childhood.

So, here, we have another instance of how a strongman is developed. There had been an opening, and the demon got in there through initiation, either by what the parents did or by what a demonic person did to the child such as molesting the child. Typically, the devil wants to get into the life of children between the ages of four and seven through molestation by close relations. It is one of the widest doors and one most frequently used. Demons can enter and will promote rejection, rape, resentment, anger, or stubbornness. All of these can enter through that initial molestation. If it happens repeatedly and undetected, when that child reaches teenage years, he or she will become promiscuous, rebellious, and impudent.

In the case of this child, Jesus clearly demonstrated discernment as usual. His primary job was to discern accurately so that the deliverance ministry would be effective. How can we emulate His example? By deferring to the Holy Spirit. By not so quickly jumping in when somebody runs to you and says they are in trouble. If you do so, you will go there and fail. It could even be a trap. The Holy Spirit is Lord! And when His Lordship is acknowledged He will produce liberty.

So, in response to the query of Jesus, the father answered, "Of a child. And ofttimes it hath cast him into the fire, and into the waters, to destroy him..." Just by that alone, Jesus got the point. And then the father added, "but if thou canst do any thing, have compassion on us, and help us." But Jesus said, "No, that is not it. It is if you can believe."

Why did Jesus say that? Why did he mention the faith of the father? If faith was necessary, which faith did He act upon when He helped the demoniac of Gadara?

Remember that when Jesus saw the Gadarene with all the demons, the man rushed forth and began to worship. By that action of worship, he was saying, "I believe you are my Creator. I am in bad condition through my fault perhaps, but you are still my Creator. I worship you." In this case of this father, it was a different thing entirely. This father apparently had gone to different places. We do not know what he had done that might have contributed to his son's condition. He did not believe his son could be healed; he only came to the disciples to try. Unfortunately, being inexperienced themselves, the disciples jumped in on trial and failed on trial. This was why Jesus became the next person for the father to try.

As soon as Jesus made the man realize that his son's healing depended on his faith, the man cried out, "Lord I believe, help thou my unbelief." That declaration was a sign of budding faith in the man. And before he could complete the sentence, Jesus had faced the demon and commanded it to depart.

This again gives me the impression that the doorway to demonic possession for the child must have come through the father. Whatever he might have done and his child took the brunt of it when he cried out like that – "Master, Adonai, I believe, help my unbelief," he opened the ground for God to step in and Jesus got ready to deal with this demon.

What do we learn from this? We have to make sure the case is ready for action. We have to prepare the case to be ready, through counseling, fasting, proper discernment, or detailed interview. Seek to reach the bottom of the situation; seek to get to the root of it by discernment or by interview so you can open the case up and get ready to kick that devil out.

"When Jesus saw that people came running together he rebuked the foul spirit and said unto him, Thou dumb and deaf spirit, I charge thee come out of him and enter him no more" (v.25).

There are two things to note here. People started running. If Jesus had allowed the crowd to gather, it would have become a circus, and there would have been distractions. Christ, therefore, decided to deal with it before the environment became unmanageable. The second thing to note is that when the father spoke, he said the child had a dumb spirit – which means that he had an idea of what was wrong with the child, but his knowledge was not complete. But Jesus, seeing much deeper, said, "Thou dumb and deaf spirit..." If He had just said "thou dumb spirit," the spirit, which was also deaf would not have heard. Instead, He said "Thou dumb and deaf spirit." Jesus got the accurate discernment, and it proved very helpful to his ministration. We should pray for discernment, and if we have it, we should nurture it by practicing the presence of God, meditating on the Word of God, and staying in the presence of God.

There are places that domesticate and regulate your life into a routine. To practice the presence of God, try to move away from such places. You need to be able to come away and be quiet. Your house may not always be a good option because there are certain routines that have structured your life into a pattern. You need to go away sometimes.

Now, look at what verse 26 says – **"and the spirit came out of him and sent him and he was as one dead, and many said he is dead."** We would have thought that Jesus would speak and instantly the spirit would leave. No. The spirit tore him, renting him sore, crying. But the order had been given, and Jesus would not repeat Himself. The anointing was compelling obedience to the order Jesus had given.

A man of God said to me recently that, if you say nothing, God will confirm nothing. You have to preach His Word for Him to confirm His Word. So, if you say nothing, He will confirm nothing. What did He say? He said, "Thou deaf and dumb spirit." But we can't go everywhere saying "Thou dumb and deaf spirit" to every other spirit. In another instance (which we saw earlier), He said, "You unclean spirit come out... What is your name?" Jesus dealt specifically; Jesus dealt precisely.

Let us summarize what we have learned so far about the strongman. He is the first demon to gain access into the spirit of a person, and he can decide to host other demons who bring reinforcement. This, in a way, tells us that even the strongman knows that he has limited opportunity. Generally, demons know that one day, God, the real owner of life, is going to show up and then they will have to leave; so they prepare by reinforcing themselves.

In my country, we have a saying, "Many days for the thief, one day for the owner." Once the owner comes and catches the thief, the thief's time immediately comes to an end. Jesus is the rightful owner of life. **"For by him were all things created, that are in heaven, and that are in earth, visible and invisible, whether they be thrones, or dominions, or principalities, or powers: all things were created by him, and for him" (Colossians 1:16).**

I believe that some of the deliverance cases we handle fall into the category of what we call "the prey of the terrible." Isaiah 49:24–25 says:

> "Shall the prey be taken from the mighty or the lawful captive delivered? But thus saith the LORD, Even the captives of the mighty shall be taken away, and the prey of the terrible shall be delivered: for I will contend with him that contendeth with thee, and I will save thy children. And I will feed them that oppress thee with their flesh; and they shall be drunken with their blood, as with sweet wine: and all flesh shall know that I the LORD am thy Saviour and thy Redeemer, the mighty One of Jacob."

Here, the mighty one of Jacob, the Lord, the Holy Spirit talks about the lawful captive and the prey of the terrible. There are lawful captives and prey of the terrible. I believe that when you look at these two high demonic cases that we have just considered, you will find the one that belongs to the lawful captive and the one that belongs to the prey of the terrible.

BREAKTHROUGH PROPHETIC DELIVERANCE PRAYERS

1. I disable the strongman and his evil strategies or enchantments to tie me down. Be exposed and expelled from my life now in Jesus' name.

2. Let the glorious light of the Living God beam upon every aspects of my life exposing the roots, tentacles and modus operands of the strongman for total divine retribution and destruction in Jesus Name.

3. Father of life, reclaim and restore every distortion and corruption of the strongman in my life in the mighty Name of Jesus Christ.

4. God of glory touch and heal me. The God of Wonders, where I have been damaged the most, release a higher level of authority in and through to bring healing to others in the Mighty Name of Jesus Christ.

CHAPTER 18

Complicated Cases in Deliverance

Some deliverance cases are very complicated, and they require mature counseling and discernment. In the course of my deliverance ministry in the last three decades, I have stumbled upon some cases that do not readily yield to a straightforward approach and may require discernment, endurance, patience, and clear instructions from the Lord. Some examples of these might be cases of mental disturbance that come in some ways. I will explain this by relating actual cases:

In 1986, in the city of Enugu in Nigeria, I was conducting some deliverance sessions and was on a long fast. One day a young man who had a mental disorder was brought for prayers. When he came, I was led to mobilize the team and engage in worship warfare. While we were worshiping and praising God, the power of God came upon this young man and restored him. For the next couple of days, we monitored him, and there were some amazing testimonies emerging from this young man. He related how these demonic powers that once held him captive tried to stage a comeback. Each time a man, he said, would come out of him and drive them away – he did not fully understand that it was the Lord Jesus through His Spirit because he was just coming into the faith. This is a very special case, uncommon compared to the regular type of straightforward counseling, prayer, and deliverance we often encounter.

INSANITY AND DEMONIC DELUSION

There are still other more complicated cases, for example, cases of young anointed believers who are not broken and in complete submission to authority but then try to engage in warfare. I have seen some of such cases result in insanity. Permit me to mention two of such cases: There was a young man whom we were invited to pray for a few years back. We were taken into his parents' home, and we tried to interview him. We could tell clearly that his speech was not coordinated. You could see a level of spiritual pride as he compared himself to great men of God and even claimed to be greater than all of them. In reality, he was in a state of demonic delusion and a certain level of insanity and inability to coordinate. This was not a case where one could readily lay hands on him and cast out the demons because the demons, to begin with, were not living inside him.

This sent me to inquire really. From my inquiry, I began to see a pattern emerging whereby sometimes people violate spiritual laws and spiritual territorial laws, particularly relating to individuals who may have had inherent occult background and abilities. Inherent occult abilities potentially exist in people who come from families who were mediumistic, who have dealt with the devil at a level of using the false prophetic or occult power to their advantage and the advantage of others. This may have happened in the past generations, and the power is transmitted down. You discover that though the individual comes to Christ, this spirit of the enemy begins to afflict the mind with illusions and begins to stir up the pride of the individual, making him feel that he is one thing or the other and also showcasing titles that appeal to the pride. If these young believers not rooted in the word or grounded in the Spirit, and who, predicated on demonic delusions and seduction, begin a quest for power and begin to fast for power, what could happen is that because of the demonic element, the occult power that are inherent and were silent at a subconscious level, will begin to surface and project themselves as the Holy Spirit. As such you may find such individual manifesting the occult or psychic power or in some other cases slip into a state semi-psychosis.

HOLY SPIRIT VERSUS PSYCHIC POWER

I know I am on a very controversial territory here, but let me quickly say that there is a difference between the Holy Spirit power and psychic power. The Holy Spirit power results from faith in Jesus Christ. When an individual comes in contact with the gospel, repents of his sins, and places his faith in the Lord Jesus Christ, and is born again, a new life is transmitted to his spirit. That new life is the life of God or *Zoe* in Greek. It is as if Jesus is born inside them like Jesus was conceived in Mary, and they begin to grow into that new life in God in Christ Jesus. This life functions by faith. For this life to function effectively, God progressively leads the new believers to the rejection of self-will or what the Bible calls the 'old man' – the old way of thinking and doing things. This new life is a life of power as well, but it is not a power that is manifested immediately at the will of man. That is why the Bible says, "They are born not of the will of the flesh nor of blood but the will of God." The Holy Spirit drives the new life as the individual responds in faith to God's word.

God controls this power and uses the believer who walks in faith to produce the supernatural life. This is different, for instance, from what I call the psychic phenomenon. In the Fall of Man, the soul powers of man – man has tremendous soul powers – was imprisoned by the flesh. Therefore any individual who seeks spiritual power and expression can begin to practice some disciplines such as fasting, and in the course of that unleash that soul power. This soul power is under the domain and the dominion of darkness, being controlled by demons that allow themselves to be controlled by man whereas the man thinks he is in charge. Hence men can be deluded into unleashing that soul power – which is at a psychic level, (Psuche the soul) – as against the (Pneuman spirit) which is the spirit life. That is where you get the psychic phenomenon. This can produce tremendous supernatural manifestations of a kind, but it is not spiritual, it is not of God, it is not of the Holy Spirit, and here men can veer off to the wrong trajectory. (Readers, please take a look at The Latent Power of the Soul by Watchman Nee)

Yes, men can veer off course: They start off being born again, and they see the manifestations and the power of the Holy Spirit, and they can veer off on what I call feel-good doorway into the spirit realm. When this happens, the principalities, the big boys, can then tap their brains and cause delusions and madness. This is in fact how false religions, false moves, and then counterfeit moves of God are started and projected. Consequently, the individual is accessing the supernatural realm but not through God and is not aware because it is usually done by people who are unbroken, still young, and are not deep in the things of God. They are not accountable to spiritual authority and so are uncovered, and the enemy can tap them. The devil will use them to corrupt the gospel, or he will disturb their brain, and people can go mad as a result.

 ## AUTHENTIC DOORWAY INTO THE SPIRIT REALM

Now let me explain a little bit as to what I mean. There are doorways into the spirit realm, but the main important doorway is the Lord Jesus Christ. He said, *"I am the door: by me, if any man enters in, he shall be saved and shall go in and out, and find pasture"* (John 10:9). In other words, *born again* Christians are to know that Jesus is the door that admits them into God's supernatural domain. So going back and forth is spiritual engagement with God's supernatural realm to be able to access the benefits of the Kingdom. My subject is not to dwell extensively on how this is done, but to just indicate that there is a right way, a gateway into the spiritual realm, and that is through Jesus and the Holy Spirit. However, there are illegal doorways.

Now someone who is *born again* but not trained in the Word and is not matured to engage meaningfully in the spirit realm, but is ambitious to manifest power can veer off course particularly if they have an inherent occult background which has not yet been identified and cleaned out through the process of deliverance. I have seen many *born again* Christians become mad because they entered into that realm of insanity.

When we handle these kinds of deliverance cases, and this also goes for many cases of insanity, we should ask that the glory of God come in and suspend the activities of the devil by the sovereignty of God. For every law of the spirit that the enemy may write, God is above all, because God is the Creator and has the prerogative. Therefore, God can step down and still do what He wants to do through His sovereignty irrespective of what exists. So in some cases, you see God's sovereignty intervene, and instant restoration of sanity takes place. However, in the majority of cases, I have found that God will trust the ministry team to provide the necessary help.

This is why I believe that for the church of God to be effective, there need to be some specialized deliverance ministries that have the facilities to admit people in distress. Furthermore, they should also have the resources and workforce of a pool of trained people who know how to combine intercession, warfare, and direct ministry into an intelligent blend of an interdisciplinary pool of God-given strategies to reach the common goal of bringing about the deliverance of many. I would even suggest that for some of these cases of madness, it may be necessary, where possible, to incorporate both the spiritual and the medical sides.

MULTI-DIMENSIONAL APPROACH

Let me expand on this. There may be various reasons why people can go off suddenly in their minds. This is not an exhaustive study on that, but many complicated deliverance cases in the church will often need more than just prayers. For instance, if there is an unbelieving person who is living with a believer goes insane. Another example could be a believing parent who lives with an unbelieving child who goes insane, and this believing parent wants his child to be delivered, and you know that child is not a Christian because he is not of the faith, how do you handle that? Right now, the individual is out of his mind; he is not coordinating, so he is not too responsible for his behavior. So how do you handle that? This is where I believe God will generate, in these final days, big ministries that have facilities to combine both the medical and ministry side such as could be found in Tulsa, Oklahoma at the Oral Roberts University that combined prayer and medical science together. Why is this necessary? People under these kinds of scenarios will need to be handled professionally so they can sleep while intercession is going on to disengage them from those principalities that have tapped into their minds.

There is an extent to which we can use authority. We can use authority on the devil or on the issues whereby the individual is reconciled to God. When they are not reconciled to God, there is a limitation to which we can exercise authority. In some cases, however, the ministry of intercession can break the siege and break through and still secure the release of this individual. But while that intercession is going on the medical side is available and can step in to provide professional help particularly as much as possible to get these people to sleep. It is very, very useful in the process of the deliverance ministration.

As stated in the preceding paragraph, breaking the siege could include some level of intercession and prayers and supplications. This is the reason real prayer warriors with a priestly ministry of intercession should be co-opted into the deliverance team. Consequently, the deliverance team is very vital. It is so vital to actually have deliverance teams who are trained in spiritual counseling, trained on how to handle people under demonic oppression, and on how to work together as a team in church groups, ministry groups to achieve maximum results. If I may say this on a prophetic level, we are in the end zone, and the devil will throw up everything he can muster in the air. This is so vital that each church is prepared to build and train her team to be effective in the work ahead. I will talk in a later chapter on what constitutes a deliverance team.

NEED TO HAVE LEGAL SAFEGUARDS

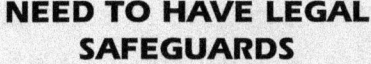

Another point that I would like to mention on complicated dimensions in deliverance cases is the legal dimension. It is very important wherever we live in this 21st Century world to understand that there are applicable laws from nation to nation, from place to place, and the enemy is well aware of those laws and he can try to blackmail us with them. While we are zealous to do good and to help the oppressed, let us not be naïve. Some of the people who will come looking for outright help are going to be the agents of the enemy. Hence we need discernment. I cannot over-emphasize that. Because of my ministry, I have had many occasions where the enemy sent his agents to destroy me without success. This would need an entire chapter to discuss. Note that they will come and pretend to need deliverance but eventually what they want is to blackmail you.

It is important to have a legal document carefully put together by a legal practitioner that gives you immunity from legal prosecution so that any person who is coming to seek help will read, understand, and sign in ink that the help they are seeking is voluntary and that they will hold the team members and the ministry harmless and immune to prosecution for anything that may come as a result of their participation in the deliverance meeting. This is so vital for the deliverance ministry or team to be safe. Otherwise, all kinds of litigations can come, and that can derail the good intentions of God for the ministry.

Now let me talk about another aspect of complicated cases. These will be just a few examples of how the enemy has sent me agents of darkness. Right from the onset of my call to deliverance ministry, I have over and again encountered agents of darkness pretending to be seeking for help. The first example I remember happened in late 1985. I was in the Northern part of Nigeria conducting deliverances and having a lot of wonderful results. I was a young bachelor, very anointed and consecrated and growing in the school of the Holy Spirit. One day, somewhere between 10:30 a.m. and 11:00 a.m., a young woman walked through the door. I was alone in the house, and she wanted deliverance. Trust me, I was ready to help, but it is something I would not do now. I was still young in the ministry in those days.

There are some principles you must have in place to avoid blackmail. I started to pray for her. While I sat with her and was trying to take her through counseling, I noticed that she deliberately popped her bust open and opened her legs. As we were talking, the issue became uncomfortable, and I had to call her to order. I said, "Sister, do you mind? I want you to close your legs and cover yourself a little better". She complied, and we talked to a point where I felt I should pray.

We stood to pray, and I stretched my hand, and she slumped. As she fell on the ground, I heard very clearly in my spirit, "Stop! Do not proceed. Tell her to come the next day." So I gave her an appointment for the next day and forgot about her. However, later that night, I suddenly felt so sleepy at just around 8:00 p.m. I dropped on my knees and tried to pray and was instantly transported in the spirit. I had a vision where I saw this young woman lying by me on the bed, and her hands were filled with blood. Instantly my sleep went from me, and the voice of the Lord came, saying that the girl is no ordinary person, but an agent of darkness sent to destroy me. The Lord said this was a test case for me and if I passed this test then I would move up in the Kingdom, but to pass the test I must carefully listen to instructions and obey. The first instruction was that when this girl returns the next day, I should not say anything to her about her deliverance but just to be casual with her and be conscious and listen for instruction.

BAITING THE WICKED

(Readers note that I was under divine instruction here)
The following day she came, and I offered her tea, talked, laughed until she left. This went on for about a fortnight, and then the Lord said to me "ok, now is the time for action. She has swallowed you." In other words, she was endeared to me, loving me, knowing that she came to kill me. So the Lord said to me, "she loves you now so begin to talk to her about God's

judgment on the wicked." I began doing just that, and as I spoke things turned. She said, "Do you know who I am"? I said, "I have an idea." She said, "Let me tell you. I am four persons in one, with millions of snakes in my belly. I was sent to seduce you to fornication and then kill you because your activities here are disturbing our kingdom." I said to her, "I am aware of who you are. My God whom I serve told me about you for the past two weeks and He told me to love you. Don't you realize that the one you are following as your god does not even love you? He only wants to destroy you. I want to invite you to test my own God who only loves you and told me to love you for the past two weeks despite the fact that you wanted to kill me." She broke down and gave her life to Christ, and the battle started.

At this point I was led by God to inform the brethren and for us to constitute a team. By the grace of God, the deliverance progressed well. I received two physical letters from the enemy through her. In one of the letters, the enemy was boasting that he would eat my flesh and drink my blood. I laughed because my flesh and my blood were not available to him anyway. The other letter threatened to disfigure the young woman because she failed her assignment. To make the long story short, it was a fight but in the end, the Lord prevailed, and the young woman was gloriously delivered by the Lord through the combined efforts of brethren at that time who came in the case. She was gloriously liberated and filled with the Holy Spirit and began to serve God in earnest. That was one case that ended well.

Case Number Two: There was a particular mission where I was serving as a young deliverance minister. There were about thirty-three of us on full-timeappointment. At a time, things began to deteriorate in the ministry very fast. However, there was this young lady who seemed to have a lot of struggles. She was also on full time. I offered to pray with her, to minister to her. As I was trying to do that, I set a time for us to fast and pray for a few days together. On the first day of the fast, as I went in to pray I saw a male-like figure with a weapon in his hands advancing menacingly towards me. I stood on my feet and rebuked. Then I noticed in the night that I had a strange dream whereby I was told that I had a gift to come and take. I was riding a bicycle and arrived at a particular bungalow. I went inside and sat on a chair waiting for the gift and realized that there was someone sitting on my lap. It was the same young woman. I was surprised. I opened my eyes and thought that this was unnatural. I had a similar dream another time and started to realize that something was wrong here. So I discontinued my effort to help her and broke off the close relationship with her.

Later on, conditions in the ministry deteriorated so badly, a few of us banded together to pray. As we started to pray, God said He was going to take the lid off and expose what was going on. One of the 'anointed' beautiful girls in the choir began to confess to atrocities and witchcraft activities that were going on. It so turned out that in her confession statements, she mentioned that this particular young lady that I had tried to minister to was one of their witchcraft team members in the ministry and that in the coven they presented my name as a request for me to be her husband. Then I saw the correlation between the dreams I was having. I cut off the relationship, and those dreams stopped. She was trying to manipulate me as I was trying to save her life. There are people who seem to be in the church but are evil agents. We have to be careful when we meet with those cases.

I will give one final case, the third case: One of my deliverance students told me that someone was coming to live with her and wanted me to do deliverance for this individual before that happened. I agreed, also offering to put this person under close observation for some time before recommending the individual to go and live with her and help in the ministry. However, I did not remember that approximately two months before this time, God had begun to talk to me about someone who would come to look for deliverance but would be an agent of the devil. I would tell my wife the message, but I would often forget about it. When this person came, I did not recognize her right away. We welcomed her with open arms and were loving her and ministering to her, and she seemed to be responding very well. I said, "Wow, she is doing so well. I will even make her a member of the choir." At that point, the Holy Spirit said "no, don't. Hold on." So I held off.

I started to look more closely, and I saw some things that did not make sense to me, but I did not say a word. One day, for our wedding anniversary, one of our children had bought a package for my wife and me to go to a hotel and rest. The following morning I saw what was like an open television. God showed me this lady who had supposedly come for deliverance. I could see her targeting various members of the church and attacking them with witchcraft. So she was not seeking deliverance, she was an agent of darkness. Her purpose was to destroy the church. There are many individuals like this who will come pretending to be looking for deliverance, just waiting for a man of God who may have a lustful spirit, or who may have one sin or the other in his life to lay hands on them. Once you lay hands on such persons, they tap you in the spirit and things that you did not reckon with begin to occur. On account of the above, it is very vital that we are conscious of these things and not make ourselves prey to the devil.

NEED TO BUILD A TEAM

All cases are not the same. Some are a little bit more complicated, and that is why we need to have deliverance teams. That is why we need to have lines of authority. That is why the church of God needs to be coordinated. We are an army. There are chains of command and lines of authority. We should never go out to engage the devil if we are not under the authority or if we are not living an accountable life. No man is an island unto himself. The moment you say you are a deliverance minister and are casting out devils, and you are not accountable to anybody and are not prepared to live a holy life, you become a joke and a disaster. God wants to use us. He wants to build us into a team so that we can do a good job for Him.

I hope to talk a little bit about the deliverance team now. What do I mean by a deliverance team? I mean a team of people who have a hunger to see individuals come to liberty and freedom. They have a burden for the oppressed and have at least a measure of desire to be used by God in prayer and warfare. These persons can be screened by church leaders and constituted into a warfare deliverance team. Among them can be people with prophetic gifts, gifts of revelations, and the spirit of prayer. The prophetic gift will bring the counsel and guidance. An average deliverance team can be from five, fifteen, twenty, forty persons depending on how big the church is. The individuals should be trained and should be taken through deliverance prayers, and should be mentored properly. What happens is that when the church, particularly a church that is ready to flow in the supernatural, engage in worship and supernatural ministry and somebody is manifesting, right away, you know that that person is going to the deliverance team. They step in so that those who are manifesting can be handled without disrupting the service.

One of the very clever strategies of the enemy is that once the man of God wants to bring the Word, demons begin to manifest and the man of God is diverted from the ministry of the Word to start casting out the devil. What happens is that we lose the Word for that time, and the drama of the devil takes full attention, and the entire church becomes a spectacle. This all can be avoided if there is a deliverance team in place. Once a person begins to manifest the deliverance team takes the person to a designated place and handles the individual. From time to time, people who are having some demonic oppression and seeking help can be referred by the pastor after initial personal counseling to the deliverance team where they will clean them up. This makes for very effective ministry. Also when you have deliverance crusades or healing crusades, and there are a lot of people who are under the power of God and require help, those who have already been trained and have been cleaned up themselves can now become useful hands to help people into liberty as the power of God moves, without having the man of God to focus on all the cases one by one then be unable to focus on the flow of the anointing.

Deliverance teams are very, very important. The work of the deliverance team is first, prayer and fasting, to generate momentum. Secondly, to counsel, under the close supervision of the spiritual leader of the church, and to follow up on people who have been delivered and ministered to – to monitor, to track their progress and to disciple them so that they can be integrated properly into the church. They are like the war room or the powerhouse of the ministry. These will help in the day to day ministering to the oppressed within the local church.

BREAKTHROUGH PROPHETIC DELIVERANCE PRAYERS

1. I boldly apply the blood of the Lamb of God to the Foundation of my Family. Any remnants of occult investitures, inherent abilities, and manifestations; be located by the fire of God's Holy Spirit and burn to ashes in the Mighty Name of Jesus.

2. Through the Blood of the Everlasting Covenant, I present my entire family line a living Sacrifice, holy and acceptable unto God. I stand in my place as the priest of God over my family line and cancel every past and present satanic dedication of my family line by anyone acting on behalf of my family in the mighty name of Jesus Christ.

CHAPTER 19

Dreams and Deliverance

Dream is a spiritual state mostly, and a spiritual gateway into the spirit. There are gateways and entry points. For instance, when you are entering the USA, there are gateways where you get checked in. Similarly, there are gateways into the spirit. You hear Jesus say in John 10:9, "I am the door." The door to where? To the authentic spirit realm. There is the illegal spirit realm. He said, *"I am the door. If by me any man enters he shall be saved and shall go in and out and find provision."* The dream state is one entry point into the spirit whereby you can benefit from a lot of information that will otherwise be out of your reach physically. However, that will be a category of dreams we call 'divine revelations' that are given by God. Not every dream necessarily proceeds from God. In this context, I am just going to look at sources of dreams and how dreams come to us.

"For a dream cometh through the multitude of business; and a fool's voice is known by multitude of words" (Ecclesiastes 5:3). Dreams come to us through the multitude of businesses. Your dreams can be related to the things with which you are preoccupied. That is why it is important to identify your dream. What am I dreaming about? Why am I dreaming about this? What does this mean? Is this something beneficial? Is this something indicative of a spiritual benefit that I need to know? Is it a warning? Is it just a reflection of what I am doing physically and what I am preoccupied with which plays out in my dreams?

DIVINE INSPIRATION DREAMS

"But there is a spirit in man: and the inspiration of the Almighty giveth them understanding" - Job 32:8

The first source of dreams I would like to address is Divine Inspiration Dreams. There are many such dreams in the Bible. Man is a spirit, and that spirit can be inspired by the Almighty to produce understanding and to give you useful information. Sometimes there is information you need, and God drops it in your spirit. If you are a spiritually sensitive person, you can pick up on it right away. But sometimes we are not very sensitive. Sometimes we are very busy, and because of that, there is a disconnect between your mind and your spirit, because everything that God is doing, He drops it in your spirit. For it to become intelligent information that you can benefit from, it has to proceed from your spirit to your mind where you have your reasoning and understanding. Preoccupation with activities can cause a disconnect between your spirit and your mind so that the flow of divine information to your spirit does not reach your mind such that even though God is speaking, you are not hearing, and then you say God is not speaking to you. However, He is talking, but you are not hearing. So as an extreme measure of love, God could decide to talk to you in dreams when you have rested yourself in sleep.

"For God speaketh once, yea twice, yet man perceiveth it not. In a dream, in a vision of the night, when deep sleep falleth upon men, in slumberings upon the bed; then he openeth the ears of men, and sealeth their instruction, that he may withdraw man from his purpose and hide pride from man. He keepeth back his soul from the pit and his life from perishing by the sword" Job 33:14-18

This is not the only reason He speaks in dreams, but this is the most frequent reason. However, there are some people who have a prophetic grace on their lives, and the last portion of it would be dreams. They are dreamers of dreams at a very high level.

"For God speaketh once, yea twice, yet man perceiveth it not." How come man has not perceived it? He is too busy. He is trying to

conquer the whole world and get his stuff done; he cannot stop and take a rest. We do not understand the whole vital nature of deliberately resting ourselves in the presence of God. We do not know how to disconnect ourselves from the company of those we love to be alone in the presence of our God. We do not do it, yet we should be doing it. So God, as an extreme measure, comes to you in a dream, because He spoke once, He spoke twice, and you did not hear Him. *"In a dream, in a vision of the night, when deep sleep falleth upon men, in slumberings upon the bed; then he openeth the ears of men, and sealeth their instruction."* What ear? Not the physical ear. He prints his instructions there, and you have this beautiful dream. Why? To withdraw man from his purpose and hide pride from man. You are going in the wrong direction, He warns you, "Don't go too close to that individual as he will bring you into some pain." Or He may say, "No. This is not the right way to go. Do not invest on this. Stop, stop, stop!"

He is busy as a father or mother watches over a child. *"He keepeth back his soul from the pit"* – the pit is demons. They are there pulling at you trying to lure you away, and God warns you in the dream.

> *While you are sleeping, your body sleeps but your spirit does not sleep, but engages under divine inspiration.*

And sometimes He will code it. Why does He do that and make it like parables? I believe that one of the reasons is that He forces you to think, because if you hear it right away, you think, "OK, I got that." It is like the movie The Lion King. The lion himself as a child was very stubborn. Now he has a daughter, and he is very protective of her. He wouldn't let the daughter step away out of his sight. So the daughter keeps asking, pleading and he says, "Alright, but you must not..." Before he could finish the daughter recites everything with him, indicating that she already knows. God does not want you to miss it so sometimes He will code it. He gives you a beautiful picture, but it is all coded, and it forces you to think. He hangs that picture in your mind, and as you wake up that picture is fastened there, and forces you to think so He can get your attention and cooperation. All the time He is keeping your soul away from the pit, from the influence of demonic powers of hell trying to activate you in the wrong direction.

He also keeps your *"life from perishing by the sword."* The sword is an instrument of death. It can come in the form of famine. Your finances can be hurt. Various aspects of your life can be hurt. He is keeping you from the power of the sword, from sickness, from bad investments. All of these kinds of things can be avoided in this way when divine inspiration comes to you through dreams. To that end, dreams are very important.

Like I said, the dream state is a gateway into the spirit realm. While you are sleeping your body sleeps, but your spirit does not sleep but engages under divine inspiration. Hence wise people who understand that God deals with them in this way will handle their body in a way that they are not too tired. They will find time to rest before the Lord and will feed their spirit with the Word of God. The more you feed your mind and spirit with the Word of God, your mind is programmed and ready for the flow of information. These are the ways you can enhance your dreams.

From the preceding, you discover that we have divine inspiration through dreams. They are all over the Scriptures, from Genesis to Revelation.

> *"And it came to pass at the end of two full years, that Pharaoh dreamed: and, behold, he stood by the river. And, behold, there came up out of the river seven well-favouredkine and fat-fleshed; and they fed in a meadow. And, behold, seven other kine came up after them out of the river, ill-favored and lean-fleshed; and stood by the other kine upon the brink of the river. And the ill-favored and lean-fleshed kine did eat up the seven well-favored and fat kine. So Pharaoh awoke. And he slept and dreamed the second time: and, behold, seven ears of corn came up upon one stalk, rank and good. And, behold, seven thin ears and blasted with the east wind sprung up after them. And the seven thin ears devoured the seven rank and full ears. And Pharaoh awoke, and, behold, it was a dream. And it came to pass in the morning that his*

spirit was troubled, and he sent and called for all the magicians of Egypt, and all the wise men thereof: and Pharaoh told them his dream, but there was none that could interpret them unto Pharaoh." (Genesis 41:1-8)

Do you see this beautiful drama? He was having a movie while sleeping. Who created the movie? God. Look at this nice, grassy place. It was beautiful. The grass was very green. Then he saw seven – pay attention to the fact that there were seven – not just cows, but seven of them, feeding, grazing, all of them fat-fleshed, beautiful. Suddenly, he looked at the other side and saw these gaunt looking cows that came after the nice looking ones and swallowed them. He woke up, sweating, got a cup of juice, and went back to sleep. Another beautiful field, this time of corn, seven again with a stalk looking rank and good, and another seven gaunt looking ones came and ate them up. He jumped up from sleep, "what is the matter?" He had his breakfast, but the dream was playing in his mind. Something was holding him in his spirit. He tried to shake it, but the dream just would not shake off. It was there, why? It was a divine inspiration. He needed to decode it because it was something beneficial.

> *"The more you feed your mind and spirit with the Word of God, your mind is programmed and ready for the flow of information."*

You have to understand, however, that at this point Pharaoh had no relationship with God. The Spirit of God is the one talking, and as against a child of God, Pharaoh had no relationship with God, but we do. He had no ability to decode it. But God had prepared a man, and that was the reason He gave it. Finally, he gathered the magicians because the dream was not going away, even after he woke up. Can you relate to that? You have some dreams, and they just keep coming back. You pray, but it keeps coming back. All day the thing just sits there in your spirit. These are divine inspirational dreams.

So Pharaoh was looking for interpreters for his dreams. He went to stargazers, and people still do that today. If I were to print a flyer right now, that says, "Come, I interpret dreams," the church would brand me a fortune teller. We now realize that the church ought to be prophesying. Do you believe that those fortune people can do better than me? Why then would the Church be mad if I should print such a flyer? Why would they call me a false prophet if I did that? But they will. Wonderful hearts and stupid heads so naïve, full of religion and they sing the devil's song – "can't do this, can't do that, can't touch that." But I can! I have the prophetic grace of the Lord Jesus Christ. I can, by His grace and I do interpret dreams!

The Bible says that none of the fortune tellers could interpret the dream. Do you know why? This dream was from God and not from demons, so God sealed off their minds and blinded them. When you stand before people that you do not know are real of God, say, "Father, if this is not you I shut down the equipment in the name of Jesus," and the lying will stop. You do not have to be afraid of it.

> *"Then spake the chief butler unto Pharaoh, saying, I do remember my faults this day: Pharaoh was wroth with his servants, and put me in ward in the captain of the guard's house, both me and the chief baker: And we dreamed a dream in one night, I and him; we dreamed each man according to the interpretation of his dream. And there was there with us a young man, a Hebrew, servant to the captain of the guard; and we told him, and he interpreted to us our dreams; to each man, according to his dream, he did interpret. And it came to pass, as he interpreted to us, so it was; me he restored unto mine office, and him he hanged."*

The butler who is talking here was not *born again*. He was an unbeliever, but Joseph interpreted his dream and left a witness there. At the right time, this Butler had still not become *born again*. He was an Egyptian in the palace. When the time came, God showed the dream to the Pharaoh, and someone in the palace said, "Oh, I remember this person, someone who should not be in jail." Divine inspirational dreams.

> *"Then Pharaoh sent and called Joseph, and they brought him hastily out of the dungeon: and he shaved himself, and changed his raiment, and came in unto Pharaoh. And Pharaoh said unto Joseph, I have dreamed a dream, and there is none that can interpret it: and I have heard say of thee, that thou canst understand a dream to interpret it. And Joseph answered Pharaoh, saying, "It is not in me: God shall give Pharaoh an answer of peace.""*

Notice what Joseph said here – "It is not in me." He is trying to say that the interpretation is not him, but that God does it through him. But I like the words he uses "It is not in me." I am going to hold on to that word and teach you something right now. But it is in you: For Joseph to interpret that dream, the anointing had to come upon him and inspire him at that moment. But for you, the anointing sits on the inside of your spirit (1 John 2:20; 27). Jesus spoke and said, *"If you love me keep my commandment, and I will send the promise of my Father upon you, the Holy Spirit, whom the world knoweth not. But you know Him for He is with you and shall be in you"*. By means of the death and resurrection of the Lord Jesus, the Holy Spirit can come to the believer and indwell him, and He is the Spirit that knows all things.

"But you have an unction from the Holy one, and ye know all things"... *But the anointing which you have received of him abideth*

in you, and you need not that any man teaches you as the same anointing teacheth you of all things and is truth and is not lie, and even as it has taught you it shall abide in you." (1 John 2:20; 27). You can discern the meaning of your dreams because you have an anointing from the Holy Spirit. The anointing you have received of Him abides inside of you. It is the anointing, the Holy Spirit. Outside of the Holy Spirit, you see legalities, lies, deceptions, which I will talk about when I begin to address the issue of manipulations through dreams. This is divine inspiration and revelation through dreams but also there are also manipulations through dreams. He says as that anointing is resident inside of you and is not lie, but truth. The counsel of the Lord is in the heart or spirit of the believer. Just train yourself to listen.

Pharaoh told Joseph his dreams (verse 25). And Joseph said, "The dream of Pharaoh is one." But weren't there two dreams? In other words, Joseph was saying to Pharaoh the two dreams have one message. I will not teach this fully but would like to mention a few points. To interpret a dream correctly, look out for the vocabulary. The vocabulary employed in this dream is 'farming,' with which Pharaoh is familiar. God will employ signs, symbols, or vocabulary with which you are familiar. Do not go to another person to interpret your dreams, unless that person is a prophet. You are in the best position to interpret your dreams. Just listen to the Holy Ghost. Neither should you look for symbols in books. They are too generic and may not apply to you. Some of these books offer symbols and interpretations that may cause you to waste your time and practice witchcraft. The Holy Spirit inside of you will give you the understanding you need. Look out for the language or the vocabulary the Holy Spirit employs.

Secondly, every dream has a storyline. Look at the story as it unfolds. He was in the meadows...green...seven cattle...fatfleshed... Look at the **storyline** and how it unfolds, and look at the **problem**. Thirdly, every dream has a **message** for you. Why is the dream coming? It is giving you a message. What is the message? It is more important than the story and the language. Then fourthly, it has a **purpose**. What is God's purpose for bringing me this message at this time? Finally, it may or may not have a **sign**. A sign is for emphasis, something to which you can relate. It may be the symbol of a person you knew when you were young. A sign is for emphasis. If you look at these five keys, you will interpret any dream with the Holy Spirit's guidance upon your life.

> *"Joseph said to Pharaoh, The dream of Pharaoh is one: God has shewed Pharaoh what he is about to do. The seven good kine are seven years; and the seven good ears are seven years: the dream is one. And the seven thin and ill favored kine that came up after them are seven years, and the seven empty ears blasted with the east wind shall be seven years of famine. This is the*

thing which I have spoken unto Pharaoh: What God is about to do he sheweth unto Pharaoh. Behold, there come seven years of great plenty throughout all the land of Egypt: And there shall arise after them seven years of famine, and all the plenty shall be forgotten in the land of Egypt, and the famine shall consume the land."

I want you to notice something here in interpretation. The first one he is breaking it, but right now, the burden rests on him as he is getting into the details now. Why? The Holy Spirit is giving the interpretation. While you are in the middle of it, BAM! It comes. I see that all the time. And when it comes you know you are talking with authority. The flow is there.

"And the plenty shall not be known in the land because of that famine following; for it shall be very grievous. And for that the dream was **doubled** *unto Pharaoh* **twice***; it is because the thing is established by God, and God will shortly bring it to pass."* That is the sign – doubling the dream.

"Now, therefore, let Pharaoh look out a man discreet and wise, and set him over the land of Egypt." This is even bigger than the dream – he is giving him counsel by the Spirit of God. This is the purpose of the prophetic to counsel and to guide. With counsel, purpose becomes established.

So we see the first category of dreams here is divine inspirational dreams. God is trying to show you something that is of benefit to you. He is trying to prevent you from disaster or from falling into hard times. He comes and inspires these dreams to reach you and minister to you and say something to you.

MANIPULATION TYPE DREAMS

There is another category of dreams. The source of this is not God. The source is the devil. It can come through men, or it can come directly to you through dreams. Anytime dreams come from the devil it can send people to prophesy to you. It is manipulation and a recipe for disaster if you believe it. Just about three weeks ago, one of my church members was about to travel to Africa. A family member called and said she had a dream that she went to Africa and was kidnapped. Another person in the family called and said, "Do not come so that you will not get into trouble." She told me about the dream and asked me if I will pray. I said, "No, I will not" because if I do, I will validate their fear. I was still going to pray but not with her. I said to her, "Go, nothing will happen to you. It is not God. God doesn't direct us with fear".

What do you notice about divine revelation? It is inspiring and stirs your faith. If the dream is from God, it will inspire you, give you faith, and will give you hope. But if it is from the devil it will make you hopeless and fill you with fear and trepidation. So after the sister left, I went on my knees and prayed for her, covering her and cutting off any satanic manipulations. That was manipulation. If she did not go on that trip, she would have bought into the fear of the devil. She would be here, and that fear would have remained in her. Any other thing she wanted to do again it would bring out that fear and she would be stuck. There are people who want to do great things for God, and if this kind of spirit functions in them, it will always give them a dream to prevent them. Such dreams will put fear in you, and you will back off. A dream that eliminates your faith in God is witchcraft manipulation. We see an example of that in the Bible, and God was very angry. Let us go to Jeremiah 23:25-28:

"I have heard what the prophets said, that prophesy lies in my name, saying, I have dreamed, I have dreamed."

Wait a minute. These prophets had a dream which they thought was from God, and they were feeding it to the people, and God was angry. Why? Because the dream obviously did not proceed from Him. So the prophets were deceived by a spirit of witchcraft manipulating them. They may have been sincere, but still, it was a spirit of witchcraft manipulation. So you have to understand how this thing can function sometimes.

"How long shall this be in the heart of the prophets that prophesy lies? yea, they are prophets of the deceit of their own heart..."

This means their hearts or their spirits are under deception. So they are prophesying, they are dreaming dreams but what they are dreaming and are prophesying, however, was a deception from the enemy and not from God. So what is wrong here is the source of their prophecy, the source of their dreams. It was not proceeding from the source which is God. If it was not proceeding from God, then it was proceeding from the devil with a sinister objective.

There are many people in the Body of Christ who just do not pay attention to dreams. Dreams are important. Why? Because they are gateways into the spirit. However, there are people in the Body of Christ who, through exposure to occult backgrounds, have a measure of existing hereditary occult bondages that function within their family lines. They always dream, but those dreams are not necessarily of God. They have not been taught, nor have they gone through deliverance. They are simply repeating doors that were not shut. The enemy blends in, and they think they are having experiences with the Spirit of God but are not. They get themselves into bondage and bring well-meaning people into bondage. There are highly anointed children of God that I have seen in shackles because they are believing and following someone who is simply telling them dreams and revelations by

Leviathan spirit. I have seen them and warned them, and they will deny it. One such person, I have spoken to is a highly anointed brother. A particular sister just cornered him with these visions and dreams, neutralized him completely, and now he is under her lock and key. She is the Holy Ghost to him. You can neither correct him nor her because they think they are hearing from God. Oh no! It is a devil with sinister motives.

God was very angry here in this passage of Scripture:
"...Which think to cause my people to forget my name by their dreams which they tell every man to his neighbor, as their fathers have forgotten my name for Baal. The prophet that hath a dream let him tell a dream; and he that hath my word, let him speak my word faithfully. What is the chaff to the wheat? Saith the LORD" (Verses 27-28).

The above category of dreams are are not from God. They are from the devil with sinister motives to make people forget the name of the Lord, that is, to neutralize people's faith in God. When you are operating under this type of witchcraft word, you enter a period of self-hypnosis. You are trapped and neutralized, and you cannot move because a dream will always come to put fear in you. Once you want to embark on something, a dream comes and says, "if you do it...!" So you stop. You are depending on dreams, and not on the Word of God. And how do you know when you are being manipulated? You live in fear. Manipulation goes by fear; God goes by faith.

If God is revealing something to you, you cannot be afraid. If the enemy is the one revealing something to you, faith is replaced by fear. He neutralizes you and puts you in bondage, and ties you up. They are very difficult to break especially if you are dealing with people who want to be known as 'prophets' without questioning the source. As a result, while you are trying to rescue them they are trying to validate their position to you by telling you more of the same kind of dreams – the ones they dreamt that came to pass. You can have many dreams that come to pass, and they are still not from God. I have had many people who have told me stuff that was deadly accurate but the source is not God, and I told them so. I told them, "I bear witness with what you say, but I reject the spirit with whom you spoke." Direct. Because I do not want to open my destiny to peeping and gazing that masquerade as prophetic but only wants to manipulate you and get control over you.

It can be a human being trying to gain control over you, or it can be from being exposed to the occult. There are churches that are occult in nature. There are many of them in Africa. They propagate a gospel of works, and they have their prophets who can tell you details of the contents of your wallet, your credit card number, your birthday, your social security number, but it is still not of God but of the spirit of divination, the snake spirit or Leviathan spirit. This is so important in deliverance. Most of the people you meet in deliverance are either people from this background or have gone through this influence. They are able bodied, but in their minds, are crippled.

There was a lady I worked with for a time in the ministry, and I wanted to help her, but because she wanted to be a prophet she refused the help. There was a day she tried to manipulate me: We had a meeting, and she said there was someone who would give an offering, but that offering will be cursed money that would curse the finances of the church. She requested that I stand up and announce publicly that whoever that person is they should not put the money in that basket. Now, I can tell you the information was correct, but it was not of God. Think of it if I should stand in the church and make such an announcement. What message would I be sending to the people of God? A message of fear? A message that there is a power in the church that I can respect? No. I do not have to say anything, but I can deal with it in the background. Just by receiving the offering and pleading the blood of Jesus and breaking every curse linked with that. I did not have to make that kind of announcement, so I disregarded it. When I got home, the young man she had crippled already called me and said, "Pastor Patrick, there was something that happened today that just disturbs my spirit. The Holy Ghost gave a message, and you did not announce it. Was it because you are afraid that you would lose the offerings of the people?" There is no need to be afraid. I said, "Brother, you do not know who you are talking to. I will see you tomorrow."

The next day, they came together, himself and the sister. Her eyes were glazed and tormented, and it was obvious she had not slept at all since that time. She said to me, "The Holy Ghost is angry with me that you did not carry out His instruction." I said, "Sister, sit here while I deal with people. Here, read Isaiah 27:1-2. I will be back with you to handle your case." After I had sent off the evangelism team, I came back to her. I said, "Sister, if the Holy Ghost gave you a message to give to me and I fail to obey, you have already delivered the message to me, should He be tormenting you? He should come after me. However, what you are dealing with now is not the Holy Ghost it is a leviathan spirit, and I am going to cast that snake out of you right now. In the name of Jesus, move!" Instantly she began to manifest, and that snake was flushed out of her. You would think that would humble her, but even after that, she continued to peddle her prophecies.

If you go to the Bible, you see patterns of this behavior. Paul was preaching to a deputy named Apollos who he was trying to reach for the Lord, and there was this Bar-Jesus standing by trying to hinder the gospel – that snake spirit. In our system, we see the same spirit, the Leviathan spirit. As they went on, there was a girl prophesying, *"These are the men of God, they come to show us the way of salvation."* The information is true, but the motive is sinister. It is a spirit of divination, a snake. It went on for some days, and Paul cast it out.

This demon has a measure of prophetic infiltration into the churches, and it infiltrates the dreams of God's people to cripple them. We are not to run from dreams and the prophetic, but we are to go for what is real. Know what truth is, hold on to it and reject what is not truth. Rebuke the enemy, withstand him, reject him, kick him around and do not let him kick you around. Have discernment of the spirit and connect with what proceeds from God your Father. Say, "I am born of God and have overcome them because greater is He that is in me than he that is in the world."

This manipulation through dreams essentially eliminates faith. Also when you are taking people through deliverance, this can be one source of trouble. People who have been bound by water spirits, marine spirits, or Leviathan spirits, who have participated in the occult to any measure have a sensitivity to the spirit world. As part of deliverance, you have to ask God to shut that door. But while they are still going through the basics of deliverance, for a time, they are seeing things and interacting with things, and the enemy can come through that door and be manipulating them by showing them dreams. The enemy writes a program and throws it on them, and in the dream they see themselves doing some bizarre things. They wake up, and he begins to accuse them – "You say you are delivered, but you are still doing this, you are still doing that, you are not delivered." The person feels discouraged and hopeless and feels they are not delivered, and they come back in. It is manipulation. You have to teach them to resist the devil.

How do you get delivered anyway? Is it by merely fighting the devil? No. It is by submitting yourself to God. When you submit yourself to God, you are delivered. Then you can resist the devil. True deliverance is to bring you to a place of submission to God, to teach people to stand on the Word of God and to dwell in an atmosphere of worship. Feeding them with the Word of God, we program their minds to line up with the Word instead of their mind lining up with demonic programs that are sent against them in dreams. Teach them to live by the Word of God and not by their dreams. I always say, "If you have a bad dream, sleep and dream another dream. If you have another bad dream, do more sleep and dream another dream. If you keep having bad dreams, wake up and read the Word of God." You do not live by dreams; you live by the Word of God.

There are demonic dreams and demonic manipulations in dreams. The source of these dreams is not God. It is the devil trying to gain control and trying to intimidate you, put fear in you, and paralyze you. They do not inspire faith; they inspire fear and hopelessness.

MANIFESTATION DREAMS

The third category of dreams we shall briefly consider is dreams from the man himself. I will call it manifestations of the state of the man. Manifestation here means bringing forth to visibility of that spiritual reality which lies hidden underneath the soul of a man. After this, we will briefly consider why it is important to reckon with dreams in deliverance. Let us look at Isaiah 29:8 which will help us to explain:

> *"It shall even be as when a hungry man dreameth, and, behold, he eateth; but he awaketh, and his soul is empty: or as when a thirsty man dreameth, and, behold, he drinketh; but he awaketh, and, behold, he is faint, and his soul hath appetite: so shall the multitude of all the nations be, that fight against mount Zion."*

God is making a statement. I am just going to lift it and use it to explain. He said it should be as a man who is hungry, and he sleeps and is eating a nice meal. When he wakes up, he is still hungry. Or he is thirsty, and he is drinking in the dream, the best kind of juice. This kind of thing will normally happen when three days fast is declared in the church. If you do not like to fast and you are fasting that day, and you are missing the food, nice food will come in the dreams. This is not serious. Or you may have been watching a particular movie, and you go to bed, and what you were watching in the movie, as you sleep, you continue the movie in your dream. It is very surface subconscious manifestation of some reality that is not a spiritual reality.

However, there can be an even deeper reality in a spiritual state that manifests in dreams. These can be indicative of an area of need. Particularly, this can happen in seasons of consecration when you are seeking God or seek to be closer to God, and something just shows up in your dream characteristically that throws confusion in your mind. By dreaming of wearing your teenage school uniform or your elementary school uniform, going to school like you use to go before thirty to forty years ago, and in the dream, you have no consciousness of your adulthood; you are just blending in. Something is wrong there. Some have dreams of oppression whereby someone known or unknown comes and have sexual intercourse with them with all the associated feelings. Something is wrong there. Some have dreams of being naked. It is indicative of an area of trouble where you need help.

This is not necessarily negative. It is for you to be able to intelligently go to God. I will not put them in the category of divine inspiration because you started doing something that provoked them. You were growing close to God, and it is as if coming closer to light, you were able to see the blemishes. It is like having a stain on your clothes, and until you see it in the light, you do know that the stain is there. God is that way. Any representation of darkness in your life, areas of your soul that have been fractured that is still being visited by the enemy, in seasons when you are trying to consecrate and seek God, they begin to flash. The light is coming upon them, and so you can intelligently go for prayer to break them. Ask God for release and healing so your life can move forward gracefully.

These are categories of manifestations that are helpful and necessary. The problem is, if you do not understand their purpose, you get frightened. For some people who are already into deliverance and are walking in the light of spiritual warfare, and then something like this comes, they begin to wonder, "Pastor, I thought I was already delivered. Why am I still having this?" Then we find out through the counsel of the Holy Spirit and some things get dealt with while some other layers are removed subsequently. I think regarding manifestations of this nature it is so important that we walk closely with the Lord, so we know what the Holy Spirit is doing in our lives so that we are not pent up, and we are not frightened. It is never an intelligent thing to react or relate to your dreams through fear. Rather, seek to understand.

Now, we have heard the three sources of dreams. So if you have a dream and you are in doubt, go before God and ask Him the source of the dream. Is it divine inspiration? Is it demonic manipulation? Is it a manifestation of a not-serious situation? Is it an unconscious situation in which God wants to help me? Anytime you have a dream; it is for your benefit. Nobody should ever have to be afraid. The Bible assures us in 1 John 2:20, 27 that we have the ability to know. We do not have to be perturbed, concerned or depressed over a dream. We can just decode it because we have the ability. *"The secret things belong unto the LORD our God: but those things which are revealed belong unto us and to our children forever, that we may do all the words of this law"* (Deuteronomy 29:29).

The things that are hidden belong to the Lord our God. You are not responsible for that. But the things that are revealed, they are for your benefit. They are being revealed so that you can taste some action that will empower your destiny to fulfill your original purpose, which is God's reason for releasing deliverance and the prophetic to help us.

In summary, why is the dream life important for the deliverance counselor? There is normally a form for collecting information for prospective clients who want to be delivered. As they fill the form, you take a close look at their dream state. Their dream state can reveal a lot of useful information that will give insight into what is happening in their lives. Usually, I would tell the person to be on fasting and to write his dream down, even if it doesn't make sense to him before coming for deliverance. Why? Dreams are manifestations of your reality. When you put it down, the Holy Spirit will flash his light, and those things come to light. If you are honest, then we can cast those things out, and they can go. We can uproot those things and clear the way out. Why? It is because the dream state is a gateway for spiritual activities.

Every demonic power that has hurt, injured, or opened a doorway to itself into the life of an individual can function underneath. As that person is sleeping, they are activated, taking the soul of the person to dangerous experiences and destroying that person. They can even use the person without his knowledge. This is the reason you find blind witches in churches. They have been involved in the occult in the past but have now come to Christ and because they are not walking in the knowledge of the Word of God and do not respect scriptural boundaries, these demons are still empowered to be taking them to meetings, and also using them, in dreams, to harass people. You find people blacklisting such individuals, and even though they declare their innocence, they keep showing up in places because the demons can use their image or their representation.

On this note, the dream state is important: It is the gateway into the spirit where a whole gamut of activities can be going on which the individual does not know. The dream state can reveal patterns of bondage, issues that need to be dealt with such that you, the deliverance counselor, can get inside. All of this information is to be collected before doing deliverance. Do pre-deliverance warfare to address these issues, so that by the time the person comes you are already hitting the target before you get to minister to them.

BREAKTHROUGH PROPHETIC DELIVERANCE PRAYERS

1. I declare this day that I am born of God and my spirit, soul and body is bought and sanctified by the blood of the Lamb. Every spiritual gate invaders manipulating my dreams is hereby renounced and destroyed in the name of Jesus.

2. I command that any satanic implants, codes and seeds placed on my life through dreams be located now by fire and burn off in the mighty name of Jesus Christ Satanic targets of my fruitful seasons shall backfire in the mighty name of Jesus Christ.

3. I invite the purifying power of the blood of Jesus to sanctify and disconnect me from any flow of evil being channeled into my life through demonically manipulated dreams.

4. Lord grant me divine insights, revelations and counsel to understand any spiritual need that I may have showing up in my dreams and teach me how to turn such experiences to my own advantage and uplifting in the mighty name of Jesus.

CHAPTER 20

Follow-Up in Deliverance

This is vital for those who are serious and want to be delivered. Some people come to waste your time. They are not serious. They do not want deliverance. But there are some who truly want deliverance. For those serious about their deliverance, how will they be able to maintain or contain their deliverance?

I am trying to be careful with my choice of words because of our definition of deliverance. Remember I said that deliverance is not just casting out a devil. To cast out a devil is a relief. It is just one of the things you do in the process of deliverance. Deliverance is total liberation or freedom from factors and agents that prevent a man or woman from enjoying the privileges of their covenant relationships or rights which they have with God in Christ Jesus. In other words, deliverance is focused on and predicated on a covenant relationship with God. Bondage, on the other hand, is focused and predicated on some covenant relationship with the devil. For somebody who was in covenant relationship with the devil but has accepted Jesus Christ and now realizes he wants to be free, they are immediately transferred from the kingdom of darkness into the Kingdom of Light.

Deliverance is a transfer of kingdom. A person who is delivered can enjoy the benefits of deliverance which we have been enumerating. Now, this person who comes, having some conflict in their walk with God based on where they are coming from, is like Lazarus who had been dead in the tomb for four days, decaying and stinking according to John 11:43-44. Jesus says, "Lazarus, come forth." Lazarus receives life but is still bound by grave clothes. Jesus says to them, "Loose him and let him go." Two things were said:

"Deliverance is focused on and predicated on a covenant relationship with God."

(1) loose him, and
(2) let him go. You find that it is not enough to "loose" him. He said, "Loose him. Let him go."

Go where? To continue with his life of freedom and liberty. So it is to break the chains and empower his destiny to succeed. That is the whole point of deliverance. Deliverance involves counseling, locating doorways, breaking of covenants, cleansing or casting out devils, and closing the doors. It is like hospital work where there are specialists who do these various things to bring this person to a place of soundness.

After this person has been brought to a place of seeming liberty, there are still other things that need to follow. What are these other things? We call them follow-up in deliverance. How will you follow up the persons to make sure they maintain the benefits of the yoke that was broken without them being re-yoked? We realize, from our previous studies, that the demons make a comeback. We read in Matthew that when an unclean spirit is gone out of a man he walks through dry places seeking rest because he has no body, and he needs that place to feel at home. He says "I will go back to my house." Do you see what he is calling the human being? His house. When he returns there and finds this person swept clean and garnished, he goes to bring seven other spirits (more wicked) than himself, and they enter in. The Bible records that the last state of the man becomes worse than the first. In other words, do not accept responsibility for ministering what you call deliverance on people who do not have the wherewithal to continue walking in that deliverance because their case will be worse off.

THE PLACE OF DISCIPLESHIP IN DELIVERANCE
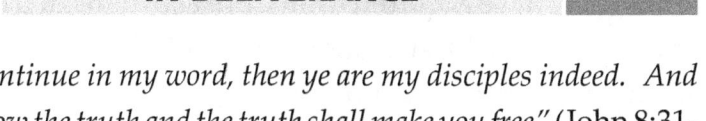

"...If ye continue in my word, then ye are my disciples indeed. And ye shall know the truth and the truth shall make you free" (John 8:31-2).

In deliverance, after people have been ministered to, they need to be *discipled*. Where does discipleship begin? It begins with making Jesus the Lord of one's life. This is where instructions come in. Remember we talked about the process of deliverance – salvation, counseling, deliverance, instruction in the Word of God. We said we have been delivered, and are being delivered, and will be delivered.

> *"I would not have you ignorant brethren of the afflictions we endured, that we pressed beyond measure insomuch that we despaired even of life, but we had a sentence of death in us so that we learn to not trust in ourselves but in God who brings back again from the dead, who delivered us from so great a death and doth deliver us and whom will yet deliver us"*
> (2 Corinthians 1:8).

We read what Paul said about the afflictions that came upon them when they were in Asia. From the Scripture, we discover that deliverance entails the past, present, and future.

With this understanding, the crucial part of continuing in that which they have acquired from Christ is predicated upon their making the Lord Jesus Christ the Lord of their lives. *"As he spake these words many believed on him. Then said Jesus to those Jews which believed on him, if ye continue in my word then ye are my disciples indeed. And ye shall know the truth, and the truth shall make you free"* (John 8:30-32). Jesus was speaking to the Jews who believed on Him.

Where does the ability to withstand the devil come from? Surrender to the Lordship of Jesus Christ, without which deliverance is not even something to think about. Their problems can drive people into a desperate desire to do anything to be freed and just want to be free from their problems. However, if that problem is demonically generated, you have a responsibility to let them know that they cannot be free from this type of problem without changing masters.

Most often you will find that people in these kinds of problems have been in places. This is what we saw Jesus doing with the man whose son was demonized. Why didn't he jump in right away? Because people have been in places and now they want to try 'you' out because they heard about you helping people and they just decide to give it a shot. When they come that way, you will notice that because they have been going up and down, the case has grown worse than it was at the beginning. We also see that with the woman with the issue of blood. The

Bible said that she had been to many physicians, spent all her living, yet her case had not improved but was getting worse.

Typically, you discerned and are seeing someone who has a situation and have been from place to place making his problem grow worse. Why? The demon knows the victim is trying to get rid of him and has been asking for reinforcement to be stronger. To help such an individual, you need to make sure he or she is properly counseled about the reality of his circumstances and the need to receive Jesus and make Jesus the Lord of his life.

When there is a mass crusade – a deliverance crusade, a healing crusade, or any gospel crusade, all kinds of people are there, and the power of God comes. You see people begin to manifest and devils cast out of lives. In this scenario, what happens? After the meeting closes, everyone goes home. Here it is very important when planning such crusades that the man of God works with local churches. Do not set up such a meeting without a network of partners. Work with local churches and ministries that will contribute people to work with you. Arrange training for these people so that once people give their lives, they move them, and they take their information and link them up with these ministries for follow-up. If that is not done, there is the danger of making their condition worse.

FIRST THINGS FIRST

"Behold, I stand at the door and knock: if any man hears my voice, and open the door, I will come to him and will sup with him, and he with me" (Rev 3:20).

The first action is to believe and surrender to the Lord Jesus. Why? Because when they do that Jesus now comes into the house. Once Jesus is in the house, and the demons try to come back, the landlord is already in the house so they cannot get in. The spirit of the man is already occupied by the Lord - the Scripture is so wonderful. Remember earlier on I asked how many demons possessed the man at Gadara and the answer was one unclean spirit. How many demons lived in the man? They were thousands in number. Many lived in him, but only one possessed him. Why? Because he did not have the Lord, his spirit man got possessed (only one spirit can possess him because the only part of him that can be possessed is his spirit man. Man is a triune being – spirit, soul, and body). That unclean spirit possessed his spirit and invited these thousands of demons to come and take residence in different parts of his soul, mind, body, will, emotions, hair, teeth, hands. They were just packed in there – it is a mystery.

When a person receives Jesus Christ, where does Jesus stay on the person? When a person gets born again, Jesus takes over his spirit, so when demons come to occupy they cannot possess him. He can come to him and can afflict him; he can live in his body if some issues have not been dealt with, but he cannot possess him.

On the whole, by just making sure the person made Jesus Christ the Lord of his life, he can no longer be possessed by evil spirits. However, the affliction means the person is dealing with oppression and outside situations.

Now, what did Jesus say to those Jews in John 8:30-32? He said if ye continue in my word. That Word is not a one day word or a two days word. It is a life-coaching process, a progressive encounter with the revelation of the Word of God. This is where many deliverance ministries are in trouble. They counsel, bring people to Christ, cast out devils, and they feel their ministry is over. Most deliverance ministries are headed by evangelists who do not have the ability to equip people. In these deliverance ministries, everybody goes there and sits week after week. They never grow past the mentality of oppression, because the man is preaching deliverance week after week and they remain at that level. I would much rather prefer they bring the individual out and send him to Pastor A's church – who is a strong teacher of the Word so that the individual can listen to the Word of God one year and is changed – deliverance is a team effort.

Deliverance is an encounter with God's revelation. Jesus says, you shall know the truth, and the truth shall make you free. It is a progressive encounter. Why? The enemy has bound different parts of the person's life. Even when the chief demon is kicked out, the person is not fully delivered but as they encounter instruction in the Word of God, it comes from their flesh which had been corrupted to fit into the demon's agenda. Remember demons are disembodied spirits powerless for evil until they can occupy a body. So what happens now? As this person encounters that revealed Word – "be angry and sin not;" "let not the sun go down on your wrath" for instance – they begin to realize their issues and repent. That Word of God brings cleansing for *He sends His Word and heals them and delivers them from their destruction,* from their waste.

If you are someone who fights the Word of God, you cannot be free. While these people are receiving instruction from the Word of God, they can still be coming for deliverance because the demons will overwhelm them in their flesh but we can kick them out again and again. A note of warning: Do not depend on this kicking out. People go to all these deliverance clubs; they depend on the kicking out to gain relief, and they do not go past it, but you should go past that demon: The Bible says that the yoke shall be destroyed because of the anointing and anointing is spiritual fatness. Because of the grooming, the individual gains fatness and the demon becomes undersized, thus the yoke breaks. That is what instruction in the Word of

God can do.

THE WORD OF GOD IS CENTRAL

Progressive revelation of God's Word will open up areas in your life. The Word of God is like the surgeon's knife. It probes into the area of corruption and decay in our lives, opening them up and cleaning them so true healing can take place. Deliverance, healing, and wholeness go side by side.

When I say, the Word of God is like a surgeon's knife: if you have a wound and it is decayed, but somehow the skin grows over it, you can no longer see the wound, but if you press the area you feel the pain. You feel pain because it is not totally healed on the inside. If there happens to be an infection inside, what do you think the surgeon is going to do? Cut it open, and you do not want that because you have forgotten that matter. In our context, there are issues about that man that continue to be a problem and the enemy builds upon it and what the knife does is go into it and cut it open.

The surgeon, the Holy Spirit, is working and He cleans that aspect of your life.

Do you see why in the process of deliverance you have to put people through interrogation and to probe of the Holy Spirit? Not just one probe, but several probes. This is the reason we need to let people know from the onset that it is not the man. The man is only a trained specialist. The real deliverer is the Lord, the Holy Spirit.

Why can't I just kick out a demon from a person but make sure they now make a covenant with God by receiving Jesus into their lives? Once they receive Jesus into their lives, they will receive one important gift – the Lord, the Holy Spirit who comes alongside to help them. He stays with you in your bed and goes with you in your car. He is even in your dreams such that while you are dreaming, He is busy working and all you have to do is cooperate with the Him.

In a moment I will tell you three areas the devil will fight back after someone has been ministered to, but first I want us to visit those cases we handled before and see how Jesus prepared for the ability to continue.

POWER OF TESTIMONY

Let us look at the case of the demoniac at Gadarene. Jesus completed this great work of deliverance, and naturally, the man wanted to follow Him. Why does the man want to follow him? He knew what he had been through and he wanted to be able to continue. He figured that "if I just follow Jesus these horrible demons cannot jump back into my life because Jesus will be there to help me." Smart! In other words, a commitment is made and established here. He not only believes now, but he also wants to follow. However, Jesus had another instruction for him which, if he obeyed, would retain his deliverance. What was the instruction? Verses 18-19 has this to say:

> *"And when he was come into the ship, he that had been possessed with the devil prayed him that he might be with him. Howbeit Jesus suffered him not but said unto him, go home to thy friends and tell them how great things the Lord has done for thee and has had compassion on thee."* Mark 5:18-19

What was the key to maintaining or working his deliverance that Jesus gave him here? He had compassion, kicked out the devil, but now to keep the devil out the man wanted to follow Jesus. Jesus said no. He gave him another key which, if he used, he would be able to maintain and retain his deliverance. Go and start testifying about what God has done for you and how he has had compassion on you.

 **POWER OF PERSONAL TESTIMONY**
(Revelations 12:11)

How does testimony help you maintain deliverance? When you testify that power is immediately provoked because the Holy Spirit is there. The Gadarene became an evangelist. He was given an important key here. Jesus gave him the key of personal testimony to the saving power of God. *"And he departed and began to publish in the Decapolis how great things Jesus had done for him and all men did marvel"* (Verse 20). Decapolis means ten cities. He turned ten cities around. As he is going, Jesus says *"go to your friends."* He decided that ten cities were his friends and he began to broadcast everywhere. The power of testimony was activated. Go and declare what God has done for you, how he has shown you compassion.

Let me ask a question. How many dollar bills, wives, cars, and houses did God give to this man? None whatsoever! He delivered his soul from the torment of hell. That was great enough, and the man embraced that call: "Figure out. Do you know me? Oh, you've never been to the tombs? You know that tomb that people could not pass because there was a mad man there who would break chains, crying and screaming? Take a look at me; I used to be that man until Jesus came along. He did this for me – He turned my life around." He was excited about it and broadcasted it. He was all over the place, covering ten cities.

While he is on that assignment, his wife will come from that testimony, his new home will come, and everything he needs to continue the great work of testifying will come. Have you seen where the church has failed? People have come to church thinking, "give me my miracle right now. This is my tithes and offering, now where is my miracle?" And pastors have lost their voices. They have to put Diapers on them to keep them in those churches. Is that ministry? This is a ministry in the Bible right here: He went all over testifying what God had done for him. This was the key that Jesus gave to him. How will you know the key to your deliverance if you do not surrender? Do people who come to church even want deliverance today? What are they looking for? Some material blessings? Not a bad idea, but unfortunately that is what they are looking for without caring about their souls. The majority of people have not yet been convinced that their soul is important. "This is my tithes, where is my blessings, where is my husband?" "Pastor, it is now January ending. I believe God my husband will come by February." You had better be sure. Stupid Pastors who are simply too naïve to walk away from the religious witchcraft. We haven't told the Body of Christ we are practicing foolishness. The whole world is laughing at us, and their laughter is justified.

Imagine the agony that this man went through in his life. Those who loved him put chains to restrain him. The demons laughed and cracked the chains like egg shells. He went about cutting himself and crying among the tombs and the mountains. Then Jesus came along and gave him back his life. So he said, "ok, you gave me back my life, so the life I now have is not my life I am going to use it to honor you." Out of love you will serve and will do anything for the kingdom. No one will need to be begging you – "come out tonight, come to church early, please, service is by 11:00, come by 11:30 at least." "Believers, let's fast, please fast one meal." Miserable church with miserable pastors lost in the crowd.

OVERCOMING THE COUNTER-ATTACKS

Every time a demon is cast out, he will do three things to launch a comeback. In the case of this demoniac on a mission for Jesus, when the demon goes around and comes back trying to jump in he found the man testifying with testifying angels around him. When those demons see that, they run. That man does not need a pastor to be guiding him. He does not need a pastor policing him not to fornicate. Do you know how many demons fornicated with him out there in the tombs before? He doesn't want it anymore. If you have touched hell on earth in your career with the devil, you get done with him. He does lead you to temptation, but you will not cross the line because you know what is on the other side.

Three things the devil does:
1. **Allurement:**
The devil allures and seduces you. Once you have broken free, he looks for the one thing you like. The devil does not tempt you with what you do not like but with what you like. It can be anything. It can be human beings, emotions, pride, anything.

When the demons come to live in somebody, they establish habits in your life, which you wrongly claim to be you. "This is my little weakness," and you begin to breast feed and nurture it. It is the demon's character. Now you kick him out, he cannot come close to you, but he comes around to find that habit, that vice in you. If you open up to that vice, you give him the opportunity to re-launch and become effective in manipulating you and oppressing you. If you fall into seduction, he moves into the next stage.

2. Blackmail:
He starts accusing you. "Look at what you just did. You are not really free." He accuses you to produce hopelessness and condemnation. You start condemning yourself and begin to feel hopeless. But the Bible says, *"there is therefore now no condemnation to them who are in Christ Jesus who walk not after the flesh but after the spirit. For the law of the Spirit of life in Christ Jesus has made you free from the law of sin and death"* (Romans 8:1). Anything that makes you accept condemnation in your mind brings you into bondage. God never condemns. He justifies us.

3. Persecution:
Most often he will use the things you used to do before to persecute you. This is the reason he establishes strongholds in people. If you were an agent of darkness before, in touch with the occult, with witchcraft or with the marine world, he would

bring your fellow people who you use to work with to torment, persecute and fight you. Those kinds of specialized cases more especially need to be handled in the community of faith – *"Not forsaking the assembling of ourselves together as the manner of some is, but exhorting one another and so much the more as ye see the day approaching"* (Hebrews 10:25). There are levels of demonic activities for which it is so important to stay in the community of faith and be in fellowship. Every time you are in fellowship, there is a portion of God coming to you. Do not be neglectful of that. Be in the services because the day is approaching. While the day is approaching what happens to the devil? His time is running short, and on account of that, he is breaking out in wrath.

BREAKTHROUGH PROPHETIC DELIVERANCE PRAYERS

Ephesians 3:10-12
To the intent that now unto the principalities and powers in heavenly places might be known by the church the manifold wisdom of God, According to the eternal purpose which he purposed in Christ Jesus our Lord.

Revelation 12:1-4 And there appeared a great wonder in

"In a way, deliverance anointing is demonstrating, in a visible manner, the defeat and the weakness of the devil."

heaven; a woman clothed with the sun, and the moon under her feet, and upon her head a crown of twelve stars: And she being with child cried, travailing in birth, and pained to be delivered. And there appeared another wonder in heaven; and behold a great red dragon, having seven heads and ten horns, and seven crowns upon his heads.

And his tail drew the third part of the stars of heaven, and did cast them to the earth: and the dragon stood before the woman which was ready to be delivered for to devour her child as soon as it was born

1. Every satanic Covenant, Allegiance, Pronouncement and evil commitment; be neutralized, broken and liquidated by the blood of the Lord Jesus Christ.

2. Every Altar of Evil, Hex, Curses and burdens speaking against me and my Family. Be liquidated by the blood and fire in the Mighty Name of the Lord Jesus Christ.

3. Merchants of Death and Your instruments of untimely Death in my family Catch Fire right now burn to ashes in the Mighty Name of The Lord Jesus Christ.... Any innocent person in my family life consigned to untimely death, I proclaim Liberty. You are free, be free indeed in the Mighty Name of the Lord Jesus Christ.

4. The power behind misfortune in my family line; your government of evil is over! Today is your hour of visitation! Your memorial has come before the Lord and the cup of trembling has come upon you........(active warfare here).

5. Demonic implants, decorations, coverings and points of contacts roast by fire.

6. Any demonic power that has seized any ground in my life or sneaked into my body, be located by fire and run right now in the Mighty name of Jesus Christ.

7. Dear Lord Jesus, I call upon your great Name for my total release and cleansing. Cleanse me, Heal my wounds, fill and Use me for your glory. Bless me, change me and set me up for your glory.

CHAPTER 21

Preparation to Serve in Deliverance Ministry

Deliverance ministry is a peculiar ministry. I cannot overemphasize that. Deliverance ministry is a frontline ministry where you face the devil head on, and he does not like it. Every time the anointing of deliverance goes forth, it confronts something. That is the reason you often see in the Bible, as Jesus functioned under this anointing, the power of the Lord present to heal, demons cry out and leave people – suddenly a very dignified environment becomes rattled.

When the power of God goes forth, demons begin to manifest. What happens is that it becomes obvious that two kingdoms are fighting, and immediately, because of the display of the anointing of deliverance, people also get to notice the superior kingdom. In a way, deliverance anointing is demonstrating, in a visible manner, the defeat and the weakness of the devil. First, he does not enjoy being in the open; he likes to function behind the scenes. Secondly, if he is forced into the open, he does not want to be defined as the defeated one. Deliverance ministry will do this damage to him directly, and he hates it and will actually fight. He fights to prevent this humiliation by using devices to try to stop you, the Deliverance Minister.

SATAN RELIES ON SMART STRATEGIES

If you are going to fight the devil, you need to pay attention to something Paul said. He said, *"we are not ignorant of the devices of the devil"* (2 Corinthians 2:11). What does he mean by devices? It means strategy, modus operandi, or how the devil functions. There are well meaning, good people serving God but who are ignorant of Satan's devices. If you do not know his devices, he can destroy you. Satan has smart strategies that he relies on. This is primarily because he has power, but he does not have authority, so he relies on these strategies. By now you know the difference between the two: power is supernatural ability to cause phenomena which are unnatural to occur; authority is the right to exercise power. Satan has no right to exercise power though he has power because he is disconnected from God. He is like a policeman who has been dismissed from service but still carrying a gun, badge and wearing a uniform. He can illegally exercise power, but he has no authority.

There is a breed of people walking through the earth that have knowledge of the fact that Satan is illegal. When he meets those people, he is totally helpless, and so he is forced to rely on his devices or strategies.

Paul said here that we are not ignorant of his strategies lest he gets the advantage over us. This means that if we become or chose to be ignorant of his devices, we can be quoting Scriptures, but he will have a strategic advantage. Strategy is a very important word because every battle is fought, won, and lost based on strategy.

As a historian, I monitored the first Gulf crisis when the bombs started landing on Iraq in 1990. Before the commencement of hostilities, Saddam Hussein had boasted, relying on the fact that he had over 5,000 Russian-made armored tanks and half a million foot soldiers trained in desert warfare. He could not see how the US military could resist or beat him. He boasted that it would be the mother of all battles. He was expecting the US military to come from the front and predicted that he would beat them soundly. They remained silent and went on the table and mapped him out. They knew what he had and decided to use aerial bombardments to cripple his air force and cut off communication with foot soldiers. Within four hours of hostilities, 41,000 tons of explosives were dropped from the air which liquidated his air force and severed communication with the soldiers dug into the desert. For the next few weeks, there was no communication and no food for Iraqi frontline fighters. The US troop did not even bring one tank but continued its aerial bombardment. After a few weeks of waiting in the desert, Iraqi army finally surrendered and tactically, the war was over. They knew his strength but decided on the appropriate strategy.

THE ENEMY IS AFRAID OF YOU

The devil does not want to confront the church of Jesus Christ frontally because Jesus said, *"I will build my church, and the gates of hell shall not prevail,"* and He gave the church the authority of His name. We have the power and authority to deploy the name of Jesus. Praying in the name of Jesus means "I command this thing to be done"; it means presenting Jesus Christ and all He is worth. This calls heaven into action to do whatever is necessary. The devil does not want to face that frontal firepower, so he works through devices to cripple the church. You have to know that he is not developing new strategies, but he relies on the same old tricks. He successfully used his evil strategies to defeat anointed individuals in and outside the Bible. Beloved, please recall the sad end of the Bible account of Samson in the Book of Judges 15-16. He is a great example of an aborted great destiny and what you might call an 'Old Testament Deliverance Minister.' The enemy could not handle his anointing, so he went behind the scene to devise a strategy of defeat for Samson.

Just to give you a little understanding of why preparation, consecration, intimacy with God, and the principle of submission and endurance, is necessary; let us look at this account of Samson in the Book of Judges 16. Samson was a man with a prophetic destiny. Before his birth, there was a prophetic utterance. God wanted to give Israel a deliverer, not just a judge, and Samson would be it.

The devil does not want to confront the church of Jesus Christ frontally because Jesus said, "I will build my church and the gates of hell shall not prevail", and He gave the church the authority of His name.

Nazarites were special people who carried a vow of consecration. Samson had to undergo special consecration; he had to be a Nazarite. No razor would touch his head; he was not allowed to drink alcohol. Even his mother had to carry that consecration while conceived with him. The Philistines found Samson to be a spiritual enigma, a mystery they could not solve. They tried so hard to overpower him, but he often beat them silly. They even threatened his kin, the tribe of Judah to get to him. The Philistines threatened to kill them all if

Satan will try to stop your consecration because if your consecration kicks in, you can become unstoppable rendering him completely vulnerable.

they did not deliver Samson to them. They went to Samson to complain, and he allowed them to bind him and deliver him to them. The Philistines thought they had him, but that was not to be as he snapped into action and killed many of them. As an anointed person, you can be weak in the domestic aspect of your life, which can be a huge problem to your ability to function in the anointing. These flesh people came to bind Samson and hand him over to the enemy because they were afraid.

FEAR AND INTIMIDATION

The enemy works through fear and flesh to try to stop you from taking some measures that will put you spiritually on the top. He will try to stop your consecration because if your consecration kicks in, you can become unstoppable, and the enemy becomes completely vulnerable. As long as you want to continue to feed your flesh, God will permit you to experience defeat even though you are a champion. So they bound Samson and took him to the enemy. When the enemy came, the Spirit of God came mightily upon Samson. The word 'mightily' in the Scriptures means an anointing of might. It is a very important anointing that you will need as a deliverance minister. When the anointing of might rests upon you, it will be as if ten lions are inside of you. You can be in a long fast, and a Spirit of might is upon you, and you can go all night long. When it leaves you, you become a normal human being again. It is divine superiority. God can drop that anointing of might upon you to accomplish certain tasks. When you are engaged in a lot of stuff, ask God for an anointing of might.

Samson broke the rope, grabbed the jawbone of an ass and beat them silly, and then wrote a poem about it.

GRACE IS NOT VALIDATION FOR SIN

They could not stop him but wondered how to find his weakness. Someone found out that he loved women. Shortly after they found out that Samson was in town doing business with a prostitute. He carried the anointing to do business with a prostitute while the enemy waited outside to kill him, but the Lord was still with him. Do not mistake the grace of God to mean validation for sin! God's grace will stay with you even if you are messing up, but it does not validate your mess. The fact that God answers your prayers when in a mess does not mean that God is saying you can stay in your mess; rather He is trying to encourage you to come out clean. The Bible says, *His goodness leads us to repentance* (Romans 2:4). The more God shows you grace, the more you should go closer and ask Him to cleanse you.

Samson later learned that some Philistines had surrounded the place where he was. He uprooted the gate of the city and marched to the mountain and dropped it. His enemies ran away. They began again to strategize on how to overcome Samson, as everything they did to destroy him crumbled. They knew they needed a plan or a device and they found that device in the Book of Judges 16. What did the enemy spot? They found out that Samson was amorous in nature and had a taste for women. Not women in the kingdom but women in the enemy's territory. He was a very romantic guy. They spotted that and decided that they could work with that. Is it an evil thing for a man to be attracted to a woman? No. It is a natural thing that God placed there. But if you are going to work for any serious thing in the Kingdom, you have to understand boundaries. One of the things the enemy uses is emotional entanglement.

SEX TRAP

The Bible says that Samson fell in love with a stranger. Do not fall in love with a stranger. Falling in love is different from loving. When you fall in love, you lose your will, and you can be taken captive. How should Christians love? They may become attracted to someone, but when you get attracted to the opposite sex, which is a small

> *"Anyone that can be used to take the anointing from you is an enemy"*

portion of it, the next thing is, can you pursue this relationship and still honor God. If you cannot pursue this relationship to a logical conclusion and honor God every step of the way, that relationship is not good for you; so you withhold your will, exercise control over your will, and do not surrender your will. You will know when your will has been surrendered and enticed when, in spite of an atmosphere that dishonors God, you tolerate and stay with it.

One of the deadly games of Jezebel's witchcraft is to fight to get your will. There are two ways Jezebel will take one's will. One of which is through emotional enticement, delicacies, and appeals. It appeals to your emotions, and if you fall for it and open up, you are entangled and trapped. The other way is through intimidation. That is the witchcraft aspect of it. These persons bully you into submission. The most important thing you have as a human being is your will to choose or to surrender to God. Anything that takes your will, other than God, makes sure you cannot serve God.

The Philistines saw a weakness in Samson and built a strategy to entice him. They trapped him by flattery and emotional coloration and reconfiguration of his mind, so he lost his will. As you read along in the text, we see how the woman trapped him. Anyone that can be used to take the anointing from you is an enemy. He is an instrument of the devil. Consecration requires radicalism. You have to be violent against yourself and other people. Do not let your love for anybody be used by the enemy to take your anointing from you because that is all you have. If your anointing is taken away from you, you will become ordinary. If you do not want to be ordinary, fight to keep your anointing; fight against your emotions; fight against your lusts; fight against your desires, because the enemy will work through them.

After several episodes of seducing Samson, Delilah finally got him to give up the secret to his strength. She put him to sleep on her lap and shaved his head, and then she called the Philistines to take him. The Bible said, *"But the Philistines took him, and put out his eyes, and brought him down to Gaza, and bound him with fetters of brass; and he did grind in the prison-house"* (Judges 16:21). Samson's glory was removed. When the glory departed from him, his vision was the next to be removed. When his vision was removed from him, they bound him with fetters. See how the deliverer is taken captive, and imprisoned, and made to grind at the mill for the enemy. His destiny was truncated and replaced – his assignment was replaced.

VOW DISHONORED BRINGS REPROACH

Your hair will never be shaved off in the mighty name of the Lord Jesus. Your hair represents your vow of consecration. What did God give you as a vow of consecration? Every anointing has a vow of consecration. That is the first thing the enemy comes to steal. Anointing is not authority. If you have an anointing, you have the potential in evidence. It is different from authorization to proceed. Before God tells you to proceed, He will put you under mentorship to be trained. There are people who come into ministry to be trained and were given the pulpit, and they thought they had it but they still "smell" inside. They are a disaster waiting to happen and do not even know it.

> *When Samson's glory was removed from him, his vision was the next to be removed*

What happened here? Why did we have this disaster with Samson? He had a great prophetic destiny; he undoubtedly was anointed; set to shake everywhere, but he did not know that there was the other side. The anointing is potentiality in evidence, and because of the anointing, you have to be dealt with by God. There is a preparation that is required for you to proceed on your assignment.

THE DESERT SCHOOL EXPERIENCE

If God brings the material to prepare you and you are oblivious to it, you are likely to take it for granted, and that means trouble. There are people that God is giving revelations of how big they are going to be, but that is just potential. It is not a done deal. For you to get even near that, God will bring people in your life to strip you. So anywhere God puts you to serve, do not go there with the air of an anointed man or woman. Even when they are calling you pastor, sit down and learn a few things.

The deserts of your life are places of mentorship where God puts you.

Luke 1:80 says, *"And the child grew, and waxed strong in spirit, and was in the deserts till the day of his shewing unto Israel."* This verse is talking about John the Baptist. His potential and anointing were evident, but he did not jump right into ministry. He stayed in the deserts – notice the word 'deserts' is plural – until the day of his manifestation. The day of his manifestation is his destiny hour. He already has the anointing and the potential, but for him to be able to rise to that time and that occasion, he was placed in the deserts.

The deserts of your life are the places of mentorship where God puts you through character training. The desert is not a place for pleasure; it is a hard place. There are certain churches where God will ask you to serve, and the tough environment of those churches are what is required to process you and bring you up to date with God's design for your destiny. It is not a subject for your criticism and rebellion. If God finds a perfect church and puts you there, you will never become the person He wants you to be. He puts you in an imperfect environment with some imperfect people because of your "smell." Anointed? Yes, but you are smelling with some bad stuff. That environment will help God to deal with your stench. Ask God to show you your smell, and you will be embarrassed enough so that you will never be able to smell anything else around you anymore.

John the Baptist was in the desert until his showing to Israel so that in those desert places, God would begin to bring out all the issues in his life. He took Israel from Egypt and anointed them to go and inherit the Promised Land, but He put them in the desert so they could be groomed and changed. As you go along your anointed path, God turns a flashlight on you to see how much uncleanness you have inside of you. After forty years, Moses begged God to look for another man, but God said, "Now you are qualified." Forty years ago when you wanted to do it, you were not qualified, but now you are asking me to look for another man, but I am telling you that you are the man. This was forty years of getting in touch with the reality of seeing how wretched he was.

God's way of developing the Fruit of the Spirit in you is first to show you how rotten you are. When you try to use the natural ability that you have in the church, it feeds your sense of pride, and you think you are very holy. That is not the real holiness. The first holiness God will give to you is to let you fail and contradict yourself like Peter. When you fail miserably and are too ashamed to speak of it, God says, "That is what I have been telling you all the time. Come, let's deal with it quietly." Men and women who are dealt with do not have pride in their heads because when you see enough of your failure, it humbles you. In Luke 3, God brought John the Baptist out of hiding and placed him on the front line. He was ready.

What then was wrong with Samson? He had the anointing, but he had not been dealt with. When Israel came out of Egypt and was headed to the Holy Land, God asked that the men born in the wilderness be brought out and circumcised. God deals with His anointed servants to preserve them. There is a desert experience that the anointed servant must pass through.

BREAKTHROUGH PROPHETIC DELIVERANCE PRAYERS

1. Heavenly Father, promote me above every satanic strategy and help me to keep in steps with your Holy Spirit.

2. Lord strengthen me and help me to overcome Fleshly, Domestic, Social and Spiritual distractions.

3. Lord sharpen my vision. Empower me to see what I can be and do to make a difference in my Family, Church, Nation and Generation. Help me to live for a cause greater and bigger than myself in the mighty name of Jesus.

4. Probe deep into my character and strip me of every self-imploding tendencies that satan has programmed into my life.

CHAPTER 22

The Deliverance Minister

A Deliverance minister is a man or woman who may be used by God in the ministry of deliverance. There are individuals raised by God who move in the deliverance anointing more particularly than others. Any person who is anointed with the Holy Spirit will, at some time or the other, have to confront evil and can only deal with it by the authority of the name of Jesus and the power of the Holy Spirit. Seeing we are at the end of the end, there is an escalation in the manifestation of evil. But thank God that where sin abounds, grace abounds much more (Romans 5:20). God has raised many people who now consider themselves more particularly trained and commissioned to handle deliverance.

Of course, when you look at the operational definition of deliverance which we covered earlier, we will readily know that every person who is a minister of the gospel is also anointed automatically to be a deliverance minister because you are turning people from darkness to light – from the power of Satan unto the living God. That makes you a deliverance minister of some sort.

I remember my first encounter with casting out a devil: It was not planned, and I was just a few months old in the faith. One of my friends and I had scheduled with a sister to minister the Baptism of the Holy Spirit to her. I had it in my heart that we were to fast, but we did not. Later that evening we met the sister to conduct the session. As we began to pray, suddenly she slumped and started to wriggle like a snake and foamed at the mouth. We recognized that it was a demonic manifestation, but we did not know how demons should leave. We just started saying, "Go, in the name of Jesus!"

For a long time, nothing seemed to be happening. She continued writhing and foaming at the mouth. We were a little concerned, fearful, and in doubt. I called the brother aside and reminded him that we were to have fasted but did not. I also reminded him that the Bible said that this kind does not go except by prayer and fasting. Essentially, we were talking doubt and talking ourselves out of the situation. We forgot about the Sovereign Lord who is so kind. The demons started calling on Lucifer for help. That shot us back into action. How dare you? God the Father, God the Son, and God the Holy Ghost is here, and you are calling for Lucifer? We began to command the demons to come out of the sister in the name of

Jesus. She was finally delivered. That was my first accidental encounter with deliverance ministry. I was not prepared, largely ignorant, did not know what to do, but I still had the name of Jesus.

God wants to raise people and train them specially and specifically. He wants to give them the skill and the knowledge to handle the special nature of this kind of ministry called deliverance. The Book of Isaiah 60 and 61 give us a clear perspective:

> *Arise, shine; for thy light is come, and the glory of the LORD is risen upon thee. For, behold, the darkness shall cover the earth, and gross darkness the people: but the LORD shall arise upon thee, and his glory shall be seen upon thee. And the Gentiles shall come to thy light, and kings to the brightness of thy rising* (Isaiah 60:1-3).

Here the Scripture is predicting that at a time of gross darkness covering the people, the light of the glory of God will rise on you and me. The Gentiles will be able to see the light and come to light to get some help. You are here for a time like this because, on account of you being on the earth, some people will get some help. In this dark hour, as I said earlier, God is raising people, specially trained to engage in this aspect of the ministry called deliverance.

It is sometimes controversial because people do not always understand the issues involved and will wonder how we can be casting out demons from believers. We have dealt with this in the earlier chapters, but I will say this again: Believers are the only people that we can cast demons from because we really cannot cast demons out of unbelievers. The whole realm of spiritual warfare, however, goes beyond deliverance (casting out of demons). It is dealing with the powers of darkness that want to engage, cripple, and demobilize the church.

THE ANOINTING OF THE DELIVERANCE MINISTER

The Spirit of the Lord GOD is upon me; because the LORD hath anointed me to preach good tidings unto the meek; he hath sent me to bind up the brokenhearted, to proclaim liberty to the captives, and the opening of the prison to them that are bound; To proclaim the acceptable year of the LORD, and the day of vengeance of our God; to comfort all that mourn; To appoint unto them that mourn in Zion, to give unto them beauty for ashes, the oil of joy for mourning, the garment of praise for the spirit of heaviness; that they might be called trees of righteousness, the planting of the LORD, that he might be glorified. - Isaiah 61:1-3

This is the anointing of the deliverance minister and part of the work we have to do. This Messianic Scripture declared by

Prophet Isaiah was claimed by the Lord Jesus Christ in the Book of Luke 4:18-21. He connected with it and claimed it, and even more importantly, He manifested it.

> "... the Holy Spirit is the only power that can dislodge and cast out devils."

From where does the deliverance minister derive his authority?

From the above Scriptures, you find Jesus pointing out that He derived His authority from the Word of God (from the Messianic Scripture) – the things that were written, which the Messiah would fulfill. He did not only claim it; He manifested it. In the Book of Acts 10:38, we see *Jesus Christ, the Son of God, anointed with the Holy Ghost and with power, going about healing all that were oppressed of the devil, and God the Father being with Him.* Jesus did not only claim the authority of the Messianic Scriptures describing His work; He actually went ahead to do and fulfill it. The Book of 1 John 3:38 declares that Christ was revealed to destroy the works of the devil. How did He do that? He did so by casting out devils through the anointing of the Holy Spirit.

Let us look at a place in the Scriptures where there was controversy over the ministry of Jesus in this regard: People castigated the ministry of Jesus. There were many things that Jesus did that they did not criticize, but they particularly castigated and criticized the deliverance aspect of His ministry. The Pharisees accused Jesus of using the spirit of Beelzebub to cast out devils (Matthew 12:24-31). However, the Holy Spirit is the only power that can dislodge and cast out devils. Nobody can cast out devils except by the power of the Holy Spirit. This is the anointing that Jesus claimed He functioned under as noted from the Scriptures before He did anything at all, He claimed the anointing of Isaiah 61:1-3. When the authenticity of His work was challenged, He gave a lengthy explanation by referring to the authority of the Holy Spirit. It is the anointing that destroys yokes (Isaiah 10:27).

Deliverance ministry is today one that is still under great controversy and misunderstanding. One of the reasons for this is that the devil hates his business being exposed, so he furiously attacks this ministry.

Clearly, there are two kingdoms in conflict – light against darkness. The Kingdom of light is superior to the kingdom of darkness. Anyone who will minister in this Kingdom of light will have to function under the same power that Jesus functioned under – under the authority and mandate of Jesus Christ. It is important for us to know that the power in charge of Deliverance is the Lord through His Spirit (the Holy Spirit). Jesus claimed the authority and the anointing of the Holy Spirit for His mandate against the devil, and this same Jesus is sending you and me. In the Book of John 20:21, Jesus said to

His disciples, *"Peace."* In other words, *"Shalom"* – Nothing is broken, nothing is missing, and everything is in order. He said, *"As my Father has sent me, so send I you."* How did the Father send Jesus? He sent Him with Divine Authority.

The Apostle Paul testified about his experience and how the Lord encountered him. He testified how Jesus said to him, *"for I have appeared unto thee for this purpose, to make thee a minister and a witness both of these things which thou hast seen, and of those things in which I will appear unto thee"* (Acts 26:16). From the Scripture, a minister is one who serves while a witness is one who produces proof of that which he is witnessing.

What kind of proof are you producing? Are you producing proof that Jesus is who He says He is – the Son of God who died and shed His Blood for the redemption of our sins and is alive right now? Can you prove it? The only way you can prove it is through the power of the Holy Spirit. Paul further testified how Jesus told him that he would *"…open their eyes, and to turn them from darkness to light, and from the power of Satan unto God, that they may receive forgiveness of sins, and inheritance among them which are sanctified by faith that is in me"* (verse 18).

Your duty is to open the eyes of people who are blinded to the activities of the enemy destroying them. This he does to keep them oblivious of his wicked activities, but you have been sent to open their eyes. Do you think the devil will not resist you if you mean business? Can you do this kind of work by just preaching and teaching the Word of God? No. You need power, and that power will not come in the place of eating and telephone gossip. It will come through prayer, fasting, and through consecration.

THE PLACE OF THE HOLY SPIRIT

The anointing of the deliverance minister is the same Spirit that rested upon Jesus Christ the Son of the Living God; the same Spirit that brought Him out of the grave. The deliverance minister, therefore, is one who is a believer called alongside Jesus by God and given the power of the Holy Spirit to confront evil and set people free. He is empowered to turn them from darkness to light; to open their eyes, and to cut off the power of Satan. It takes power to confront that power. You are mandated and authorized by God to go ahead and confront the enemy without fear. Are you willing?

When we examine the Book of Mark 16:15-20, we see that the anointing of the deliverance minister is the preaching of the gospel, the Great Commission. It is not merely to cast out devils, but to preach the gospel and bring the benefits of the gospel, which includes freedom from sin, freedom from the power of the devil, freedom from the agents of Satan, and freedom from all entanglements with the pollutions of this world. Just by being a believer in Christ Jesus, you become a deliverance minister. Jesus told His disciples *"you shall receive power after the Holy Spirit comes upon you; and, you shall become my witnesses in Jerusalem, Judea, in Samaria and to the uttermost parts of the earth"* (Acts 1:6-8). He promised them the empowerment of the Holy Spirit.

Once you receive this empowerment that comes through the Holy Spirit, you are already on the battle line. Jesus clearly said that if we believe in Him, obey Him and do His works, then the works that He did we shall also do, and greater works we shall do, including waging war on the enemy, because He goes to the Father (John 14:12).

 THE POWER AND PRESENCE OF THE HOLY SPIRIT

I want us to examine a few Scriptures and break them down. Let us take another look at Isaiah 61 – the Messianic Scripture in the Old Covenant referring to Jesus said, *"The Spirit of the Lord God is upon me."* Why will the Spirit of God come upon you? Because you have been anointed or mandated or separated with responsibility. Let us look at the example of Jesus when the Spirit came upon Him from the accounts in the Books of Matthew and Mark:

And Jesus, when he was baptized, went up straightway out of the water: and, lo, the heavens were opened unto him, and he saw the Spirit of God descending like a dove, and lighting upon him: And lo a voice from heaven, saying, This is my beloved Son, in whom I am well pleased (Matthew 3:16-17).

And straightway coming up out of the water, he saw the heavens opened, and the Spirit like a dove descending upon him: And there came a voice from heaven, saying, Thou art my beloved Son, in whom I am well pleased. And immediately the spirit driveth him into the wilderness (Mark 1:12).

Where there is no prey, the lion will not be running. A lion that is well fed will not be running after food. The church is like a well-fed lion that is sleeping. Once there is prey, the lion will rise to the occasion. You never see your real self until there is real trouble – then the real self-comes up. Straight away, the Spirit drove Jesus into the wilderness to have a confrontation. When the Spirit comes upon you, God stops hiding you from the devil and exposes you to the devil. The preparation of a deliverance minister begins when God exposes you to evil to get you ready. God will never send a naive man or woman to confront the devil, and before you are mandated, you have to have a confrontation.

When God said, *"This is my beloved Son,"* He was introducing Jesus to the devil. Verse thirteen of the Book of Mark 1 tells us that Jesus was in the wilderness for forty days, tempted by Satan and was with the wild beasts and that the angels of God ministered unto Him.

THE CHURCH NEEDS THIS POWER

The church that is running from the devil and the wild beast will sit comfortably in the cathedral listening to nice music and hymns, rocking themselves to sleep and cannot be a threat to the devil in this generation. Such a church cannot produce fire or flame and cannot produce miracles. Members there will mostly be in church gossiping, fighting each other, quarreling over the color of the chairs and the carpets and who should sit in the front and the back. They are no threat to the enemy. Once in a while, they speak out about the gay movement, but they have no power. Beloved, God wants to move us past this level.

The presence of the Holy Spirit does not automatically translate into power, and that is where many Christians who have been filled and baptized with the Holy Ghost for over twenty years have remained.

How do you transit from the presence of the Spirit to the power? Let us go back to the Book of Acts 10:38. *Jesus Christ of Nazareth was anointed with the Holy Ghost and with power.* You can have the Holy Ghost and not have power. The presence of the Holy Spirit does not automatically translate into power, and that is where many Christians who have been filled and baptized with the Holy Ghost for over twenty years have remained. The Holy Spirit is not the same as the power of the Holy Spirit. Jesus had the two – **He was anointed with the Holy Ghost and with power.** Once you have these two in place, there is no need to sit down anymore which is why Jesus went about doing good. Why? Because the lion is stirred up, and now, he must seek the prey. How do you transit from being a prey to the devil to becoming a predator of him? Move from the presence to the power. THAT TAKES PROCESSING, PREPARATION, GOD TAKING YOU THROUGH SOME EMOTIONAL SLAUGHTER AND BRINGING YOU TO A PLACE OF STURDINESS IN THE HOLY GHOST. Jesus went about confronting and healing all who were oppressed by the devil. Wherever He went, the Father went with Him.

The presence of the Holy Spirit within you will bring you comfort, but the power of the Holy Spirit in you will bring changes to people's condition. The presence of the Holy Spirit is the ministry of the Holy Spirit to you, but the power of the Holy Spirit is the ministry of the Spirit through you. To move from the presence to the power requires consecration. Romans 12:1-2, *"I beseech you by the mercies of God to present your bodies a living sacrifice..."*

BREAKTHROUGH PROPHETIC DELIVERANCE PRAYERS

1. Spiritual and Physical projections, Torments and Vexation against My Anointing, Life, Family and Church; wither, be destroyed and die off in the mighty name of the Lord Jesus Christ.

2. Every Ministerial Head hunter and Associates against my life, Ministry, Destiny, and Family, be liquidated, scattered, shamed and disgraced in the Mighty Name of JESUS CHRIST whose I am and whom I serve.

3. Oh God remember where I am and raise up intercessors and prophetic helping hands for my destiny where i am in the mighty name of the Lord Jesus Christ!

4. Oh God deliver me from the sleep of death, disappoint the evil expectation of the wicked and release my destiny to shine for you in the name of Jesus Christ!

5. Father of lights, let the light of your glory in the face of Jesus Christ shine in every prison of my life right now (physical health, emotional, mental, marital, financial, career and ministerial shackles...be shattered in the name of Jesus).

CHAPTER 23

The Deliverance Team

The deliverance team is a body of people who have been called out by the Lord to do warfare in the area of deliverance and spiritual warfare. They are those who have sensed a calling and have the commitment and dedication to serving the church of the living God in the ministry of Deliverance. They are spiritual gatekeepers and gate invaders. They keep the gates of the church and invade the gates of hell. They stand in a consecrated commitment to do the work of the deliverance ministry. These are the kinds of people who constitute a deliverance team.

Let us look at deliverance teams in their different types. Broadly speaking, I will categorize those working in deliverance ministry in three areas:

THE LOCAL CHURCH TEAM

There are Charismatic/Pentecostal churches that understand that warfare or deliverance requires some skills, training, and proficiencies and that not everyone can truly function in that capacity. What they do is put together a team of warriors within the local Church who will make up the deliverance or spiritual warfare team. They can then be given some level of training and authorized to function under the pastoral authority of the Church. These individuals can be made to stand in the gap and handle the deliverance needs of the local Church under Pastoral supervision. They are also prayer warriors, standing as spiritual warfare counselors. They understand spiritual territories and can appreciate the delicate nature of human beings at various levels of brokenness. They are trained to properly discern and tackle demonic oppression and spiritual violence occurring in the lives of congregants who require a specialized type of help. The Bible says in Isaiah 28:5-6, *"in that day the Lord shall be for strength to them that turn the battle to the gates."* They are trained spiritual warriors under a local mandate who understand spiritual protocol and submission to spiritual authority. This is the most effective way to handle spiritual warfare and deliverance business in a local Church setting.

THE PARACHURCH DELIVERANCE MINISTRY TEAM

This is a higher level of deliverance team. The parachurch ministry is a ministry that services several churches in a given territory. It is usually led by an anointed, mandated man/woman raised by God and authorized by the Holy Spirit to function in the ministry of deliverance and spiritual warfare. The ministry can also be led by a group of trained generals who are led by God to submit to one another under a corporate mandate. Where there is a ministry like this, it serves as a spiritual clinic or hospital for the local Body of Christ in that region and beyond. They provide insights, detailed help, an enabling environment for the ministry of deliverance and spiritual warfare, and they can also provide training to the Body of Christ at large. They are specialists, generals, called to this aspect of ministry to service the Body of Christ.

Sometimes, though, there may be controversies because of their emphasis in this area of ministry. Also, they are easily criticized by prideful, ignorant church leaders as unbalanced and might even be accused of preaching another gospel, but this is not the case. However, at other times there are persons called into this area of ministry who have not been properly mentored and tutored, and as a result, they over-emphasize the power of the enemy and neutralize the faith of God's people. It does not mean that they are deliberately injurious, but it just means that they need help to be more accurate.

People are called, anointed, and raised by God in this way to service the Body of Christ, and they should be properly appreciated, supported, and held to proper accountability. The devil takes delight in hitting ministries in this area with scandals, but if they are accountable to the leadership of the larger Body of Christ, then the larger body can provide safety, build integrity, and give the necessary support. These are the kinds of ministries the devil wants to attack and discredit so that their ability to help the Body of Christ will be undermined.

CHARACTERS OF AN EFFECTIVE DELIVERANCE TEAM

1. All members must be truly saved – born again. People can be attracted to the anointing and request to be a part of the team. They must be truly born again and be true disciples of Jesus Christ, ready to follow and continue in the Word of Life.

2. All members must love the Lord completely. Their love for the Lord must be the overriding theme in their lives. To love the Lord means that you have to allow the Lord to love you and bring you past yourself.

3. All members must be people who do not prosecute hidden personal agendas. To be in a deliverance team, you must

be someone who has an abhorrence for sin. You must be prepared not to breast feed sin in your life. They should not have any hidden plan or idea to promote themselves or their personal agendas. They should not even come to the deliverance team because you hate the devil. They must come because they are called to it and because they have submitted to the Lord totally.

4. All members must be completely yielded to God and available to be used in the ministry of deliverance for spiritual warfare.

5. All members must receive at the least the basic training in deliverance, counseling, and spiritual warfare. If they do not, how can they handle human beings? They will mismanage people and cause destruction.

6. All members must understand and appreciate the flow of authority and chain of command, and be prepared to be submitted to one another in the fear of the Lord. They must have a clear idea of who is in leadership and have an appreciation for it. This will eliminate self-seeking. Ultimately, everybody, including the leader, out of reverence must appreciate and submit to one another.

7. All members must have love for the sinner and the oppressed. That love must at least match the devil's desire

to destroy them. This love must be genuine, holy, and pure. They must love people and desire to help them. *"And others save with fear, pulling them out of the fire; hating even the garment spotted by the flesh"* (Jude 23).

8. All members must have discernment. No matter how you love people, if they are not yielded to God, ultimately, you cannot help them. Team members should not allow their love for any person they are trying to help become emotional because the devil will use the person to attack them. Discernment ensures that their love for people do not cause them to be manipulated during the deliverance process but to know when to stop when this begins to happen and wherever necessary.

MAINTAINING A SUCCESSFUL DELIVERANCE TEAM

There are some things that will enhance your success with a deliverance team or in the ministry of deliverance.

1. Know the God you serve very well and how to relate to Him:

The Bible says, *"...but the people that do know their God shall be strong and do exploits"* (Daniel 22:32). What does God require of you and me? Love and submission – that is all. He will not use us and discard us. He wants us to be safe while He is using us, so we need to love Him and submit to Him.

2. Know yourself:

Know who you are in Christ Jesus. Your personal identity comes into everything. The reason Jesus succeeded was that He knew who He was and had a clear picture of His identity and was thus never vulnerable to the devil. If you do not know who you are, you will have a crisis while trying to minister to other people. When the devil came to Jesus after He had completed forty days of fasting, what the devil was doing, in essence, was to make Jesus question His identity – *"IF THOU BE the Son of God..."* (Matthew 4:3-6). If Jesus had to prove who He is, then that would mean He was in doubt of who He is. This is so important. Throughout your life, as you do things, you will be challenged by circumstances, by your environment, by the dynamics of ministry always to prove something. If you are trying to prove stuff, you have moved away from where you are or from your subject line. Be confident about who you are in Christ Jesus. You are holy, unblameable, and unreproveable in the sight of God (Colossians 1:22). Anytime you do not see yourself like that; you are having an identity crisis which empowers the devil to assault you.

3. Know your enemy:

This is a crucial point. That is why training is important because if you do not know your enemy, you become vulnerable through ignorance. *"Lest Satan should get an advantage of us: for we are not ignorant of his devices"* (2

Corinthians 2:11). Satan has devices or strategies, and we are not to be ignorant of them. This is the reason every member of the deliverance team has to be trained. Ignorance is destructive and gives the devil an advantage over the deliverance minister. Relate with the devil only through your authority that you have been given by the Lord Jesus Christ. Never relate with the devil through fear, through doubting your identity, or through doubting God's love for you. All of these things will cripple you and make you unable to function. Relating to the devil through your God-given authority makes him inferior to you (Luke 10:19).

BREAKTHROUGH PROPHETIC DELIVERANCE PRAYERS

1. Lord God of glory, in the mighty name of Jesus Christ, we set up our banners on the earth today and always. Help us to raise an army of men and women who are trained and skillful in Deliverance ministry and warfare

2. I Pray Lord for the reader here that together we will all be relevant members of God's glorious end-time Army of spiritual warriors.

3. Let the cry of the blood of Jesus for my life and destiny come before you right now. Look down and be angry at my spiritual, emotional, career, mental, marital, financial,

and ministerial imprisonment today, right now!!!

4. Oh my God, prepare me in a hurry and release the angels of my release into the place of the next level blessing.

5. Thou iron gates that leads to my city what are you still standing there for? Your time has expired; move, swing open. Angels of god in my destiny escort me out into the next level blessing! My portion today is songs of deliverance.

CHAPTER 24

How to Answer The Call to Deliverance Ministry

There are individuals who may sense a call to this area of ministry. They may have a level of anointing and are at a certain place within the call of God. These individuals are viable but most vulnerable. If you sense that God is calling you into deliverance work, you must define who you are accountable to. Get under some authority but go ahead, grow in your anointing and fulfill the call of God. You will be opposed, and fire will test you, and directly by God Himself. The enemy will tempt you with different vices such as lust, pride, to seduce you. You have to know where you are in ministry and find a godly example that you can submit to and be accountable to for your good.

I think the issue of submission and accountability to authority cannot be overemphasized for any ministerial calling. We are in a war, and that means you need a winning strategy, and a part of this strategy is submission and accountability.

The Call, Stages, and Levels of Responses.

And that servant, which knew his lord's will, and prepared not himself, neither did according to his will, shall be beaten with many stripes. But he that knew not, and did commit things worthy of stripes, shall be beaten with few stripes. For unto whomsoever much is given, of him shall be much required: and to whom men have committed much, of him they will ask the more
Luke 12:47-48.

Whatever you feel called to do, particularly if you sense an anointing for deliverance, you need to understand where you are in the call of God and how to appropriately seek avenues of support, training, mentoring, submission, accountability, integrity, credibility, and effectiveness. I want you to notice the stages in ministry in the above passage of Scripture.

Knowledge
"And that servant, which knew his Lord's will…"

The first stage of the call is knowledge. You know something is beckoning to you either by revelation, prophecy, dream, encounters, laying on of hands or by the pull or prompting of the Holy Spirit. You begin to sense something. Knowing is the first stage, but it does not mean that you are immediately ready to do what you know. At the age of twelve, Jesus knew. He was found in the temple when he went to Jerusalem with his parents and went missing as they were returning home. It took three days to find him, and they found him in the temple disputing with the doctors of the law, both questioning and answering questions. His parents said, "Wow, child, why have you treated us this way?" He replied, "Don't you know I must be about my father's business?" (Luke 2:41-52). At just the age of twelve, He knew His calling and ministry He was called and committed to the business, which is the Father's ministry. He had started studying to the extent that he was proficient in answering questions, but he was not ready, and would not be ready for another eighteen years. Then at the age of thirty, He went into Baptism, entered into forty days of fasting, and was then ready to do ministry. The Bible concludes that His fame spread abroad among the people.

Preparation
"...and prepared not himself..."

The second stage is that of preparing to do what you know you are called to do. I will also call this the training period. This process also corresponds with the stages of the divine call.

The first stage of the divine call is general works or good works. As you move from good works, you go to what the Bible calls in Philippians 3:12-14, the high calling of God. The high call is your purpose; general or good works is for everybody who is born again. Some may say, "I do not know my ministry." You can start by doing any work that is assigned to you. Anything your hands find to do in the house of God, do it. That is general or good works and is acceptable to God. The Bible encourages us to do it with all our heart. *"For we are his workmanship, created in Christ Jesus unto good works, which God hath before ordained that we should walk in them"* (Ephesians 2:10).

First, there is knowledge of the master's will. Then, because you are not yet immediately capable or available to carry out what you know, you are not ready. Jesus knew that at twelve years old He was not ready. The Bible says of John the Baptist, *"And the child grew, and waxed strong in spirit, and was in the deserts till the day of his shewing unto Israel"* (Luke 1:80). What was he doing in the desert? He was undergoing desert training in the training schools in the desert. Therefore, the second stage in the divine call is training. There are two levels of training.

Theoretical level of training: This may involve you reading books, buying materials and studying them, or going to a Bible college or some training program in your area of calling. It is important. The Bible says "Study to shew thyself approved unto God, a workman that need not be ashamed, rightly dividing the word of truth." You study to be knowledgeable about your subject. Anointing on a knowledgeable mind is good. It brings refinement and confidence.

Character level of training: God does not work merely by your level of head knowledge. God chooses His servants on the basis of character. He puts you on the burner, and you begin to go against stuff you never knew. You may at times feel afflicted and scandalized. He is processing you. He does not protect you from the devil; He exposes you to the hostilities of the heavenlies. Sometimes you beat the devil silly and other times he beats you silly, but in all, you learn.

When God took the children of Israel out of Egypt, their destination was the Promised Land, but He walked them through the wilderness. He was training them and imparting to them the character that would enable them to possess the Promised Land. It is so important that you, who sense the call and anointing of God. Understand that anointing is not authorization. **Anointing means potentiality in evidence.** You can do certain things, preach a certain way, and everyone can see that you have a call. But that is not authorization. It is not a mandate. Authorization will come when God has burned His nature into you. God will refine you, bring out the best and the worst and separate them, and then mandate you. There is a further place in anointing where you are authorized and mandated by God. This happens when He moves you into the third phase of your ministry.

Fulfilling Purpose

"...For unto whomsoever much is given, of him shall be much required: and to whom men have committed much, of him they will ask the more.
Ye men of Israel, hear these words; Jesus of Nazareth, a man approved of God among you by miracles and wonders and signs, which God did by him in the midst of you, as ye yourselves also know."
- Acts 2:22

The third stage is when God approves of you and can publicly associate Himself with you. God may not be able to stake His reputation on us if our character has not been proven. You get to discover His purpose at the second stage and are admitted into the divine processing and character refinement.

Paul said, *"I have not reached maturity, but I want to get hold of the reason why Christ Jesus got hold of me."* That was his purpose. He further said, *"...forgetting those things which are behind, and reaching forth unto those things which are before me ..."* (Philippians 3:12-14).

What is the gateway to get into your purpose? Forget about the past successes and failures. There is a present emphasis of God now. Find it. What did Paul propose to do? He said, "I will press towards the prize," the bull's eye, the trophy of the high calling of God in Christ Jesus. There is a high call, and in that high call is a target point, the trophy. You are trying to get the trophy. That is what you will be giving to God. If you do not fulfill your original purpose, you have no trophy to offer the Lord. When you get into your high calling, you enjoy what you are doing. You feel in the right place, doing what you are called to do. Everything about you flows with it your make-up, your character, who you are, everything flows together. It is what He designed you for.

When you have an anointing of deliverance moving in you, it is important to identify where you are in this call. A knowledge of what stage you are in will help you to get the appropriate help. One of the hardest lessons of an anointed man or woman is to understand the necessity of identifying your divine placement and submitting to authority. The authority under which God wants to train you may have many weaknesses, and you will get to see them. However, that is where your training is, and God is not interested in those things. He is interested in killing 'you.' He is choosing the best environment to take you out of yourself because if you are not dead, you cannot survive the battle.

People do not understand that, maybe because we do not instruct on spiritual soldiering, so people come to church and are filled with religious pride and criticize everything. Most often anointed people come into church trying to fix problems, but they are the problem. The best problem you can fix is yourself. Submit yourself unto God appropriately, intelligently. That is what the Bible says: *"I beseech you, therefore, brethren, by the mercies of God, that ye present your bodies a living sacrifice, holy, acceptable unto God, which is your reasonable service"* (Romans 12:1). It is a sacrifice, which means it will not be easy. So do not be discouraged, address it.

You need to urgently find what stage you are in in the call so that you can determine what kind of help and levels of submission and training you will need. The Holy Spirit will choose for you appropriate mentors to disciple you, grow your gift, and release you.

BREAKTHROUGH PROPHETIC DELIVERANCE PRAYERS

Ephesians 1:17 - 23 That the God of our Lord Jesus Christ, the Father of glory, may give unto you the spirit of wisdom and revelation in the knowledge of him: The eyes of your understanding being enlightened; that ye may know what is the hope of his calling, and what the riches of the glory of his inheritance in the saints, And what is the exceeding greatness of his power to us-ward who believe, according to the working of his mighty power, which he wrought in Christ, when he raised him from the dead, and set him at his own right hand in the heavenly places, Far above all principality, and power, and might, and dominion, and every name that is named, not only in this world, but also in that which is to come: and hath put all things under his feet, and gave him to be the head over all things to the church, Which is his body, the fulness of him that filleth all in all.

1. Lord of glory, I desire to know you with a deep revelation knowledge of your investments and full inheritance in me. Beam your light on my spirit; brighten and awaken the understanding of my mind.

2. I want to know your power intimately and in that knowledge be filled with all boldness to arise and fulfill my destiny. I embrace my destiny and full potential capabilities in Christ Jesus.

3. Help me to appreciate and make room for mentors and destiny helpers You position in my path and to thrive in conditions and circumstances you pre-arranged to fit me for my purpose in destiny

4. I receive grace to know and fulfill my high Call in Christ Jesus. Thank you, Lord and all glory and honor to your name.

CHAPTER 25

Some Deliverance Terms Explained

Covenant

The word covenant is foundational to Christianity and most religions. Covenant presupposes a need for a coming together of two or more parties to form a binding relationship (with mutual obligations and privileges) in order to, more effectively, reach a common goal. A covenant between God and man empowers man to draw upon the unlimited resources of the Almighty God who has all the power but still needs a man on the earth to do His business. When a man comes into such a covenant with God, that covenanted man enjoys benefits of all the resources and the power of God while serving the purpose of God on the earth.

"He is central and the superior claims of the Blood of Jesus will break the curse of any type of satanic covenant"

There are different levels of the covenant but the highest form of covenant is Blood Covenant because blood is life and is unchanging. The whole Bible is a revelation of two covenants, namely the first covenant which was between Jehovah God and Israel, and the new covenant that God has made with all mankind through the Lord Jesus. The Bible calls it the everlasting covenant (Hebrews 13:20).

God cannot deliver people without a covenant. It is His covenant that causes him to act on behalf of believers. He said, "When I see the blood, I will pass over you. I will cover you". Now the enemy perverts the righteous ways of the Lord, so he also seeks to enter into covenants with people, families, and nations, and based upon that covenant, he expects to receive worship and bring the benefit of his evil power for the temporary use of people entering those covenants with him. Remember, however, the devil's original aim is to kill, steal, and destroy. His covenant is not to give but to take. What we find in deliverance is that on the basis of even forgotten covenants the devil had with the ancestors of a particular person or individual family that is not known to the children, or that the children are not willing to carry on because they are now Christians, he seeks to enforce the terms of those covenants bringing curses and destruction. These are the things we locate in deliverance and through the application of the blood of Jesus Christ the curse can be broken and the oppressed is set at liberty.

SOME DELIVERANCE TERMS EXPLAINED

God had warned His children not to enter into those evil covenants and that the effect of it can last four generations. However, there is the Blood of Jesus. The Bible says, *"Neither by the blood of goats and calves, but by his own blood, He entered in once into the holy place, having obtained eternal redemption for us"* (Hebrew 9:12). The Blood of Jesus is eternal in scope. He is the Lamb slain from the foundation of the earth. The Blood of Jesus dates back and forth in history; before Calvary, all of history was looking forward to Jesus. After Calvary, all history dates back to Jesus. He is central and the superior claims of the Blood of Jesus will break the curse of any type of satanic covenant.

Curses

Curses refer to an expression of ill will by a superior power. Curses occur when somebody who has a higher authority is displeased and opens his or her mouth in a violent expression of an ill will to another. Again, curses have sources and reasons. *"As the bird by wandering, as the swallow by flying, so the curse causeless shall not come"* (Proverbs 26:2). A curse can come from God through the broken laws of the Almighty God. The Book of Deuteronomy 28 outlines certain blessings and curses that are consequent upon obedience and disobedience respectively. However, Jesus came to redeem us from every curse. The Bible has this to say: *"Christ hath redeemed us from the curse of the law, being made a curse for us: for it is written, Cursed is every one that hangeth on a tree: That the blessing of Abraham might come on the Gentiles through Jesus Christ; that we might receive the promise of the Spirit through faith"* (Galatians 3:13-14). Jesus has paid the price for us to be free from all curses due to our disobedience to the Almighty God.

Another source of curses could be the devil. When his covenants are violated, the consequence of that violation is a curse. There are demonic debt collectors that come to afflict, destroy, kill, and sometimes steal people's opportunities, or strike them with mental illness. These are things we apply the Blood to in order to set people free. The Bible has given us a way out of curses. It is the Blood of the Lord Jesus Christ. The Bible further says that all handwritings of ordinances that were working against us, Jesus has blotted out by His blood, taken it out of the way and nailed it to His cross (Colossians 1:14-20). Our debt has been paid; therefore Satan can only try to collect from people illegally. This is why the power of the Holy Spirit anoints men and women to break the curse.

There also can be other hidden sources of curses. For instance, curses through an improper relationship with your parents. The Bible says we are to honor our father and our mother, which is the first commandment with a promise (Ephesians 6:1-3). If you are a child and you defy your father and mother, you are incurring curses. Improper relationships with parental or other authority can be a source of devastating curses.

Improper conduct during your work when you cheat your employer while you still collect your salary can incur a curse. Another source is bad relationships: When a relationship is broken, for example, and one of the parties feels violated, cheated and bitter if the bitter person expresses ill will towards the one that walked away, it can bring a curse. There are hidden curses in the Bible that men do not know and they fall short and incur negative results. During the battle for the land of Canaan and conquest of Jericho, Joshua placed a curse on whoever would rebuild the city.

And Joshua adjured them at that time, saying, *"Cursed be the man before the LORD, that riseth up and buildeth this city Jericho: he shall lay the foundation thereof in his firstborn, and in his youngest son shall he set up the gates of it"* (Joshua 6:26).

Five hundred years down the line, a man called Hiel (1 Kings 16:34) not knowing there was such a curse, rebuilt the city and as he laid the foundation, his firstborn died and as he set up the gates, his last born died. Curses can last a long time but thank God, the Blood of Jesus breaks every curse.

Spiritual Marks

The concept of spiritual marks in the Bible was started by God when He judged Cain in the Book of Genesis 4. Cain complained that his punishment was heavy because he would be a vagabond and a fugitive and anybody could slay him. God then placed a mark of protection on Cain so that anybody who slew him would bear the consequences of killing him. This was actually a mark of protection on him. The Lord repeats this again in Ezekiel 9:4. He mandates the angel to set a mark of protection on those praying for the sins of the City and thereafter released the Angel of Judgment to go through the City and slay those without the mark. Finally, in the New Testament believers in the Lord Jesus Christ are sealed with Holy Spirit of promise:

"In whom ye also trusted, after that ye heard the word of truth, the gospel of your salvation: in whom also after that ye believed, ye were sealed with that Holy Spirit of promise, (And grieve not the Holy Spirit of God, whereby ye are sealed unto the day of redemption) (Ephesians 1:13, 4:30).

In the coming Tribulation, God will place a seal (mark of protection) on Jewish remnant before judgment falls (Revelation 7:3-8).

On the other hand, the devil who has no originals but merely copies and then perverts the right ways of the Lord puts marks of destruction upon people. When he places a spiritual mark on someone, that person is actually identified spiritually to witches and other satanic agents for persecution. Wherever the person goes about their normal life, he or she will be identified

SOME DELIVERANCE TERMS EXPLAINED

through that mark and the agents of the devil will begin to persecute and waste the person's life. This can be very terrible, especially if the person does not know that he or she carries such evil mark. This is a sign of satanic curse for non-performance, affliction, and subjugation so that anywhere the person goes that mark will begin to cause disfavor. Thank God, again, the Blood of Jesus is capable of destroying every satanic mark. The ultimate mark of destruction in the Tribulation times is the number 666.

Tokens

Tokens are symbols that denote a covenant. For instance, during a wedding ceremony, people exchange rings. That exchange of rings indicates that a marriage covenant is in place. There are tokens that the enemy can use to represent his presence in the life of people. God gave Abraham the father of faith circumcision as a token of His covenant with the Jewish people. Most occult groups have rings, materials, and occult paraphernalia that the initiates put on or hide in secluded parts of their homes. Certain types of philosophies that people carry into Christianity are a mere carry over from demonic bondage. I have heard people say that when they feel itching on their hands, it indicates money is coming to them. Question, where is the Bible and verse for this? The answer is none! These philosophies constitute tokens that the enemy will flash in your face when he wants to rob you.

There are lots of products in the marketplace in the form of rings, earrings, necklaces, bangles, that when you buy them and wear them, you invite demonic persecution. I bought a lamp once that was so beautiful and could be dimmed while I was sleeping. As soon as I put it on I could notice demonic activities in the air. I instantly traced it to the light and removed it and of course, the devil shipped himself away.

Points of Contacts

"Hereafter I will not talk much with you for the prince of this world cometh, and hath nothing in me" John 14:30

Another thing that looks like tokens is points of contact. How do these work? I will explain it this way: I once watched a movie about some American GIs who invaded a Vietnamese camp while they were sleeping and planted bombs in the camp and in their vehicles. As they drove off, the bombs began to go off and everyone in the camp got up just as the Americans vehicles left. The Vietnamese entered their own vehicles and pursued. As they got closer, the American GIs simply pressed a button corresponding to a bomb in the enemy's vehicles which then caused explosion and destruction. The Vietnamese vehicles were getting blown up remotely.

The point here is that the American GIs were not in the Vietnamese vehicles, but they could still destroy them through

SOME DELIVERANCE TERMS EXPLAINED

what they planted there. Therefore, residual pollutions that have not been cleaned out can become points of contact from where the enemy can successfully launch his attacks. One of the severest forms of point of contact is that when demons have lived in somebody, they do not come to play. They leave their character in the person. When the demon is cast out that is just the first step. The character of the demon spirit which is programmed into the person becomes the point of contact for them and they will stage a comeback unless the individual is taught to embrace the Word of God, live a crucified life, and overthrow that demonic character.

Another point of contact is through works of art. People go to different nations and acquire these things and they take them to their homes for decorations and for memorabilia. If those items were actually dedicated to strange gods, when they bring them into their homes, they subject their homes to persecution and things will begin to go wrong. They are points of contact for the enemy to gain entrance into that place and cause pain. Invisible altars can exist in homes formerly used by witches, mediums, diviners and occultists. If you move into such places without spiritual cleansing those secret altars become points of contact for demonic powers to maintain their evil presence and destruction.

The Strongman

The strongman refers to the first spirit to gain entrance into the person. He is the landlord of the house. That spirit can invite other spirits that are even stronger than him to maintain his position in the life of the individual but because it is the predominant spirit that first gained entrance, we call him the strongman. Another term for strongman is 'ruling power' delegated by Satan in a particular family or region. It is a strongman or the delegated ruler. The word 'strongman' can refer to the authority level of that demon as well as the duration a demon had been in a person.

In deliverance, we need to identify, through the help of the Holy Spirit, who the strongman is. Once he is eliminated, the tenants have to leave. You cannot be doing deliverance, binding and loosing and releasing the tenants while the landlord is still sitting there until you get to it. That will take much longer. The best route is to ask the Holy Spirit to identify the strongman, bind him and cast him out. When Jesus, the Stronger Man, comes that strongman bows and leaves and the smaller demons which are merely John and Jane Doe will have to go as well.

Ancestral Spirits

In certain societies, the dead is worshiped and considered relevant to the day to day life of the living. In African cosmological orientation, for instance, the family has two dimensions the physical and the spiritual. The physical dimension of the family is comprised of those members who are still living. The spiritual dimension comprises those who have transited. Africans do not generally believe that their fore parents have left and are no longer relevant. Instead, they believe they have transited to a higher plane where they actually represent the family at a spiritual level. To remember them, various forms of sacrifices are done; libations are poured and sacrifices of food are seasonally given to appease them and solicit their help in the well-being of the family.

Of course, the Bible says *it is appointed unto man once to die and after that the judgment* (Hebrews 9:27). The concept of ancestral spirit worship enables Satan to put his delegates to rule in the family to receive the worship on behalf of Lucifer and perpetuate generations of waste and torment on the family. When dealing with families that have peculiar problems, it is important to identify the ancestral spirit and address it.

Monitoring Demons

Satan will often attach demons to every person born in the family. That demon serves both as a monitoring spirit as well as a familiar spirit on the specific child. Jesus said that little children have angels who always behold the face of our Father God and they should not be offended. *"Take heed that ye despise not one of these little ones; for I say unto you that in heaven their angels do always behold the face of my Father which is in heaven"* (Matthew 18:10). This means that for every child born into this world there is an angel that petitions God to take care of that child. Satan also delegates his demon spirits to monitor the life of that child, and if the child is not being raised according to the Word of God, the demon begins to train and program the child according to the program of the prince of the power of the air, Lucifer. The enemy then uses those things to create some appetites and behaviors, giving that child a unique character trait that they will use to monitor and limit that child.

The work of the monitoring spirit is to serve as Satan's delegate and to groom the child in certain satanic appetites and predispositions which are then employed to limit and contain the individual from ever seriously developing their God-given potential and capabilities.

And you hath he quickened, who were dead in trespasses and sins; wherein in time past ye walked according to the course of this world, according to the prince of the power of the air, the spirit that now worketh in the children of disobedience: Among whom also we all had our conversation in times past in the lusts of our flesh, fulfilling the desires of the flesh and of the mind; and were by nature the children of wrath, even as others (Ephesians 2:1-3).

This is why the Bible says to train a child in the way he should go; and when he is old, he will not depart from it. Notice it says to train, not to advise! Training means securing the future of your child by getting him or her used to the hard and proper way now as against pampering with endless toys that end in shame.

Familiar Spirit

Then said Saul unto his servants, Seek me a woman that hath a familiar spirit that I may go to her, and enquire of her. And his servants said to him, Behold, there is a woman that hath a familiar spirit at Endor 1 Samuel 28:7

The term familiar spirit is the practice of seeking supernatural information by contact with the spirit world through a medium. This is a form of WITCHCRAFT (rebellion against God) whereby the medium who is possessed with a familiar spirit is able to give the seeker secret information by supernormal means. In reality, it is a counterfeit prophetic which constitutes an illegal doorway into the spirit realm and, a practice forbidden to the children of God.

"Regard not mediums and familiar spirits; do not seek after them, to be defiled by them: I am the LORD your God" (Leviticus 19:31)

The terms, monitoring spirit, delegated demon, informant demon and familiar spirit are closely related but the concept of familiar spirit is more directly related to divination or pretended prophetic ability. It is not the authentic prophetic ability. In divination, a medium, that is, a human being anointed with satanic power having the spirit of divination or fortune-telling, communicates supernatural information from satanic source to the individual seeker. How is this done? Remember every person has a delegated demon, which I will call the familiar spirit in the life of the person. When you go to a medium, for example, a palm reader or a tarot card reader, what they do is summon the familiar spirit in your life and it downloads your information to the familiar spirit of the medium who then begin to tell you things about your life. This person knows nothing about you and you begin to wonder how he could have known those things he or she is saying. It is the combined effort of the familiar spirits, the delegated demon, and the informant demon that gathers your information. The medium, through the familiar spirit, can pretend to recall a dead person and communicate information from the dead to the living and when this is done, it veers into another branch of satanic counterfeit prophetic called necromancy. This is what the Witch of End or attempted to do with the backslidden King Saul of Israel (I Samuel 28:1-25).

In the year 1993, I had a Christian worker who had a direct experience of this phenomenon. An untimely death occurred in the family and they needed the help of a medium to identify the killer and other information known only to the dead. The

SOME DELIVERANCE TERMS EXPLAINED

story goes; the medium wanted the family to supply a virgin to act as a medium (another level demonic initiation) so this particular girl who I here refer to as Mary, was chosen for the medium. According to Mary, the medium collected some ritual items in a clay pot and invoked the power of the spirit. In the meantime, she was told to fix her gaze on the contents of the clay pot and while the invocation was going on, she went into a trance where the dead person appeared to her with a message for the family outlining how he was killed and other information about some family possession and how to locate them. Reader, please be aware that the power of the wicked is both real and very dangerous. Can they get the dead to return to life like this? The answer is no, but through demonic manipulation, Satan is able to tell a smart lie, deceive, and eventually destroy all who follow this pernicious way to the end.

Demonic Cycles

God Almighty operates certain spiritual cycles. I will refer more to this in my other book *Prophetic Gateways*. God has a time frame within which He does certain things, and they are secret to him. Then there are prophetic cycles in which God invites human beings to participate in His process and He reveals things to them. Then there is the appointed moment which completes the cycles of God where certain things in your life are supposed to move up.

A demonic cycle is in the reverse. Demonic cycles institute times and season when the devil comes to collect from the family or from an individual. In those seasons, certain disasters happen. Maybe when someone reaches a certain age he suddenly dies, or when someone attains a certain level, he goes down and never goes up again. It could also be that at a certain time of the year there are sicknesses, afflictions or reverses that occur and are unexplainable. What you do as a child of God is to map them out and begin to do warfare to break their power.

Demonic Reverse

This is the concept of a negative consequence of covenanting or contracting with the devil. If your ancestors covenanted with the devil in order to use this benefit to advance their lives, the devil will walk with them, binding them and their souls and subsequently binding their future generations. The devil waits for some generations and then he starts to collect on the family. Demonic reverses will set into the family and if the family was rich, waste and poverty will set in. On the other hand, if an individual entered a covenant with the devil and he empowers the person to be rich, there are certain things he must do in return. If he does not do those things for any reason and defaults, the devil will send demonic collectors, and demonic reverses will set in.

Spells and Enchantments

These words are used interchangeably to describe certain words said by demonically anointed individuals to bind people and to interfere with their will. The human will is very important and God intends for the human will to function freely as your will is what makes you a human being. Through demonic spells and enchantments, witchcraft powers are able to bind and manipulate their victim and take away their will power. The ability to freely choose is an important divine attribute that God placed in every man without which a person becomes a robot and unable to function. That is why God does not want us to have a passive mind but He wants us to intelligently choose to submit to the Almighty God so He can use us.

Divination

Divination is fortune telling; seeking knowledge of the future without and apart from the Spirit of God. Satan and his gang have some measure of ability to predict things ahead. When people who do not know or are careless go to such demonic sources, they open their destiny to satanic delusions and deceit. What happens is that they will tell them some thrilling stuff, and they, in turn, unwittingly give the devil authorization to begin to reprogram their life to follow the dictates of Lucifer. The best way to know about your future is to read the Bible, connect with a church of the Living God where the power of the Holy Spirit is in function, hand yourself over to the Lord Jesus, and walk closely with Him. God, Himself will reveal things that you need to know. He says, *"Call unto me, and I will answer thee, and show thee great and mighty things, which thou knows not."* God has made a commitment to show us things. We do not have to go to secondary sources that will only harm us.

Soul Ties

Soul ties are the deep intermingling of two persons in a very intense emotional interconnectedness. There is a beneficial positive soul tie as well as a harmful demonically engineered soul tie. I firmly believe that God Himself is the author of spiritually healthy and beneficial soul ties in order to facilitate His purposes in two individuals. The love, commitment and extreme loyalty derivable in this type of relationship would never dishonor God but instead grow the purposes of God in the respective individuals. On the other hand, negative soul ties are facilitated by the devil between two individuals to disrupt their emotional stability, cripple their willpower, and render them non-viable to pursue or prosecute their God-given dreams.

Soul Ties in Marriage

Therefore shall a man leave his father and his mother, and shall cleave unto his wife: and they shall be one flesh.

SOME DELIVERANCE TERMS EXPLAINED

And said, for this cause shall a man leave father and mother, and shall cleave to his wife: and they twain shall be one flesh? Wherefore they are no more twain, but one flesh. What therefore God hath joined together, let not man put asunder. Genesis 2:24; Matthew 19:5-6

In marriage, the man leaves his parents, the closest people to him, to join and cleave to his wife. Notice in verse six, it says, "what God has joined together, let no man put asunder". God literally ties up the two souls in the spirit. This is where genuine marital bond originates. The Scripture here states that they are no more two but one. In the marriage soul tie, the two souls intermingle in the spirit and they become one. The Bible calls it a mystery or deep secret in Ephesians 5:31-32.

Soul Ties In Covenant Friendship

Based upon the call and purpose of God for our lives, He would often draw certain people to us who would absolutely commit to us and help pursue God's agenda for our lives. Sometimes they may do certain things in our lives at great personal cost and sacrifice. *"A man that hath friends must shew himself friendly: and there is a friend that sticketh closer than a brother"* (Proverbs 18:24). The popular story of David and Jonathan readily comes to mind (1 Samuel 18:1-3). This supernatural relationship began by God between David and Jonathan on this occasion empowered and protected David from many years of Saul's demonic jealousy and rage.

Jonathan literally emptied himself even rejecting the throne to ensure that David both lived and succeeded. In the course of my ministry, men and women of goodwill have been stirred up by God to invest their love, time and personal resources to ensure my sustenance and viability in the cause of ministry. These kinds of people are God's direct investment to ensure the fulfillment of His plans and purposes. However, every such privilege imposes a moral responsibility to ensure that the relationship formed is held above reproach and continue to honor God. Genuine love at any level is a platform to sacrificially dedicate oneself for the good of others without dishonoring God.

Negative or Demonic Soul Ties

I briefly stated earlier on that negative soul ties are facilitated by the demonic spirits between two individuals in order to disrupt their emotional stability, cripple their will power and render them incapable of pursuing their God-given purposes or dreams. This is usually when the door of sex or improperly defined emotional connection with the opposite sex is activated. This can be by married or unmarried people. What happens is that the door of illicit sex or deep ungodly emotional attraction is primed to open by seducing spirits against two Christians in close proximity who may be careless and undiscerning, thereby permitting the devil to move in and tie their souls together in the spirit realm. This is a powerful avenue for interpersonal demonic flow. We see this type of situation in the life of Dinah, the daughter of Jacob. In this particular case, the young lady violated a spiritual territorial law by trying to fraternize with the ungodly (Genesis 34:13).

Samson the Deliverer

And the lords of the Philistines came up unto her, and said unto her, Entice him, and see wherein his great strength lieth, and by what means we may prevail against him, that we may bind him to afflict him; and we will give thee every one of us eleven hundred pieces of silver.

And it came to pass, when she pressed him daily with her words, and urged him so that his soul was vexed unto death... - Judges 16:5-16

The life of Samson, the anointed deliverer of Israel, is another very sad example of the crippling effect of negative soul ties. The man of God fell in love with an enemy and the devil unleashed a powerful strategy of destruction on him.

The entire story line runs from verses three to thirty-one. While Samson was busy falling in love with her, she took out a contract on him and actually went forward to deliver and collect on him even at the cost of his anointing and life. What more, as she worked hard to deliver Samson, it became obvious she would go through with her devious plan yet

Samson seemed helpless and stuck with her; why is this? She had enticed him. This is the Jezebel witchcraft component of negative soul ties. The man of God had lost his will to her, and this is the dangerous end of negative soul ties — loss of the human will. Without a healthy and unimpeded human will, we cannot serve God.

In positive soul ties, we yield our human will to God and by the revealed or known will of God, we commit to another person and service the purpose of God in the individual and this kind of love will never dishonor God. The erosion of the human will in negative soul ties is the reason a severely abused spouse will stay loyal and dedicated to their abuser and may continue to live in denial and self-delusion until killed by the person to whom they have committed.

Deliverance from negative soul ties is possible through:
(1) genuine repentance,
(2) deep Deliverance Cleansing,
(3) counseling and in some cases, prolonged counseling and guidance,
(4) deep inner healing through the ministry of the Holy Spirit,
(5) destruction of all images, tokens, photographs, gift items and deleting of phone numbers, and
(6) have accountability person(s) to whom you can be transparent and who can pray with you and monitor your

progress. Finally, the Lord will cleanse and heal based on your reverence for Him. Read 2 Corinthians 7:1-2.

BREAKTHROUGH PROPHETIC DELIVERANCE PRAYERS

1. Lord God, in faith, I open my mind and heart to embrace what God has done in my life. I have the spirit of faith and declare it is already done. Am willing and obedient to eat the good of the land of USA.

2. God is about to cause a public stir with his miraculous hands of performance in my life. Every supervisor of evil in my life shall die off and be buried. Law of divine exchange go into effect.

3. Every satanic agents of opposition of wickedness be eaten of worms. You do not advance the glory of God in my life; be eaten of worms and let your memorial perish in the name of Jesus.

4. Word of the living God, grow, multiply. Increase and flourish in my life in the mighty name of Jesus Christ .....glory, glory, and glory!

CHAPTER 26

Seven Important Messages to the Church

Some time ago, the Lord called my attention and gave me these seven points to deliver to His Body, the Church. According to what the Lord said, if these seven things are not handled carefully, then the charismatic Pentecostal church will become like semi-occult churches. So, we are to pay attention to these, so that the devil, our enemy, will not be able to destroy the Church from within.

Jesus Christ Is the Message of the Entire Bible

From Genesis to Revelation, God the Father, through God the Holy Spirit, is presenting revelations of His Son. The Lord Jesus Christ is who God wants to reveal. He wants us to see His Son who He loves so much and is willing to deliver up for our sins. Whatever topics we preach - whether salvation, prosperity, deliverance, healing or breakthrough - we must reckon with the fact that the revelation of Jesus Christ is the message of gospel.

If Jesus Christ had not come in the flesh to be born, suffer, die and be raised again from the dead, there would have been no message to preach, no ministry, no church, no minister. The Person of the Lord needs to feature prominently in our messages and songs. God wants the whole world to know His magnificent Son. This is the burden of the Almighty! How desperately today's Church need to return to that simplicity of the gospel and present Jesus Christ and Him crucified.

Redemption Is By the Blood

The foundation of true Christianity is the testimony of Blood of the Son of God. He is the Lamb slain from the foundation of the world. We are not dealing with blood of a mere human being; not blood of animals, but the Blood of the Son of the Living God. The Blood of Jesus is central to the Gospel message, because without the shedding of Blood there is no remission or removal of sin.

It is the Blood of Jesus that enables God Almighty in His glory and holiness to be able to look upon a vile sinner and remove his sin. Without the Blood, the Church will fall into the trap of New Age thinking. The Bible says that without the shedding of blood there is no remission (Hebrews 9:22). More particularly in these days when there is a surge in wickedness, evil, and satanic activities, the Church of God needs to bring forth the testimony of the Blood, as it is by means of this Blood we overcome the evil one (Revelation 12:11). Without the Blood, the message of repentance will be lost, as it is the Blood that encourages us to come into a place of humbleness, brokenness, and repentance. The shedding of the Blood of Jesus presupposes that man is a fallen creature and helpless to save himself so the Son of God paid our ransom

The Cross

The Cross as a message and lifestyle is at the heart of the Gospel. If the Church of the Living God does not pay attention and bring back the message of the Cross, we become a generation who will be mostly emotional but cannot take a stand for righteousness. By means of that ugly Cross, God's Best was crucified. By means of that Cross, we are crucified to the world and the world is crucified to us. The Cross brings us to the place of self-denial. If we do not come to the place of self-denial, we will only have an academic Christianity that cannot be respected by God and which cannot impress the devil. God doesn't mind how much we sing about His love for us (which is real anyway), but He just wants us to be like Him and the Cross forces us to embrace the narrow way in our lives. *"For the preaching of the cross is to them that perish foolishness; but unto us which are saved it is the power of God"* (1Corinthians 1:18). The Church must return to simple messages on the Cross.

Intimacy with God

God not only loves us; God is in love with us. The Lord God wants to be with His people. At one point, He told me that He would allow the Holy Spirit to take the love between Himself and Jesus and transmit it to the Church. When He said that, all the glory of heaven was unleashed upon me; I was melting where I was.

God wants us to hunger and thirst for Him. David cried out, *"O God, thou art my God; early will I seek thee: my soul thirsteth for thee, my flesh longeth for thee in a dry and thirsty land, where no water is"* (Psalm 63:1). We must return to a place of intimacy with our God. It is a privilege for us to love Him, because He first loved us. The message and lifestyle of intimacy with God will open the door to new possibilities in the supernatural realm of Almighty God. We at the church of God must return to the message of intimacy and the pursuit of God. Let us love Him, let us chase after Him. He delights in it.

The Power of the Almighty

When we become intimate with God, we enter into the power side of the Almighty. The gospel is not in mere words. It is also in demonstration of the Spirit and of the power. This generation cannot be saved with philosophy and sound doctrines alone. This generation must be confronted with the raw power of God. That is what God is calling us to to embrace

His power. As we get intimate with Him and He begins to adjust us, we will move into the realm of power. The age in which we live has seen an upsurge in counterfeit power in all shapes and forms invading all religions. The devil is anxious to take over, but it is not his time. This is the time that God wants to raise a glorious Church, put His seal of authority on the sons and daughters of the Living God who will be able to give this generation a demonstration of the resurrection power of the Lord Jesus. This is the desire of the Lord. Go for the power of the Holy Spirit. It will take power to break shackles, to bring changes, to transform societies and nations. God said to tell His children to desire power. He warned me in a revelation that the power of the Holy Spirit would be decisive and that those who do not pay the price to walk in His power would live as beggars, because all His provisions would flow from His power to His children.

Evangelism

Power is for purpose. Power without purpose is abuse and ultimate destruction. God wants us to evangelize, to craft ways and means to reach the lost, to spend our time and our money to reach the lost. If the Church of the present day does not rise up to reach out to the lost the consequence will be that we will be hardened in our consciences. We will be practicing self-hypnosis, that is we will be so concerned about our own needs to the point that we will not see what God has done. In the wilderness, God sent the Israelites manna every day. When that day's supply was done, they forgot about it. He had to send it again the next morning, and by the evening they had forgotten again and rebelled. Miracles without focus on the purpose of evangelism will lead to hardness of heart. God wants His Church to return to the purpose for which he came, which is to seek and save that which was lost.

Eternity

Most Christians are living from time to eternity, and that is wrong. God invites us to live in eternity now. Once you are born again, you do not wait to die to enjoy eternity. You are in eternity now. What is the advantage of living from eternity through time? That way, you are judging yourself day to day. People are so blessed today that they enjoy the blessing and forget that heaven is their home. What will it benefit us if we gain the whole world and lose our souls? By living in eternity, we will be able to shun sinful behavior and avoid the traps that Satan puts all over the place by way of temptation. We will be able to live an accountable life, always cognizant that we are pilgrims on the earth, hasting unto the day of the Lord, putting all our energy knowing that heaven is real. Sin will not be able to overtake us.

These are the seven urgent messages the Lord wants the Church to reckon with. If you are reading this, God bless you!

BREAKTHROUGH PROPHETIC DELIVERANCE PRAYERS

THE GREATEST PRAYER OF A LIFETIME

The greatest prayer of a lifetime is to be reconnected back to God in a living relationship. A relationship is a basis for asking. You cannot pray to a God whom you don't know and who does not know you. God wants to be intimate with you. This type of relationship is available to each one of us when we sincerely repent of our sins, ask for God's forgiveness, and receive His Son, Jesus, as our personal Lord and Savior. If you have never surrendered your life to God, or if you have turned away from God and you want to return to Him, now is the time. God is waiting for you. His arms are open wide to receive you. Just pray this simple prayer right now:

O Lord, be merciful to me, a sinner. I realize that I am a sinner. I need a Savior and you are my savior. I repent of every sin, every wrongdoing, and I ask for your forgiveness. I receive Jesus Christ, Your only begotten Son, as my Lord and my Savior. I believe that Jesus went to the cross for me and paid the price for my salvation, and now I receive Him into my heart. I declare that I am born again. I am a child of God. Old sins are gone, and I have a brand-new life in Christ in Jesus' name. Amen.

Appendix
Practical Deliverance Encounters

Case Encounter 1

A Case of Spiritual Confusion

Mr. T was a young convert having just given his life to the Lord in less than six months. He was growing and enjoying his Christian faith until he started hearing voices. This voice claimed that he was God Almighty and was giving him messages to relay to his fellowship members – other young Christians with whom he associated. Each time he delivered them a message purportedly sent by "this God Almighty," the believers were conflicted by it and decided that it could not be God based on their study of the Scriptures. He went back to his closet and this voice, speaking as God, came back to him again, told him not to mind his friends, and reiterated that he was Almighty God speaking to him. "To prove that I am God," the voice told him, "go out to a particular place and you will see some individuals discussing this particular subject which he gave him." He went and checked it out, and the voice told him "see, I am God Almighty. Go back again and relay my message to those stubborn children of mine," which Mr. T did.

Each time Mr. T delivered the message purportedly sent by God through him, the believers were conflicted by it and decided that it *could not be God based on Scriptures. He went back to his closet and this voice speaking as God, came back and said, "Don't mind those my children, I am Almighty God speaking to you. To prove that I am talking to you, go out now to this particular place and you will see these particular individuals speaking, and this is what they will be speaking about." He went and checked it out, and the voice reiterated, "I am the Lord; don't mind those my children. Go back to them and say, "I, the Lord, says..." Again he went back to relay the messages purportedly given by God and as in other instances, they declined them saying that they were not from God based on the Scriptures.*

It got to the point of personal frustration and to a point where he said, "Before I gave my life to Christ, I had a relatively peaceful life. Now I am in just so much confusion and I want to break out. I don't want God talking to me anymore. I just want to have a normal life." But the voice continued to speak different things to him so Mr. T sought the help of a Christian counselor. The Christian counselor got in touch with me and invited me to come into the case and take a look. As my habit was in those days, I usually go around with some of my trainees – people that I have trained in deliverance and the prophetic. So I had this young woman who accompanied me. We went to the school and I invited the young man to relay his experience. I said, "Okay, let us pray." As I lifted my hand towards God, the power of God slammed him. He fell down, his eyes dilated, and he became like a snake with his tongue darting back and forth. The spirit in him started speaking, challenging me that if I cast him out, the boy would lose his intelligence. *(It turned out that the boy's mother and a certain false prophet had gone to their river, performed rituals to seek help for the boy's academic performance and that was how this spirit entered him.)*

God opened the eyes of the young woman (trainee) that accompanied me. She saw that when I stretched out my hand, a huge, muscular being came out of the boy and was coming behind me to strangulate me from behind, but lightning flashed from my body and knocked him down – that was when the spirit started talking through the boy. This muscular spirit with dreadlocks (Leviathan spirit) called itself by the name Araya, and made some confessions that were both interesting and very telling.

The Bible says, "Greater is He that is in us than he that is in the world." I did not even see these things in the spirit. I was addressing the issues in faith but God opened the eyes of this young trainee to see the battle that was raging in the spirit. That huge being had dreadlocks. I can attest based on all the information that was put together that this was the Leviathan spirit that entered him. After the demons were cleared out, I conducted further counseling with him to check things out, and found out that Mr. T was in what Nigerians call Junior Secondary School (11) when his academic performance went sharply down. His mother took him to a church in Nigeria which is renowned for combining the Bible and some occult practices. He went to see one of their prophets for help. This prophet recommended a ritual whereby they took this young man to the river, performed those rituals, and bathed him in the river, after which his academic performance went soaring. But unknown to them, this was a demonic covenant that they entered and, as a matter of fact, in the process of the ritual and bathing him, the Leviathan spirit entered him, temporarily helping him with his academics but with another grand design for his ultimate destruction. The demon confessed that already, he was putting the spirit of immorality in him and his intention ultimately was to take the boy with him to hell.

The manifestations of this kind of spirit begins with a state of confusion and if help does not come soon enough, a situation of psychosis will develop, landing the individual in the mental institution.

IMPORTANT LESSONS

What happened here was that without knowing, both the fellowship and the young man were fulfilling the Scripture, which says, believe not all spirits but prove them. Readers please note that the fellowship did not simply take the supernatural experience at face value; they checked it out and found that it did not line up with the Word of God so they rejected it. If prophetic experiences or supernatural utterances do not line up with the Word of God, we are NOT to accept them. Without realizing what they were actually doing, they were essentially proving the spirit. The young man ultimately delivered a deadly blow to the spirit when he said, "I do not want any more instructions." But because this was a demon spirit, it continued to speak. The devil's aim is to break or erode the human will whereas God would not violate the human will. The devil constantly applies pressure on the human will but God on the other hand works through a surrendered human will. If it was Almighty God, when the young man stated that he did not want to hear any more voices and is not ready, Almighty God will stop because God has given to mankind a free will and He will not override man's free will. However, when the young man stated that he wanted the instructions to cease, the demonic counterfeit refused to stop, thereby violating the young man's will. In reality, demons do not have control – they are intense with their evil objectives and will apply pressure.

Thus the young man also tested the spirit without knowing. By going to a Christian counselor, the final blow was delivered because that channeled him into the right kind of help from an anointed man of God like myself who stands on the Word of God. We were able to provide help and clean him up out of that demonic situation. Thank you Jesus.

Case Encounter 2

Confronting a Lifeless Young Woman

I heard the sound of a bang, bang, bang, on my door, and before I could respond, shouts of Pastor, Pastor followed. I opened my door only to be confronted by Sister A., mother of sister D, the latter of whom was approximately 18 or 19 years old at the time. It is not unusual for those desperate for help to come to the parsonage in this way. (This was when I Pastored in a city called Ibadan, Nigeria). This mother was crying, "My daughter, my daughter, my daughter." "What happened to your daughter, Madam?" I asked. The mother reported that her daughter went limp and lifeless and the mother did everything she could but there was no response. We both rushed to her home to call on heaven for some urgent help. For poor folks in developing nations, your first line of emergency responders and helpers is God because that is all you have available and heavenly 911 works. As a trained counselor and also a prophet, I know that I do not have power of my own. [People do not seem to realize this when they ask a prophet or deliverance minister to come and pray or conduct deliverance. They generally think that these ministers have all the answers within themselves since they are God's oracles]. I am trained to listen. As I was running alongside her, I asked the Lord, "What do you want me to do? Exactly what is going on here?" Light broke out in my spirit: I was to speak one word in the daughter's ear: JAMB (Joint Admissions and Matriculation Board). This is a Board in Nigeria that does testing to determine suitability for admission into universities and colleges and is equivalent to the American SAT. When I went into the room, I met her sprawled out on the floor. I bent down and did as the Holy Spirit instructed: I whispered JAMB into her ear. All of a sudden the young woman shot up — she came alive. As she was crying, I held her. I started to investigate the case and found out what happened. She had left the high school four years earlier. For four successive years, she took this JAMB testing and failed. All of her friends who graduated high school with her were now finishing college and here she was still trying to get into college. When she took this last test and failed, she became depressed. Added to her depression was the fact that there were already some demonic conditions – marine spirits which were responsible for knocking her unconscious. (Demons of death can sometimes get hold of their victim's spirit and this will produce a temporary sense of lifelessness). The Lord later revealed this to me and I went ahead to disciple her for some years and in that *time, took her through thorough and proper deliverance. She was not really dead but seemed lifeless – knocked off. Readers should please note that the temporary cessation of life was not a medical condition. A lot of complications can result from this, and could finally lead to actual death. Her mother being there was able to cut into it and quickly ask for help. Demons specializes in producing death and near death conditions in their victims and if proper discernment is missed the opportunity to help the victim back to life can be lost and this would result in actual physical death. Timely intervention and correct action are vital to success in these cases.*

IMPORTANT LESSON

The Holy Spirit gave us the key. This is very important. To be successful in deliverance, we have to understand that the final authority does not lie within us. We do not have the answers. Everything does not immediately yield to your authority. Had I gone there and shouted the name of Jesus, I probably would not have had results. On the contrary, I was not led that way. I received a specific word from the Lord, which was the key to revive her. That meant that you, as a deliverance minister, must know that you DO NOT have the final authority or the final say. You have to defer to the Holy Spirit and in each particular instance, He will tell you or give you the key that would be the answer to the case with which you are dealing.

Case Encounter 3
Case of Delay in Marriage

S is. W was a 36 year old, anointed believer and she approached me and said, "Pastor Patrick, what is my problem? Here I am at 36 years old. I have been a dedicated follower of Jesus for 19 years and all these years, no man has ever proposed marriage to me so that I have the opportunity to say yes or no. What is wrong with me?" I have had many people say that to me but on this occasion, I knew that Sis. W was very serious and needed answers. I scheduled with her to go on a 3-day fast together, seeking the Lord to find out what was wrong.

On the set day of the fast, I went before the Lord on my knees to present the case and I drifted away in a trance. I saw four huge, ferocious dogs advancing menacingly towards me. Speaking with a human voice, they asked me, "Is it by power? Is it by power?" I responded by saying, "It is not by power nor by might, but by My Spirit says the Lord. I take up the authority of the name of Jesus and come against you." I opened my eyes. I was shocked and said, "My goodness! Lord, what is this?" He said that these are Abaddon powers in charge of her family. The word Abaddon means Destruction. It is a principality in charge of lawlessness and *immorality. This was the power that was in charge of her family and was hindering her from getting married.*

On the third day we met to pray. She was kneeling before me and I was praying in the spirit to the Lord for intervention and deliverance. All of a sudden I got carried away and transported into the future to witness her marriage. The marriage was a powerful, gorgeous marriage and I came back to myself speaking in tongues. I said to her, "Sister, open your eyes. I just attended your wedding." Then I started prophesying: "Sister, you have two months to take the veil from your face or you will miss it." A veil means spiritual blindness of some sorts. Satan uses them to blindside us and abort our seasons. We prayed and ended the session. Of course, in a short time, she disconnected from me. I understand that when she realized that I was a bachelor but was not the one God chose for her, she became angry. (Lord could that have been part of the veil?) I did not know that she was looking towards me. Exactly two months after this, a very important military officer who lived 400 miles away came and proposed marriage to her.

IMPORTANT LESSONS

1. Here we can see that sometimes people struggle because there are unseen powers, causing delays and are blocking them. It will take deliverance warfare to dismantle such barriers. When knowledge of deliverance is lacking, people just endure painful delays thinking that they are waiting on

the Lord.

2. **Wrong thoughts or Focus:** *Our own thought patterns can sometimes hinder or cause us needless delays. The fasting provided us the opportunity to take care of this. The Lord then warned her to take off a veil that was standing in the way or again miss a marital miracle that was on God's calendar for her within two months. This brings me to a third issue which is missed opportunities and aborted seasons.*

3. **Missed opportunities and aborted seasons.** *We see from the above that God had scheduled an appointment for her breakthrough and that appointment was just eight weeks away. Had I not taken her into fasting, she could not have known about it and such ignorance will be used by the enemy to their own advantage. How? Remember that the Lord said she had to take away the veil! A form of spiritual blindness imposed by the enemy to blindside her and rob her by then aborting her season. Painful delay blows from the evil one are frequently inflicted on God's people who mostly walk in ignorance of their times and seasons thereby failing to prepare for the blessings and opportunities that God programmed into those seasons for their promotions. "My people are destroyed for lack of Knowledge" Hosea 4:6.*

Case Encounter 4
A Misleading Voice

Here is a similar case to the one referenced above. We were conducting a deliverance crusade in a particular city in Lagos, Nigeria. The Word of Knowledge came and the man of God said, "There is someone here whose life is going in the wrong direction because you a listening to a misleading voice." Once that word went out, the power of God hit a particular woman. I noticed that some of our pastors were trying very hard to get the demons out of her. This normally infuriates me, and I walked over to them and asked, "Why are you working so hard? Step aside." I said, "In the name of Jesus, I command the manifestations to cease." This is how I was led. I normally listen in my spirit. I commanded that the sister's spirit should take charge over her body. She sobered up and I said to her, "Sister, do you want deliverance?" She said no! I was shocked. I said to the pastors, "this sister said that she does not want deliverance, and this is why you are struggling." I asked her, "Why, then, did you come here?" She answered, "I didn't come for myself; I came for my friend. Maybe God will answer her. I have been waiting on God for many years pleading with Him. I came out of an Islamic family. Everyone is laughing at me. I was pleading with God, just for His own namesake, to please give me a husband and He would not do it. So I don't care about myself anymore. He is not going to answer me." Oh no! This was not God denying her the blessing but rather a spirit of delay and a misleading voice causing her frustrations. The word of God says that every perfect gift, every good gift comes from heaven. God wants to bless. But when a spirit of delay and a misleading voice combine together, and deliverance is not known, the strategy of the wicked becomes effective.

IMPORTANT LESSONS

To be successful in Deliverance cases we must carefully listen to the Holy Spirit instruction and follow His strategy accurately. Let's do a little analysis of the above scenario. The word of knowledge started off this Deliverance and notice that the Lord said there was the presence and work of a misleading spirit/voice. The power of God's Holy Spirit immediately interacted with the woman in question and the demons were rattled and violent manifestations began as the demons struggled for their very lives under the weight of God's power. The Pastors jumped in and started attempting to get the demons out of her. This was right but they failed because they did not yield grounds to the Holy Spirit for complete discernment but instead relied only on their God given authority of the name of Jesus to cast out the demons. Indeed they had that authority and the demons stood inferior to them yet it appears they were mostly reacting to the manifestation and in this way allowed the devil to gain the upper hand. In all *circumstances, we are to reverently yield consciously to the Holy Spirit's instruction even when moving in commanding authority against the devil. We should be reverently responding to the active leading of the Holy Spirit and not excited in the flesh and reacting to the devil's drama. Without the Lord, the Holy Spirit, we can do nothing. Moreover, this individual had swallowed the devil's lie thereby validating his presence; merely using your authority to cast out the demons will not last and they could easily jump back in. She needed some good teaching in the Word of God regarding her wrong notions about God's love for her. I merely interrupted the drama, corrected the Pastors and allowed them to continue while I moved on to other cases. Yes the demons were eventually cast out but first a brief counseling to secure her understanding and brokenness was required to re-engineer things in the correct direction.*

Case Encounter 5

The Case of Demonic Manipulation

This case has to do with the author himself. I once lived in the mission with fellow full time ministers with various degrees of breakthrough and issues. We all have baggage. Sometimes people don't realize that even as ministers, and as children of God, we are all, to one extent or another, damaged goods, badly needing the repair work of the Good Shepherd the Lord Jesus Christ. There was this case of a particular sister, called Sister E. She seemed depressed. One could see her an atmosphere of rejection around her. I became interested in her case and I offered to help her. I called Sister E to have a conference with her. She told me about her woes and I said, "You know what? Deliverance is possible. Let us go before the Lord and fast and pray together. We set a date.

The first day, as I was going on my knees to present her before God, I saw a male-like figure in my vision with a lethal instrument advancing towards me to strike me and my eyes opened. I knew I was getting into some dangerous territory so I pressed further praying and interceding for her. I asked her if she saw anything, to which she responded that she had seen a broken bottle. As the bottle broke, she saw a duck come out of the bottle and was eating raw blood. My understanding of that was that it was a group of dangerous witchcraft. She was actually into witchcraft herself but I was naïve and out of goodness, was trying to help her. As I pressed on with her case, presenting her before the Lord, I began to have some bizarre dreams. In one of the dreams, somebody told me I had a gift and that I should come to get it. I was riding a bicycle going to get this so called gift. I arrived at the location; it was a ranch styled house and sat down waiting for the so called gift to be delivered. All of a sudden, I realized that someone was sitting on my lap. I looked and saw that it was this same young woman I was trying to help. I reacted in shock and I woke up. I thought this to be bizarre but then I said, "It was just a dream." When I saw her the following day, there was such a look about her face that suggested that something was wrong. I still did not reckon much with it. Later on, maybe a week later, I had a follow up dream. I was still interested in working on her case. In this dream, I saw that we were moving towards what looked like a chapel. She came behind me and touched me inappropriately. I reacted and woke up.

Again, the following morning when I saw her, there was that foreboding guilty look on her face. I had no clear evidence as to what I was doing but something told me to withdraw from her. I did! Later on, the conditions of the ministry deteriorated and some of us banded together to pray and intercede. While we were praying, the Lord told us that the ministry was in trouble but if we were faithful to pray continuously, He would expose everything. Boy did He expose *things! ALL HELL BROKE LOOSE!*

One of the most beautiful ladies in the choir started confessing to witchcraft atrocities that a group of them in the ministry, including this lady, were carrying out against the ministry. In their confessions, it came out that this lady I was asking God to deliver, had requested that I become her husband and in their coven, they granted her wish. This is why I was having those dreams. Had the Spirit of God not been mercifully strong with me, my mind would have become manipulated and I would have entered into a marriage covenant with a witch. God delivers! His mercy endures!

IMPORTANT LESSONS

Compassion must be balanced by the judgement of matured counsel. Sometimes we see people with a lot of issues and we just want to help them. Well, it is okay to want to help. We should show compassion. The Bible says, **"And of some have compassion, making a difference: and others save with fear, pulling them out of the fire, hating even the garments spotted by the flesh (Jude 1:22-23).** If you are not careful, your own flesh will put dark spots on your garment and the enemy will take you in. The people you may be trying to take out of the fire can be used of the enemy to take you into the fire. For young people who are in the ministry, it is good for you to be compassionate but not emotional. You can try to help people and you should have love for them but if they do not yield to God, that love will become a risk factor for you. Particularly in dealing with the *opposite sex, be aware that you can be manipulated.*

The spirit of Jezebel aims at the human will. There are two ways that the human will can be subdued
1. By seduction and
2. By Intimidation.

If someone of a higher authority or some type of influence, whether it be financial or aesthetic, starts to appeal to your emotions or sentiments, they can erode your will if you do not understand or respect boundaries. They can erode your will just through that emotional appeal and you can become seduced to do what you normally would not do because your willpower has been eroded. As one of my leaders used to say, "Close proximity can break down your resistance."

Another way is through intimidation. A person in leadership standing over you can intimidate you until you lose your will. You are so scared to be wrong, you lose your will. Without your human will, you really cannot serve God. You need your will to surrender to God. If something else takes your will, it can make you go against God. In conclusion, this woman was responsible for her own delay and stagnation. She was not sincere with the Lord.

Case Encounter 6

Blood of God: A Case of Deception

This case involves a very dangerous spirit of deception. It happened many years ago, around 1995 in the city of Ibadan, Nigeria. Some of my financial partners had reached out to a certain unique couple in their own evangelism efforts who wanted to receive deliverance ministry and they thought that I could help. This couple was strange in the sense that the man was a Marine medium. A marine medium is someone who is in touch with Marine spirits and professes some type of false prophetic. Mermaid spirits can manifest divination through python or serpentine spirit and in this way, develop clients people who come for prophetic visions and insights.

This man was some type of demonic Prince, practicing his evil craft and obviously doing good business for himself and his master Satan, until Jesus came calling and he gave his life to Christ. There was a young woman he wanted to marry and both of them had become involved in that trade and by the time they came to me for deliverance, their story began to develop an interesting twist. Quite interestingly, as I counseled them, some bizarre things started happening. Every time they came to me for counseling, the demon spirit they were in touch with told them, "That man is a true man of God. The things he is telling you, you must take seriously. Go through the prayers and get married so that I can enter your womb and you can give birth to me. I want to be born as a human being so that I can escape the judgment of God. Only the blood can save." This spirit claimed to have originated in the Mediterranean. It told them of experiencing Noah's Flood. In their kingdom, according to the spirit, there was pandemonium as they were rattled by the fact that time is very short; the wrath of God will soon begin, and he wanted to be saved before it begins to rain fire and brimstone. The only hope for it (the demon spirit) to be saved was the couple (Medium) to get married and give birth to it (the demon spirit). The whole scenario was very confusing to me for a while. I had never had a demon spirit advocating Scriptures like that. I went before the Father, and told Him that I did not understand, and that I needed Him to clarify my thoughts. I did not want to get into error. Why should this spirit be validating? Where in the Scripture does it say this? As I started to ask the Lord, I was at the point of near confusion. The Lord came to me mercifully and said, "Ask them if the spirit is saying the blood of God or the Blood of Jesus." When they came for counseling again, I inquired what the Lord told me to ask. When they said the blood of God, I realized that it definitely was a demon spirit who could not say "the Blood of Jesus"

I asked the Lord, how come the demon spirit was confirming His Word and He said that there is a general desperation and this demon *was so desperate that even though it knew that a demon spirit cannot be saved, was trying to see if he could get a human body through them and therefore probably be saved. I do not believe that this is possible but it shows a level of desperation in the spirit world.*

IMPORTANT LESSONS

As we go deep into deliverance work, we will encounter things that ears cannot even comprehend. People may think that we have gone out of our minds. The couple were eventually set free but the lady was a bit difficult and emotional about the spirit once I concluded it was a demon and needed to be cast out and the door shut against it. The man, the would be husband intervened and called the lady (his spouse) to order in the following words; the beautiful, graceful woman you have come to know and love as the (Mommy spirit) is not the original image and look of this spirit. The original state is a hideous and fearful looking creature with snake heads. The lady gave in to reason and the demon spirit was evicted.

We will encounter what the Bible calls the depth of satan but let's be clear, the Word of God is settled forever. We are to hold the written Word above experiences and judge everything and everyone on that basis. If we do this, we will not fall into deception and demonic delusion. This is partly why we are to be under authority and be accountable.

Case Encounter 7

The Case of the Boy without Father and Mother

◆◆◆◆◆◆◆◆◆◆◆◆

In August 1986, the Lord constituted myself and a couple other brethren into a Deliverance Team in the City of Enugu, in the Eastern part of Nigeria and a great deliverance work was accomplished with many testimonies. During this time, the Lord promised to send us a young man without earthly Parents. We had no idea how he was going to come to us but we simply believed and waited. Not long after a particular couple came to bring my team and me provisions and they were a bit hurried. I questioned them as to why they were in a hurry to which they explained that there was a young man who had come to visit them without earthly Parents. We naturally got excited based on the promise that the Lord had given us and we wanted to know more about him and invited this couple to bring the young man to us. He came the same night and after a brief chat we tried to impress him with the need for Deliverance Prayer but he resisted apparently thinking he has already surrendered to the Lord and consequently could not see the need for that type of prayers. One of my Team members queried him about his struggle with pride and anger and managed to get through to him. He then humbled himself and requested for Deliverance Prayer. We merely formed a circle around him and engaged in intensive worship of the Lord. While the worship was underway, he collapsed under the power of God with nobody touching or laying hands upon him. Less than one hour into this Worship encounter, he got up with a look of shock in his face explaining to us that something was emptied out of him making him feel so light and joyful; he event requested for some food as according to him, he became very hungry.

His Story

He story which was published at the time by a secular local news outlet (The Statesman) was mind blowing and a great testimony to the saving grace of our Lord and Savior, Jesus Christ. He suddenly appeared one day in the commercial city of Onitsha in Eastern Nigeria, asking for the Queen of the land. People felt that he had psychological problems so they took him to the police station. He was told that there was nothing like a Queen in the Federal Republic of Nigeria and they took him for a psychiatric analysis. He was declared to be of a sound mind but his search for the Queen of the land remained bizarre. A Christian policewoman took him under her wing, accommodated him in her home and started trying to reach him with the Gospel.

They brought Brother G to me. Brother G, according to his story, grew up in the Marine world (the underwater world) among mermaid spirits. The Queen of the Coast was his mother. In their world, they worshipped Lucifer who would sometimes appear in the sky. He claimed that the place was called Eukay, which had a more *superior standard of life than the natural world. They had some form of aristocratic system where some of them saw themselves as being more privileged and superior to others. He was given the impression that he was a prince sent there to be trained and would one day return to his nation as a ruler- a specially trained elite trained to fight Christianity. They used to show videos of Christianity and Jesus as deranged people who were corrupting the world. Himself and others like him in the place, were selected princes from palaces around the world who were there to train and go back and have particular power and influence, and be used to fight Christians.*

Once in a while, they (Young Princes) stopped by a black man called happy, whose job was to build coffins to joke about him. They used to laugh at him for being weird and doing the odd job. One day, Mr. Happy finally reacted and fired back saying; "I am actually better than you. You are not the son of any president or king. You were an abandoned baby picked by the beach in Lagos Nigeria. At some point you will be sacrificed." Brother G asked for instructions on how he could escape but the black man told him that he could not. He told the black man that if he did not tell him how to escape, he would report that he gave him false information. Mr. Happy told him that he should go into a well secured lab, drink a certain measure of a particular chemical, and once he drank this, he would appear in Lagos where he was originally picked up as an abandoned baby.

A black man called happy, whose job was to build coffins to joke about him. They used to laugh at him for being weird and doing the odd job.

One day, Mr. Happy finally reacted and fired back saying; "I am actually better than you. You are not the son of any president or king. You were an abandoned baby picked by the beach in Lagos Nigeria. At some point you will be sacrificed." Brother G asked for instructions on how he could escape but the black man told him that he could not. He told the black man that if he did not tell him how to escape, he would report that he gave him false information. Mr. Happy told him that he should go into a well secured lab, drink a certain measure of a particular chemical, and once he drank this, he would appear in Lagos where he was originally picked up as an abandoned baby.

The place was heavily guarded but the guard slept, and so Brother G was able to sneak into the lab. He got the chemical but the guard woke up and Brother G became afraid. Instead of measuring the chemical, he drank a lot of it and found himself instead at the head of the River Niger Bridge in Onitsha in Eastern Nigeria. He thought the place should naturally be ruled by a Queen like where he just emerged from which is why he was asking for the Queen of the land. This was how the Christian policewoman took him under her wings and was teaching and preaching the Word of God to him. When the policewoman started teaching him the Word of God, he was very offended by it but his background had taught him to respect authority so he never argued. After a while, he saw her love and believed it to be true and made a profession of faith. It was after this that the Marine spirit tried to get him back but it was too late.

When the couple brought him to my team and me, he looked to be 18 years very bright young man. When I told him that he had to undergo deliverance prayers, you could see his arrogance: "Delivered from what? I am fine." Mrs. B, one of my team members at the time, said to him, "Now what about this pride and anger you struggle with?" The Lord would often give a direct discernment which can be a key to unlock a complicated case; that humbled him a little. I said, "Let's pray for you." He consented. The team gathered around him and worshipped. We did not lay hands on him. We just surrounded him and worshipped the Lord. The power of God slammed him; he fell down and was disoriented. He later got up delivered and then said that he felt empty and was hungry. God filled him with the Holy Spirit and he became our team member. He was blessed and a powerful prophetic gift came upon him. There are people who cannot be reached by ordinary means: they are cut off from human civilization because they were smuggled into and trapped in the spirit world. The spirit world is a reality. There are some who are smuggled from the natural into the spirit world and you can never find them again. The Bible says God should have respect unto the Covenant because the dark places of this earth is filled with the habitation of cruelty.

Psalm 74:20 Have a respect unto the covenant: for the dark places of the earth are full of the habitations of cruelty.

IMPORTANT LESSONS

To the average western mindset, the reality of a real spiritual world of spirits actively involved with and influencing the material physical world of human beings sounds at best like a remote possibility. The truth is there is vast array of superior spiritual world of both Positive and Negative realities exerting powerful influence on our material universe. Physical earthly life is merely an offshoot of that unseen supernatural world holding sway, controlling and often times dictating conditions in the material world. There are indeed underwater world of Marine Powers, Celestial demonic cities where evil powers scheme and spew their devious plans and pollutions upon mostly ignorant humanity. Earthly life in the realm of politics, commerce, entertainment, academics' and finance are all manipulated and controlled from this realm of reality. Thankfully, that is less than a fraction of the Glory, Power and Splendor of God's original Supernatural we are called to walk in. We must seek to know the crucified and resurrected Christ. To know and be established in His love; the fellowship of His sufferings and to be conformed to His death and be planted in the likeness of His resurrection. This way, we will be fully prepared to engage the powers of darkness. Saints of God, the evil one is yet coming with his worst because they are very desperate knowing that they have a very short time left.

Case Encounter 8

The Case of
Vanishing Pregnancy

This happened in the Ibadan city, Nigeria several years ago. I was teaching a Bible Study session and the prophetic unction came upon me. The prophetic can be dramatic. I found myself taking the hand of a woman and her maid a young maid of about 9 years of age. I took the hand of the maid and the mistress and I said, "Tell your mistress what you have done to her." I had no evidence of why I was saying this. All of a sudden the young girl was shaking. She said, "Mummy", do you remember the time you were pregnant before? We ate the baby in the coven and this pregnancy you are carrying right now, we ate the baby last night. The mistress was shocked. She said, "Pastor, no, no, no, no, no." She turned to the maid and said, "You did not eat my baby last night; you ate yourself. In the name of Jesus, I am going to have my baby." The mistress then related a bizarre experience she had some years earlier. She told us that a couple of years back, after she had two boys in quick succession, she got pregnant again. She was depressed about it and did not want it. So in the fifth month of the pregnancy, the pregnancy vanished. She just said, "Wow! God took care of this." She said I did not know it was a *witchcraft situation. But of course this pregnancy I am carrying, I want this baby, and I reject their evil counsel in the name of Jesus. I want this baby."* She carried the baby to full term; it was a beautiful baby girl, and she named her Faith.

So what do I mean by vanishing pregnancy? There have been cases where people have been pregnant, their pregnancies grew, and all of a sudden their bellies become flat, and people think that there is something wrong with them. Well, it so happened that the Lord showed me a vision while I was pastoring in the Delta State of Nigeria in 1998. He brought me in the spirit realm in the prophetic anointing to a Marine witchcraft market. The sight was bizarre. I saw a long line of people waiting to buy something. What were they buying? There were some old women laying eggs and these people were lining up to buy the eggs. I was shocked! God told me that the women laying the eggs were Marine witches. The people who were lining up to buy these eggs were Mediums on the earth who had promised babies to their clients. The Lord told me, "Those eggs that you see them selling are the stolen fetuses from the womb of pregnant women. These are women who do not have a covenant relationship with Jesus or do not know how to cover their babies so that the babies are not stolen."

Some would say that the devil does not have power. Well, there are a lot of mysteries that go on. He does have power but he has no authority, the right to exercise power. The devil does not have babies to give. He cannot create life but he can actually steal babies from the *womb of a woman and give to another through mediums. How do they effect this?*

Through witchcraft manipulation, a baby can be stolen from the womb of a pregnant woman and transmitted to another and of course, demons are added in the process. *This way the mediums who promised their clients children, can deliver on their promise but the person is giving birth to a baby stolen from another person's womb and with some demons that will bring trouble later on. These are the mysteries of darkness thank God for Jesus. In him there is life and the life is the light of men and the light shines in darkness and the darkness comprehends not the light.*

IMPORTANT LESSONS

Some would say that the devil does not have power. Well, there are a lot of mysteries that go on. He does have power, but he has no authority, the right to exercise power. The devil does not have babies to give. He cannot create life, but he can actually steal babies from the womb of a woman and give to another through mediums. How do they effect this?

Through witchcraft manipulation, a baby can be stolen from the womb of a pregnant woman and transmitted to another and of course, demons are added in the process. This way the mediums who promised their clients children, can deliver on their promise but the person is giving birth to a baby stolen from another person's womb and with some demons that will bring trouble later on. These are the mysteries of darkness – thank God for Jesus. In him, there is life and the life is the light of men and the light shines in darkness and the darkness comprehends not the light.

Case Encounter 9

A satanic Covenant of Destruction

This other case has to do with what I call a satanic covenant of destruction. I was in a city in the State of New Jersey conducting a deliverance service. On a previous night, we had broken some covenants and the following day, I had been determined to do some teachings. Before I could actually get into the teaching, I had a deep impression within me to call out people who were going through real painful difficulties. Those whose lives were full of pain, depravation, lack, and suffering, and I perceived that some of the cases were actually demonically generated. When I called for them, people were coming out for prayer. I noticed a well-built young man coming out to the Altar area for prayer. As he was approaching the altar, the power of God was interacting with the demons and he could not hold himself. He was knocking things over so I called for the pastors and the church to get hold of him.

All of a sudden he shook them off and was moving menacingly towards me. His eyes were blood shot, and he said this to me with his finger pointing at me, "How dare you! How dare you! How dare you! Do you think you can just end a 200-year-old covenant like that? *How dare you!"* So I responded in quite the same manner as the young man with my finger pointing at the spirit within him, *"How dare you! How dare you! How dare you come into the house of the Living God?"* The church was fired up and started praying. The young man collapsed. I told the musicians to come over andlead in worship and I stepped aside to observe and listen in on the Lord. It is always better to see God in action instead of initiating our own actions. Sometimes when there are manifestations, some zealous immature believers jump into the fight. Do not let the manifestations drive your emotions. Listen, see God at work, and follow as the Holy Spirit leads. As I watched things unfold, and the Choir were doing their worship, I saw an angel of the Lord standing where this young man was laying lifelessly, pouring oil from a golden pot into him. When I thought that the entire thing was done, I went and picked him up. He was a very different person broken and crying, and I led him to Jesus.

The following day he gave his testimony. He had been a Christian for a long time but one destruction after another, one disaster after another was following his life. There were untimely deaths which afflicted his family. One of the nephews that was looking up to him, was released from the hospital and as they celebrated the victory, he died suddenly. So he had come to church saying to God, 'This is my final week in Christianity. You don't appear to be able to help me. I will attend church for this week and then quit.'

Then the help came.
So what was the situation here? There was a hidden covenant and the enemy was relying on that: he was administering doses of Satan's prescribed punishment for the family. This is one of the reasons why bad things happen to good people.

IMPORTANT LESSONS

A lot of wonderful people of faith do go through really bitter and painful experiences. We are to look out for one another as the Word of God admonished us to bear one another's burden, and so, fulfill the law of Christ. Sometimes, folk's subjective negative experiences of life can rob them of the value of God's Word. It is important to understand that the Word of God holds all creation, including the devil together in a divine order and balance of all things. Such awareness will help us to navigate difficult times and what we call, "dark night of the soul" when evil seem to prevail against good. In this particular case, there was some hidden demonic Covenant dating back to at least four generations and the enemy relied on this to inflict great damage on this family. Let me quickly add that this could have been prevented because the superior claims of our Covenant with God in Jesus Christ have already nullified this evil Covenant and the Curses resulting from it. Unfortunately, this family endured needless pains and loses due to the lay back attitude of many Churches about Deliverance and Warfare. The truth is light and that light must so shine for darkness to recede.

Case Encounter 10

The Luciferian Marine Agent

♦♦♦♦♦♦♦♦♦♦♦♦

Sister G and I encountered one another when I was still very young in the ministry of deliverance. I was conducting deliverance services in my room day and night hardly resting myself. One of those days, around 11a.m., this young girl walked in and said she needed deliverance. We were alone in the entire complex. I said, "Okay, let's talk about it." She sat across from me in a rather sexually provocative manner. After a while, I felt uncomfortable and I asked her, "Do you mind sitting properly?" She complied. We talked for a little while and then I said, "Let us pray." I was feeling a little tired. As she stood up, I lifted my hands and she slumped. Immediately I heard the voice of the Lord saying, "Stop! Wake her up and tell her to come back the next day." I complied, and told her to please come back the next day. She left.

That night, around 7:45p.m., I suddenly felt very heavy with sleep. As my habit was, I wanted to pray before I went to sleep so I went on my knees to pray and instantly I was transported away into a trance. I saw myself in the room with this girl laying across the bed. I saw that her hands were filled with blood. All of a sudden, my eyes opened *and the sleep vanished. The voice of the Lord came to me saying, "This woman is an agent of the devil sent to kill you. But I have plans to use her. She is a marine Lucifer agent. Marine Lucifer agents are specific agents through the marine spirit working directly for Lucifer. The Lord said to me, "When she comes, do not preach the Gospel to her. Just interact with her, listen carefully for my instructions, and follow them."*

So the next day she came, I offered Sister G some tea, and chatted with her as I would a friend. We did this for two weeks, and then the Lord said to me, "She is in love with you now, so begin to talk to her about the judgment of God on wickedness." At this point, I began to preach to her on God's judgment on wickedness. She was confused. She was sent to kill me but after two weeks of interaction but she was in love with me and now I am preaching about judgment. She could not go away because she liked hanging around me. She broke down and started confessing. She said, "Do you know who I am?" I told her that I had an idea as to who she was. She said, "I am four persons in one with millions of snakes in my stomach. I was sent to kill you because you are disturbing our kingdom. All you had to do was to sleep with me one time and you would fornicate every day until you are dead." I said to her, "I had an idea as to who you are. My Lord told me about you 2 weeks ago, and He instructed me to love you. You have served the devil and at the end, he will destroy you. But my own Lord, whom I serve, loves you and He gave His life for us. Would you like to give my God a try? If He doesn't satisfy you, you can always go back." She indicated in the affirmative so I led her to

Christ.

When this happened, the kingdom of darkness was stirred in anger. I received two direct letters from the kingdom of darkness: one from Lucifer and the other from the marine spirit. I kept them for many years (though I do not know where they are now). One of the letters boasted that they wanted to eat my flesh and drink my blood. I simply laughed. Of course at this time I knew that I should no longer proceed alone. I invited the brethren in, and we jointly counseled her, and she gave her life to the Lord and we handled her deliverance.

IMPORTANT LESSONS

I was attacked during the process but this will be discussed at a later date. All I can say now is that we are not to be emotional but we are to be very careful and yield to the Lord. Only in the Lord do we find our strength. The Bible says to be strong in the Lord and in the power of His might. His might is His superior power: His Superiority that is the part that He displayed when He raised Jesus from the grave. The might of God makes Him superior to everyone. We must be strong in that might and in the power. We can actually ask God to strengthen us. We should not act independently. I want to add that we should not be conducting deliverance when we are very tired or exhausted.

If you are tired and not mentally up to it, please excuse yourself, set up an appointment for a later date, give yourself time to rest, and pray and fast so that you can be sensitive to the Holy Spirit. Praise the Lord!

ABOUT THE AUTHOR

Dr. Patrick Odigie is a man graced with prophetic insights, revelations, and his ministry is marked by signs, wonders, and demonstrations of the Spirit. The Ministry of this Apostolic Prophet, spanning three decades, has taken him to four Continents and he is mandated by God to mobilize the Praying Power of the Church to unleash end-time revival and Healing of the Nations. Patrick Odigie functions under a powerful anointing of Counsel, revelations, dreams interpretations and encounters in the spirit realm.

He is a trained Deliverance minister, substance abuse counselor and a consultant/participant at World Forum of Drug Demand Reduction, Bangkok, Thailand, in December 1994 under the auspices of United Nations Drug Control Program for Non- Governmental Organizations. Brother Odigie is an alumnus of the prestigious Haggai Institute of Advanced Christian Leadership, Maui, Hawaii.

He presently resides in Uniondale New York where He and his wife, Rev. Mabel Odigie, Oversees the Prophetic Power house Ministries; and travels extensively throughout the Nation mobilizing churches and Christian fellowship groups to unleash the power of the praying churchfor end-time healing revival. The three cord focus of his message is Prayer, Sacrifice, and Intimacy with the Holy Spirit as pre-requisites for accessing the power of God for the end-time healing revival.

He sees himself as an extreme lover of Jesus, and seeks to promote a spirit of bridal love for the Lord everywhere. Patrick is married to his best friend, Pastor Mabel Odigie, and is blessed with three anointed and prophetic children; Praise, Honor and Favor.

BIBLOGRAPHY

Watchman Nee, (January 1980) The Latent Power of the Soul. Christian Fellowship Publishers Inc., New York

Derek Prince; (1998) They Shall Expel Demons (Your Invisible Enemies) Bakers Publishing Group, Ada Michigan.

John Simpson and Edmund Weiner (Editors) Oxford English Dictionary Online. Oxford University Press Publication. 1989

Eto Victoria, Lesson Notes on Deliverance; (1986) Shalom Christian Mission, Ozoro, Delta State, Nigeria.

Hinn Benny, (2011) Angels and Demons, Bookmark Publishing Dallas, Texas USA

Obode O. Jerome, 90 Keys to Effective Praying AuthorHouse, UK

Other Books by
THE AUTHOR

Overcoming Delay Factors in Deliverance

Foundations for True and Complete Deliverance

Warriors Guide on Effective Deliverance Ministry

War is Normal

Deliverance That Works

Destiny Under Fire

The Anointing of The Curse Breaker

Prophetic Gateways

www.ingramcontent.com/pod-product-compliance
Lightning Source LLC
Chambersburg PA
CBHW060102170426
43198CB00010B/742